Offices **Butterworth Architecture Briefing and Design Guides**

OFFICES

Stephen Bailey

A Briefing and Design Guide   Series Editor: Fred Lawson

Butterworth Architecture
London Boston Singapore Sydney Toronto Wellington

Butterworth Architecture is an imprint of Butterworth Scientific

PART OF REED INTERNATIONAL P.L.C.

First published 1990

British Library Cataloguing in Publication Data

Bailey, Stephen
Offices : a briefing and design guide.–(Butterworth Architecture design and development guides).
1. Offices. Buildings. Interiors. Design. Implications of electronic office equipment
I. Title
725'0105

ISBN 0-408-50016-6

Library of Congress Cataloging in Publication Data

Bailey, Stephen.
Offices / Stephen Bailey.
p. cm. — (A Briefing and design guide)
Includes bibliographical references.
ISBN 0–408–50016–6 :
1. Office buildings. 2. Office layout. 3. Office decoration.
I. Title. II. Series.
NA2750.B69 1986
[NA6230] 89–23944
725'.23—dc20 CIP

Printed and bound in Great Britain by Courier International Ltd, Tiptree, Essex

Acknowledgements

The author is indebted to a number of people for their help in the preparation of this book, in particular Allan Konya for his always pertinent and helpful comments and suggestions, and Tony Barnes of Brook, Barnes, James (Chartered Quantity Surveyors) for his contributions to the sections on cost planning and control.

Thanks must also go to a number of specialist manufacturers of furniture, equipment and interior elements who generously provided information and photographs.

Contents

Appendices

Introduction

1. Who is this book for?

The main purpose of these *Briefing and Design Guides* is to provide all those involved in the initial stages of the building process – clients, users and members of the design team – with a set of tools. These tools, or resources, will help them communicate more effectively so that they are able to work together to develop rich design briefs which will, it is hoped, culminate in the best solutions to their particular problems.

There are a few points to be stressed. First, for every building within each major type covered by this series there is a wide range of variables: the building may be large or small, simple or complex; the client may be a public body, a large private organisation or a small firm, a family or an individual; those involved may be experienced or inexperienced in building; the design team may be big or small, may or may not have experience with the relevant building type; and every team will have its individual method of working. It is impossible to cover all the likely combinations and to provide an ideal set of guidelines for all clients, users and designers in all situations. There will obviously, therefore, tend to be a bias in these *Guides* towards a particular briefing context that is not the most simple nor the most complex, but rather a fairly uncomplicated middle range. In spite of this it should be possible to use each *Guide*, if one realises and accepts its limitations, as a basic tool not only for the simplest but also for the most complex of projects.

Secondly, there is no one way of approaching the design process – and this is also true of briefing. Procedures will vary, for example, between those used by and for different types of client, and by and for the public and private sectors. Although the contents of each *Guide* are organised and presented in a specific linear sequence, as demonstrated in Fig. 0.1, they should not be seen or used as a rigid set of sequential instructions but rather as a loose framework, or flexible tool, which can be adapted to suit individual requirements.

Fig. 0.1 *The main phases and steps of the complete briefing and design process. This book is specifically concerned with phases 1 and 2. (Based on stages A to D of 'Plan of Work'; see Appendix A.1.a.)*

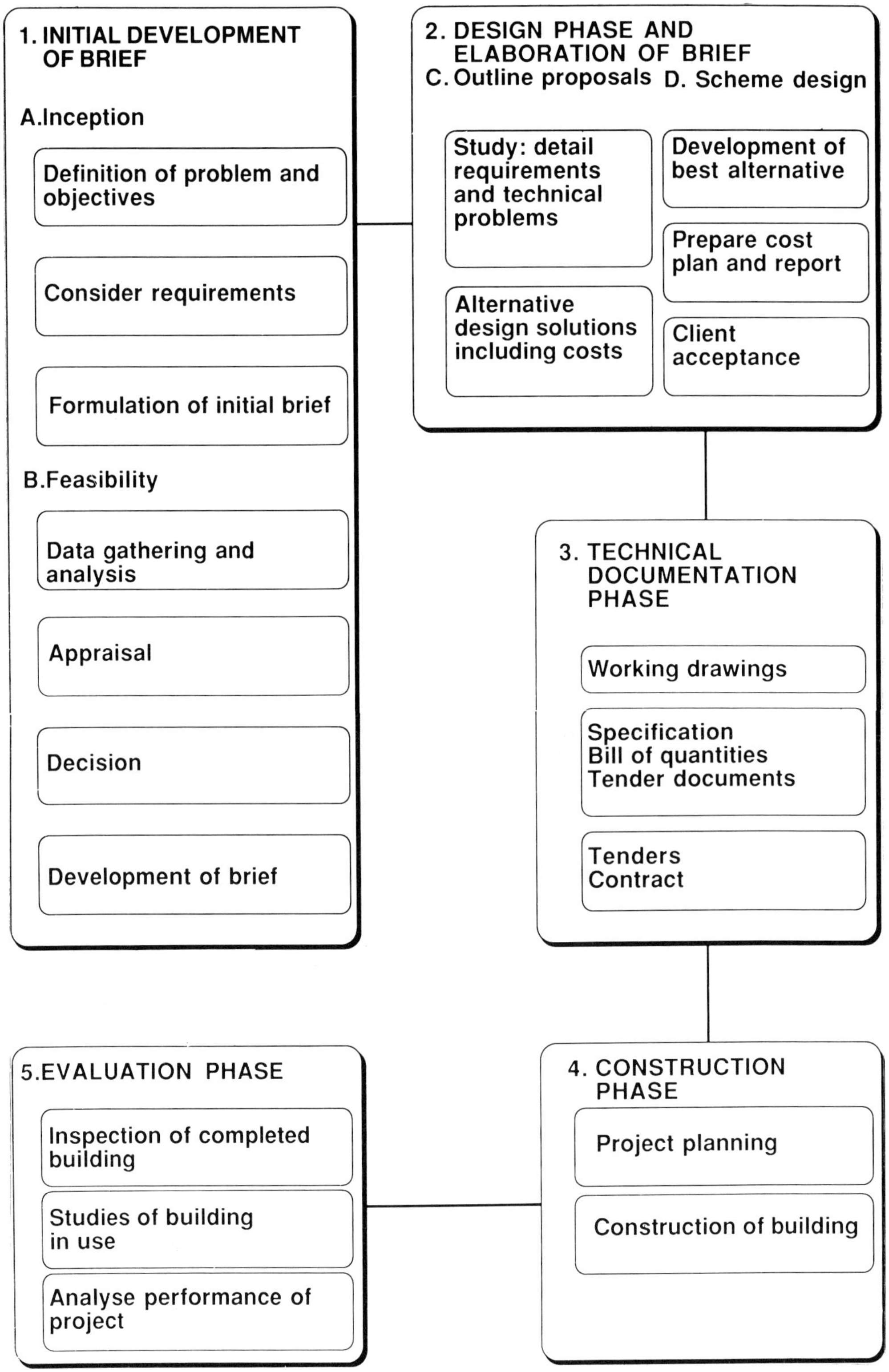

Thirdly, the guidance contained in these books is intended for the main participants in the process of briefing and design, but it is not always possible to distinguish clearly between that which is, for example, specifically the role of the client, and that which is the responsibility of others. It is not advisable to generalise about who should undertake each and every task: this is something to be determined by those involved in each individual project. Wherever possible, however, an indication is given of who is most likely to be responsible.

2. What is design?

The design of buildings is, at its simplest, the creative development of an idea – in three-dimensional form – to solve a specific problem. This problem-solving activity is called the 'design process'. This term is generally used to describe everything that happens from the time a problem is first outlined to the finalised design. The methods used can range from those based on intuition and experience on the one hand, to extremely formal and inflexible logical or mathematical approaches on the other. Whether consciously applied or not, virtually all of the procedures will include the following actions in one form or another:

— recognition and definition of the problem and objectives and consideration of the component sub-problems.
— observation and collection of data relevant to the problem.
— analysis of requirements and data collected.
— development of alternative ideas and solutions. Design can never produce the one correct answer, and from the innumerable possibilities those that seem most suitable for the specific problem will be sought.
— synthesis, or the putting together of ideas to form complete designs.
— evaluation, or the testing of alternative designs against requirements, and optimisation.

The process is not a simple linear sequence of logical steps leading neatly from one phase to another – of finding the right answer at each step or phase before progressing to the next – but rather a series of actions comprising steps grouped for convenience into phases, some or all of which may occur simultaneously. As new information becomes available ideas that seemed perfectly adequate at an earlier step or phase may have to be changed. Indeed, the complete cycle of actions may have to be reconsidered several times.

3. The importance of the brief

In a world of increasing complexity and rapid technological change, the whole process of design and building has become ever more difficult. There has been an increase not only in the number of different types of buildings needed, but also in the size and complexity of projects. The number of alternatives has also increased: more feasible solutions, more materials, systems and technologies available, more experts and specialists, and a greater number of schools of thought than in the past. In addition, there are countless other problems to be contended with: bureaucracy, controls, regulations and standards; new imperatives such as energy conservation and changing social needs; the explosion of information; economic constraints and a growing demand for guaranteed performance-in-use. Also, as the process becomes more involved and susceptible to delays, time becomes a scarcer commodity and developments are expected much faster.

The increasingly complex operations to be performed, the mass of information to be collected, the involvement of many people who have contributions to make, and the number of decisions to be taken in the design of even the simplest of buildings, have all made it more and more difficult to rely on intuition and experience alone. As a result thorough briefing has, in recent years, rightly come to be seen as an integral part of the design process.

4. How to use this book

Each *Guide* covers a major building type. Section 1 is relevant to all projects: it provides an outline description of the briefing process and the main participants and gives detailed guidelines for the initial procedure that is basic to any project. It stands as a checklist for the architect, as well as supplying clients with a framework within which to consider their requirements.

The main body of the text is contained in Section 2. This is specific to the building type and includes aids to concept-selection and basic design information. It is divided into five parts: introduction, inception, feasibility, detailed brief and design. The text is in the form of instructions and checklists with comprehensive source and detail information, and is backed up by the appendices. The first three parts of Section 2 are for all concerned with the briefing/design process. The last two parts are intended mainly for the design team but can usefully be referred to by clients and users so that they are aware of the type of information required by the design team for the later design stages.

SECTION ONE
GENERAL

Introduction

1.1 Buildings

Buildings represent, amongst other things, energy, labour and materials. These either cannot be replaced or can only be replaced at great cost. The need for economic prudence and energy conservation, coupled with a growing awareness that resources are finite have led to the realisation that existing buildings are a valuable commodity to be conserved, regardless of their historic or architectural merits, and in addition, that new buildings must be designed and built to last.

Building development today is increasingly concerned with the recyling of space in one way or another. This may be done by:

— extension or addition to a structure owned by the client to provide more space or new facilities.
— alteration of, or modification to, existing premises, which does not lead to a change of use.
— maintenance or refurbishment of an existing structure to improve its appearance and prolong its life.
— conversion of existing premises involving a change of use, for example, from a warehouse to offices or an hotel.

Conversion and rehabilitation are important not only from the point of view of physical resources, but also as a means of revitalising older, densely built, run-down inner-city areas.

In the case of new work and of many conversion or extension projects, a major goal is to provide a building of 'long life, low energy usage and loose fit' – in other words, to reduce capital turnover by making it continually viable with low fuel and maintenance costs as well as easily adaptable to changing use. On the point of changing use: although it is important to identify and design for the specific users, there is an increasing emphasis on flexibility so that the building created will be adaptable to the extent of being able to accommodate changes in activities and requirements during a lifespan of 50 years or more.

1.2 Design and construction methods

There are two basic approaches, each with variations, which a client can adopt for the design and construction of new building work, and an early decision has to be taken on which general method will be most appropriate for the project.

One option is to employ independent consultants for the design and then, at a later stage, a contractor to build the project. This method is used for many projects of all types and sizes undertaken by private clients, and has several advantages. For example, it allows the freedom to choose a briefing and design team most suited to one's specific needs from the large variety of consultant firms. It also allows the freedom to obtain competitive tenders for the construction, based on the same drawings and specifications, although it is possible for the design team to negotiate with a single contractor.

The other option is to employ a single firm for both the design and the construction of the project, a method also referred to as a 'package deal' or a 'turn-key' operation. There are a variety of construction companies offering this type of integrated service. Some supply standard buildings only, some undertake one-off projects, some do both; some specialise in building types, for example, warehouses, factories, offices, hotels, schools or housing; some produce building systems which they use in their projects; some specialise in simple single-storey structures, while others undertake complex and multi-storey projects. These companies employ their own professional staff, either in-house or outside consultants, who develop the brief and design for specific projects. Although it is possible to approach different companies and have each submit a proposal, it can be difficult to compare prices as they will not be based on identical designs and specifications. The client may, furthermore, have to bear the costs of the proposals submitted by the unsuccessful firms. While this method may save time and/or money on certain types of projects, a disadvantage can be the lack of advice from the consultants of one's own choice.

Increasingly adopted by some clients is a compromise solution whereby design consultants are employed to produce scheme design proposals only, and contractors bid to complete the design as well as construct. This approach can avoid many of the pitfalls of standard design and build procedures.

Which of the two basic methods is used will depend largely on the nature of the problem, the type, size and complexity of the proposed project, as well as the time available for its completion. It is ultimately up to the client and his initial advisers to investigate alternatives and make sure that participants, whether independent consultants or design/construct firms, are carefully selected.

1.3 The brief and the briefing process

Once the client has decided to investigate the possibility of altering, extending or converting an existing building, or erecting a new one, the first phase of the proposed project begins. This is the development of the brief through the process of briefing.

A brief is usually a document which can vary considerably in length, content and form depending upon the nature and complexity of the project. It is, amongst other things, a recorded statement of intent and a set of criteria and instructions, including proposals by the design team approved by the client. It is influenced by and derived from the consideration of many factors such as budget, climate, site, legal constraints, user requirements, the way things are used and change through time, and the trade-off between cost and feasibility. It states a set of desired

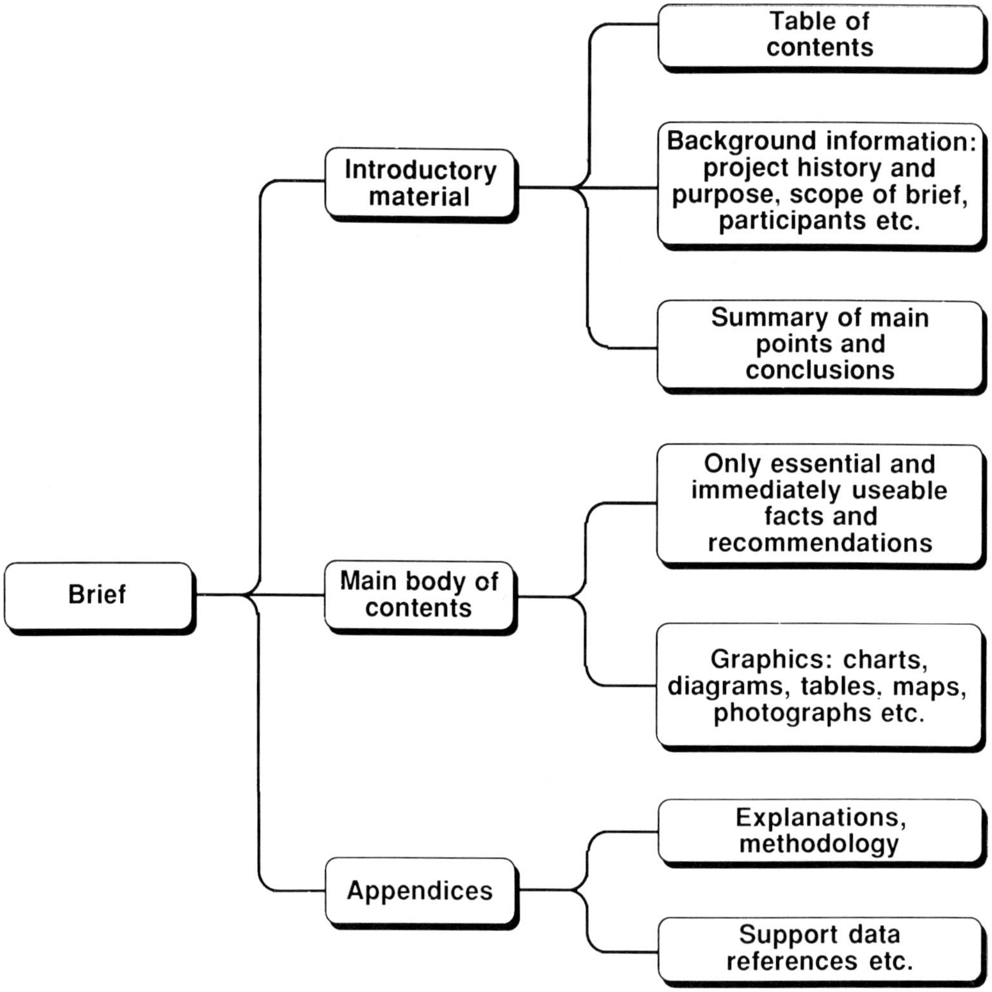

Fig. 1.1 *Different forms of brief: this may be either one of the four shown or a combination of them (e.g. 1 and 4), and typical organisation of contents.*

conditions and it is a way of defining, ordering and specifying objectives, requirements and intentions systematically, as well as outlining the methods for achieving them.

Rather than being an end in itself, the brief is a tool that can help those involved to achieve certain desirable ends. It can be used in different ways depending on the problem. For example, a preliminary brief can assist the client to select the right designers and other specialist advisers; a more developed brief (interim or final) may be used as a competition document or a contractual document forming part of a legal agreement between the client and other parties. Although the ultimate goal is usually to provide the specific information and recommendations that are needed and can be used for designing the building, the brief is also used to determine feasibility and may lead to the abandonment of the project.

Starting with a preliminary statement prepared by the client (possibly with professional help), the brief is developed and constantly refined through a process

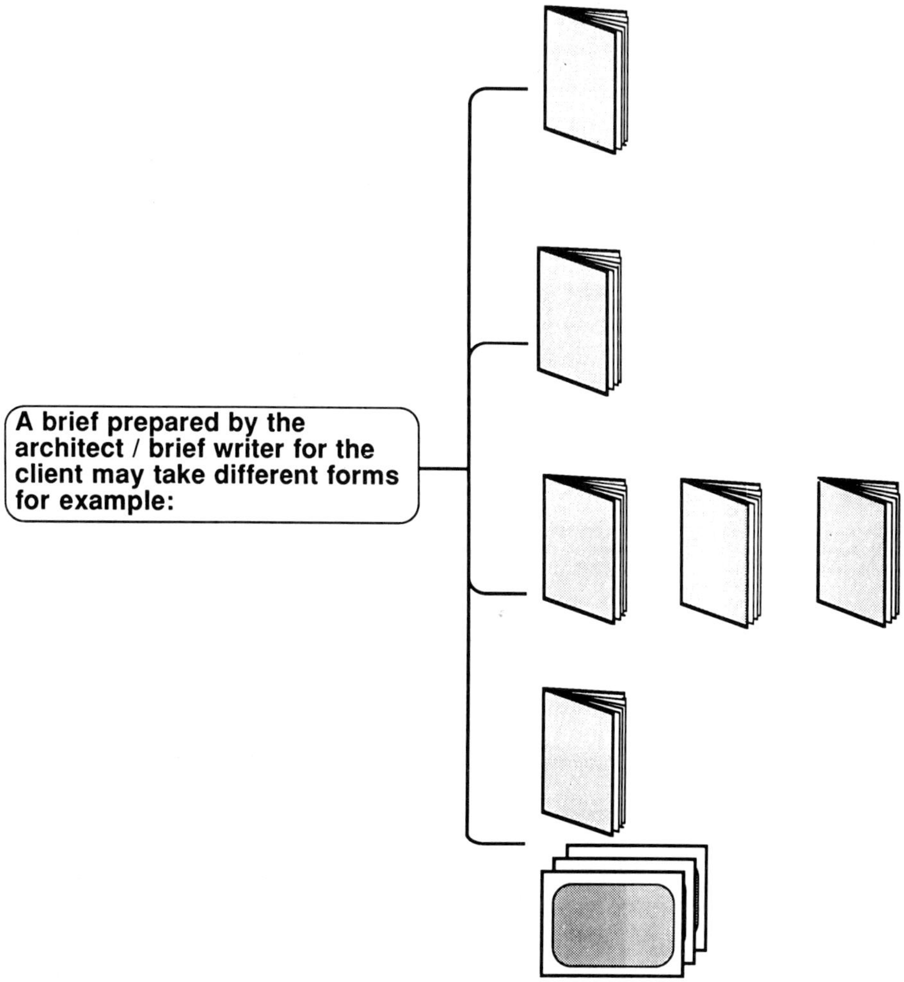

1. *A short preliminary report.*

2. *A comprehensive document covering all aspects of the building design.*

3. *A series of reports relating definable issues or phased accomplishments.*

4. *A special purpose report covering a specific aspect such as energy conservation or site analysis/survey. This may also take the form of an audiovisual presentation.*

of communication, investigation, analysis and evaluation. The process of briefing is, in other words, one of dialogue between all concerned; a process of finding as well as solving problems; of determining and defining objectives, constraints, resources, subjective and objective criteria; of determining and exploring what is appropriate and possible, evaluating proposals and making recommendations. Briefing is often controversial since, while technical requirements can usually be quantified, this is often not possible with other more abstract criteria. It should therefore be a process of debate and a means of decision-making, encouraging participation by, and feedback from, all the participants.

The brief, therefore, changes and grows continuously as the design proceeds. The design solution evolves from the brief and can, in turn, clarify and expand it through early design work which helps to identify problems, objectives and criteria. When it is realised in the completed project, it also has a role in post-construction evaluation. After a certain point in the design process, which will

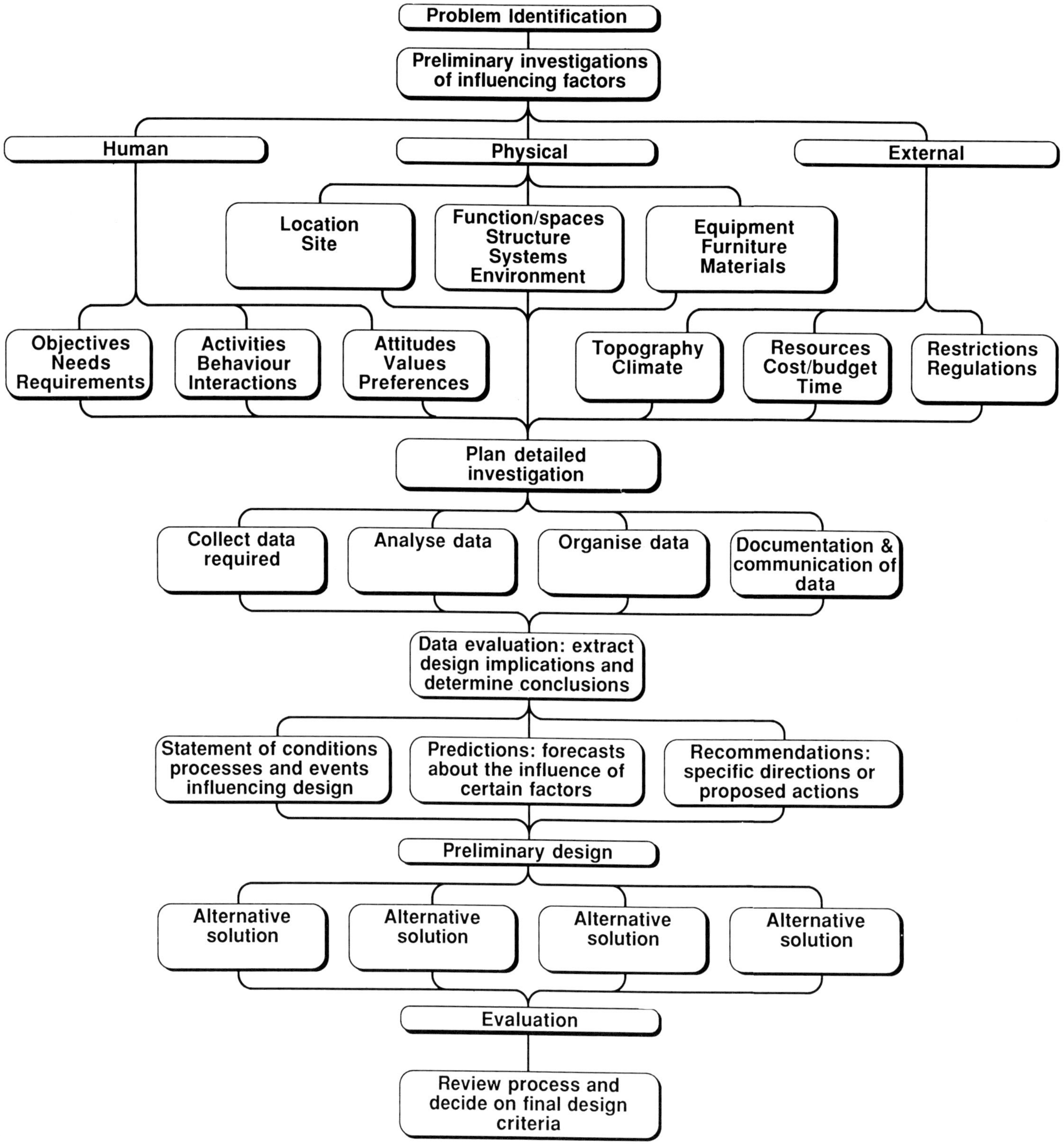
Problem Identification
Preliminary investigations of influencing factors
Human
Physical
External
Location Site
Function/spaces Structure Systems Environment
Equipment Furniture Materials
Objectives Needs Requirements
Activities Behaviour Interactions
Attitudes Values Preferences
Topography Climate
Resources Cost/budget Time
Restrictions Regulations
Plan detailed investigation
Collect data required
Analyse data
Organise data
Documentation & communication of data
Data evaluation: extract design implications and determine conclusions
Statement of conditions processes and events influencing design
Predictions: forecasts about the influence of certain factors
Recommendations: specific directions or proposed actions
Preliminary design
Alternative solution
Alternative solution
Alternative solution
Alternative solution
Evaluation
Review process and decide on final design criteria

vary from project to project, major changes to the brief can lead to abortive work and have cost implications for the client or the design team.

Although, as has already been stressed, there is no one way of approaching briefing, it always forms the foundation of the design process and constitutes an integral part of this process. For these reasons and because there are usually so many factors and variables involved in the design of even the simplest building, it is important that the brief be objectively, imaginatively and comprehensively developed whatever the method used.

Fig. 1.2 *Although the briefing process can be approached in different ways, the flow chart at left outlines the common activities involved in developing the required information.*

1.4 The main participants

The main groups involved in the process of briefing and design are the client, the users, the professional brief writer and the design team.

The client

The client is the person or organisation initiating and paying for the project. There are many different types of client ranging from private individuals to complex private and public organisations. Not only is the nature of each type different but so also are their needs, objectives, values, priorities, resources and restraints. Some build for their own use; others are providers of space rather than users of the building; yet others act for and on behalf of the actual users; for some, building is a commercial venture, while for others the basic motive may, for example, have to do with welfare, education or culture.

While clients in the public sector are controlled by predetermined rules and procedures affecting organisation, approval, financing and time-scale, private clients have relative freedom. Client responsibilities also tend to differ. In the public sector, the client departments are very often responsible not only for initiating the project, selecting the site, instructing the consultants and monitoring progress, but also for gathering and co-ordinating information from various departments, producing the initial brief and preparing the documents required for outline planning applications, loan sanctions, and so on.

Private clients, on the other hand, often leave some of these responsibilities, for example, the gathering and organisation of basic data, and preparation of an initial (or preliminary) brief, to the architect. Alternatively they may appoint a professional brief writer to assist them. At an early stage the client must determine the extent of his personal involvement which should, at the very least, be sufficient to ensure that responsibilities delegated to others are being adequately discharged.

It is not difficult for individual clients or small organisations to have a simple, ideally single, line of contact between themselves and the other participants. However, the more complex the client body – the greater the number of people, departments and sections involved, and the greater the levels of hierarchy – the more difficult it becomes to determine just who is the client. It follows that in this case it is important for the roles and responsibilities of all those involved, in management, professional and advisory capacities, and for the channels of communication (particularly on a day-to-day basis), to be clearly defined to avoid delays and confusion.

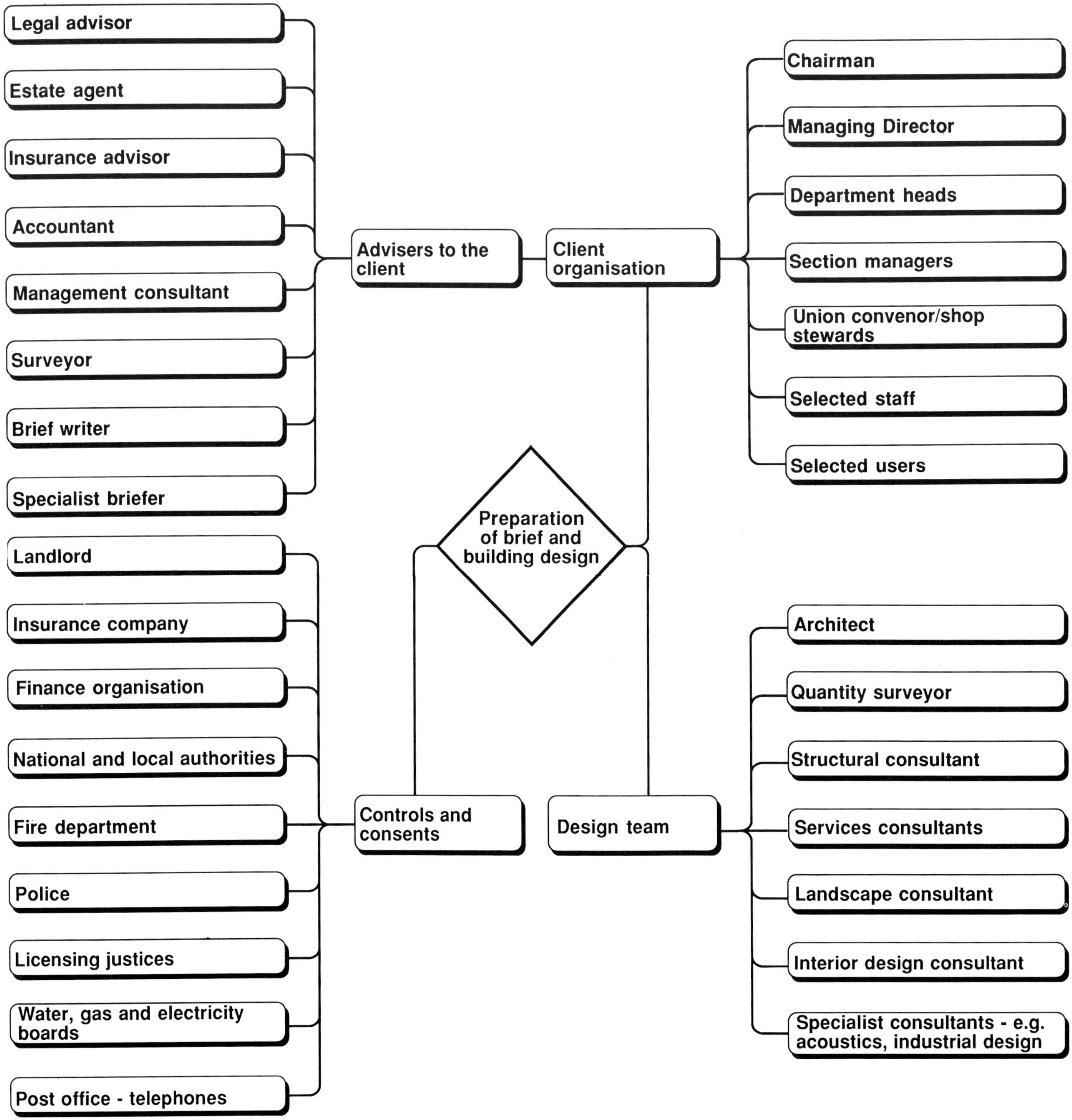
Legal advisor
Estate agent
Insurance advisor
Accountant
Management consultant
Surveyor
Brief writer
Specialist briefer
Advisers to the client
Client organisation
Chairman
Managing Director
Department heads
Section managers
Union convenor/shop stewards
Selected staff
Selected users
Preparation of brief and building design
Landlord
Insurance company
Finance organisation
National and local authorities
Fire department
Police
Licensing justices
Water, gas and electricity boards
Post office - telephones
Controls and consents
Design team
Architect
Quantity surveyor
Structural consultant
Services consultants
Landscape consultant
Interior design consultant
Specialist consultants - e.g. acoustics, industrial design

The users

The users are those who will actually use the building: they may live, work, play or relax in it; they may be permanent inhabitants or employees who use it daily, or members of the general public who visit it regularly or occasionally. Clients and users are very often different bodies: public authorities and speculative developers are examples of clients who, together with their professional consultants, brief and design on behalf of the eventual users. As a result, few users have the opportunity of influencing the original design, and all too often their requirements and likely use of the spaces are based on assumptions.

In many building types there is the problem of different kinds of users. In hospitals, for example, nurses, doctors, patients and visitors are all users. They may have different or even conflicting requirements. The various categories of user must be identified at an early stage as it is important to understand the implications of their requirements, and to be responsive to them. How this is done will depend on circumstances and vary from project to project. One or more of the following methods may be used:

— direct involvement and participation: permanent staff or regular users may be represented or consulted through unions, local organisations and pressure groups. This encourages an active role in the process by helping to define problems and objectives, to generate concepts and evaluate alternatives. In some instances this might be essential, while in others it might hinder the process or be impossible.

— social science and other user studies: a helpful source of data, but care should be taken because such studies may be generalised and in the planning of a building specific requirements are necessary. On the other hand it must also be borne in mind that the very specific data which are often provided in these studies may not necessarily be relevant to any one particular problem. If studies are to be carried out specifically for a project by surveys, interviews, questionnaires or observation, for example, the designers' limitations must be taken into account and collaboration with suitable consultants from the field of human sciences should be considered.

— surveys of similar building types in use to provide feedback on user requirements. Many of the building studies published in architectural journals tend to concentrate on visual aesthetics and technical aspects, lacking sufficient information on actual usage. If private surveys are undertaken, the method of study and appraisal should place emphasis on evidence from various users: on the deficiencies and advantages they find while living, working, playing or relaxing in the building in question.

The professional brief writer

The professional brief writer specialises in helping clients determine and describe their building needs. This person is, generally speaking, qualified not only to carry out analytical, objective, unbiased and creative studies of the clients' and users' needs, but also to understand their implications for design. He may be:

— a member of the client organisation.

Fig. 1.3 *People who may be involved in the briefing and design process. Just who will participate will depend, amongst other things, on the size of the client organisation and on the type and complexity of the project.*

— an architect who provides a briefing service either separately or as part of design services (see also Appendix A.4).
— a professional brief writer, who may or may not be an architect, but who specialises in the process of briefing and the preparation of briefs.
— a briefing specialist who provides a service for a particular building type.

The professional brief writer may only be involved with preparing an initial policy-briefing document or may be retained, with the approval of the architect and other members of the design team, to help develop a detailed brief, and possibly to help evaluate plans and proposals, as the work progresses.

The design team

The design team is made up of the architect together with various other appointed consultants each of whom specialise in one aspect of the design process. The team may include a quantity surveyor, structural, electrical and mechanical engineers, an interior designer, a landscape architect, as well as other specialists from various disciplines, possibly used on a short-term or *ad hoc* basis as dictated by the project. The responsibilities of this group include advising the client and users of the options available to them, assisting with the development of the brief, and carrying out the actual designing and managing activities.

In very large or very complex projects it may be necessary to include an experienced project manager or project controller who would be responsible for the overall co-ordination and monitoring of the total project from inception to completion. This person may be an architect, surveyor or engineer specialising exclusively in this service, and usually also acts as the liaison officer between all the parties involved.

All these consultants are generally in private practices, and although some large consultant firms may include a variety of specialists under one roof they are certain to need outside help on occasion. The same is true of the public sector and large private client organisations that have their own design offices.

1.5 Approvals

Another group of people who, although not directly involved in the briefing and design process, exert an important influence on all phases of the work, are the representatives of the various public authorities responsible for applying the appropriate legislation and regulations. There is a vast amount which governs new building work and involves discussion with and formal application to various public authorities. For example:

— planning applications – for new developments, changes of use and certain extensions – to the appropriate local planning authority. These are usually in two stages: the first is an 'outline' application giving information on the general intention; the second is a 'full' application accompanied by drawings illustrating the scheme in detail.
— application to the local authority responsible for administering the Building Regulations. Detailed drawings, specifications and structural

calculations must be submitted and approval obtained before any construction work begins.

— the local fire authority must inspect and approve premises before issuing a fire certificate; the local health officer and the district surveyor will need to be consulted on requirements for fire precautions, lighting, ventilation and the provision of sanitary conveniences.

— other individuals or organisations may have to be consulted or give their approval: for example, the local gas, electricity, water and telephone authorities; the landlord or lessor; the insurance company; owners of adjoining properties.

It will be evident from this introduction that the statutory implications of embarking on new building work can be daunting to say the least. The exercise of attending to the requirements is a time-consuming and often a frustrating one, usually taken care of by the architect and other members of the design team. However, some applications, such as special licences, have to be attended to by the client himself, possibly with legal help.

Inception and the preliminary brief

The aim of this phase is to prepare a general outline of requirements and to plan future action. The procedure is a sequence of actions, listed below, which, generally speaking, is standard (in basics only) for all projects irrespective of building type. These steps are supplementary to those given under Section 2, 'Inception and initial brief', and should be used in conjunction with them.

The client must take certain action, possibly with professional help, before any real work on the brief commences. The problem must be defined: the questions who? what? why? where? when? and how? must be considered.

1.6 Client to define problem

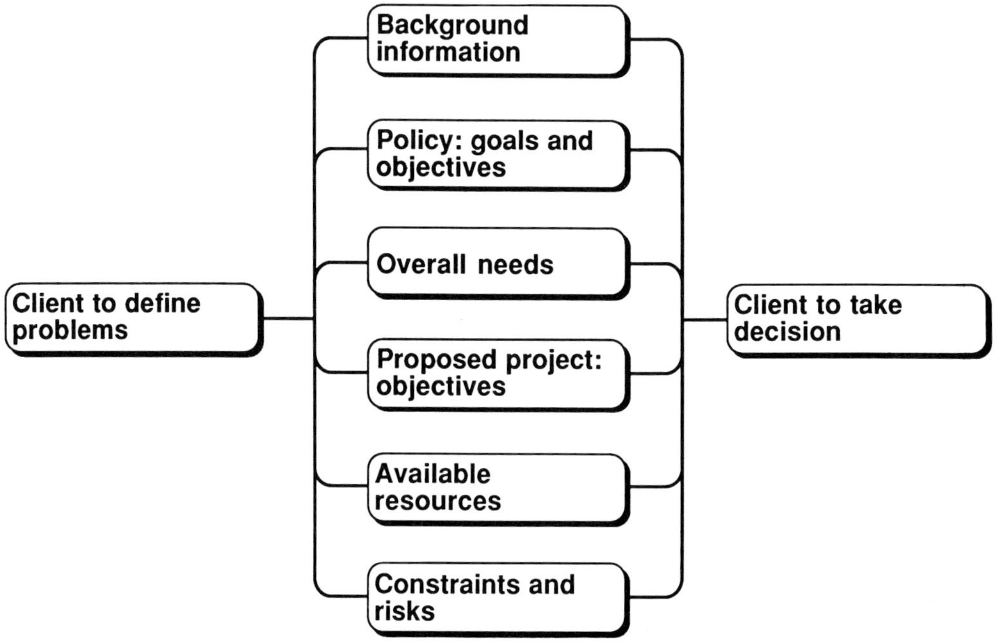

Background information

Describe the client enterprise/body as fully as possible, for example:
- function or purpose for existence, and activities.
- philosophy and history.
- structure and method of operation.
- characteristics: whether conservative or experimental, formal or informal.
- existing facilities with information on problems.

Members of the client body (for example, management, department heads, key staff) should be brought in and encouraged to assist with the various aspects of problem definition and formulation of objectives.
Although it may not be appropriate to set up a briefing and design team at this stage, preliminary general advice may be needed on various aspects such as legal, estate, management and financial which will vary with such factors as the experience of the client and the size and complexity of the proposed project.

Policy: goals and objectives

Determine what the aims and policies are for future growth and change in terms of:
- overall functions to be fulfilled.
- size, achievement, performance, organisation.
- short (2-year), medium (5-year) and long (10-year-plus) term.

Consider:
- why these objectives are important. What the alternatives are. Who will benefit from the achievement of the objectives.
- other parties involved (for example, user groups) who may have different or conflicting objectives.
- what the overriding priorities are.

Overall needs

Estimate present and future overall needs in terms of:
- number and type of staff and/or users.
- activities and equipment to be housed.

Estimate need for additional building space over short (2-year), medium (5-year) and long (10-year-plus) term.

Proposed project: objectives

Formulate in general terms (not detail) objectives for, and broad scope of, proposed project: What is required of it? What will it include and exclude? What are the priorities?
Consider:
- location, site, relationship with other buildings, landscaping.
- size of proposed building: number of people, type of process and equipment, activities it must accommodate. What floor area is required?
- special spaces or facilities required and special equipment to be housed.
- internal environment: ventilation, lighting, heating and services.
- energy use/conservation.
- maintenance.
- lifespan and flexibility: probable changes of use over time.
- prestige level externally and internally: appearance, height of building/spaces, quality of finishes.
- timing: How important is completion date? How urgent is starting date? Can project be done in phases?
- cost implications within a time-frame.

At this stage all that it requires are broad guidelines rather than rigid details; there must be flexibility for continual development and change – for additions, omissions and revisions.
To generate and develop ideas, and establish priorities, techniques such as brain storming may be useful. See Appendix A.5 for a summary of these and references to useful sources of more detailed information.

Fig. 1.4 *Defining and ranking objectives.*

1 = objective in row is preferred to objective in column
0 = objective in column is preferred to objective in row

It is impossible to start the process of briefing and design without first defining objectives which are, because of the nature of the problem, difficult to separate from the ways of achieving them. One way of exploring and clarifying objectives is to construct an objective 'tree'. Start by listing the known objectives. For example, when considering the design of fire protection for a building the broad goals might be to:
— reduce likelihood of death or injury to occupants and users.
— protect the building fabric.
— protect the contents.

Each of these can be expanded into sub-objectives that can be further sub-divided:

The first basic objective, to reduce likelihood of death and injury, can be analysed in the same way. The objective 'tree' itself does not provide any answers and these are most likely to come as a result of working through the process itself: as a result of asking oneself the questions what? why? how? The exercise should provide a starting-point for discussion that will help to identify which objectives really are essential, which are compatible with each other, and how each relates to the resources available.

Once objectives are identified a matrix can be used to help determine objectives. The value of this method becomes more apparent when there is a large list of objectives to consider making it more difficult to rank them intuitively. One disadvantage is that comparison by pairs can result in illogical responses, for example, choosing B over A, A over C and then C over B. If such a matrix is filled in by a number of people the results should be randomly checked for such responses to ensure that they are valid.

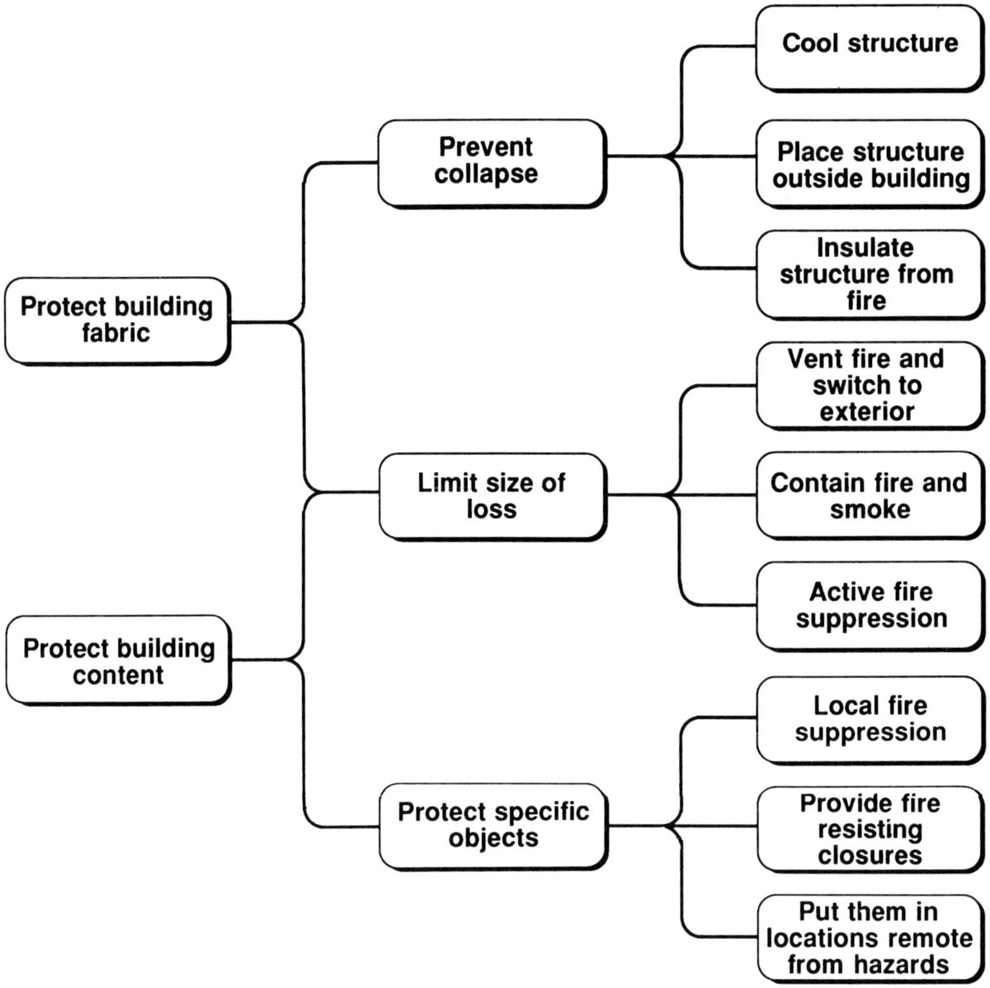

Objective	A	B	C	D	E	Row totals	Ranking
A		0	0	0	1	1	4
B	1		1	0	1	3	2
C	1	0		0	1	2	3
D	1	1	1		1	4	1
E	0	0	0	0		0	5

Available resources

Estimate your own and all other available present and future resources, for example:

- own finance, manpower, time, building space and land.
- access to other finance: share issue, grants and loans.
- availability of materials, manpower, energy and land.

Constraints and risks

Determine all possible constraints:

- shortage of resources, for example, finance and time, and/or cost of capital needed.
- site.
- legal and consents: special licence required, planning consent.
- tax implications in terms of time-scale.

Consider various ways of reconciling need and objectives with available resources without undue risk, for example:

- cash flow and commitment of resources.
- risk assessment, spread and sharing.

1.7 Decision

In terms of the foregoing consider reasons for and against building:

- is there really a need or demand for the type of facility under review?
- relate potential need/demand and stated objectives to resources, constraints and risks: What does one wish to accomplish? Will it be possible to achieve this?

Consider which of the following will be most appropriate:

- decrease demand or need for building space.
- rent space.
- buy building suited to needs.
- buy and convert building.
- expand or adapt present accommodation.
- build new building.

This is a preliminary decision only: it is a decision to proceed to the next stage, that is to invest time and a predetermined sum of money to start the formal process of briefing and design in order to investigate in detail the feasibility of the proposed project.
A decision to go ahead may be the correct one at this stage. The briefing and design process extends over a period of time, however, and as new information becomes available at a later stage it will be necessary to review the decision.

1.8 Initial procedures by client

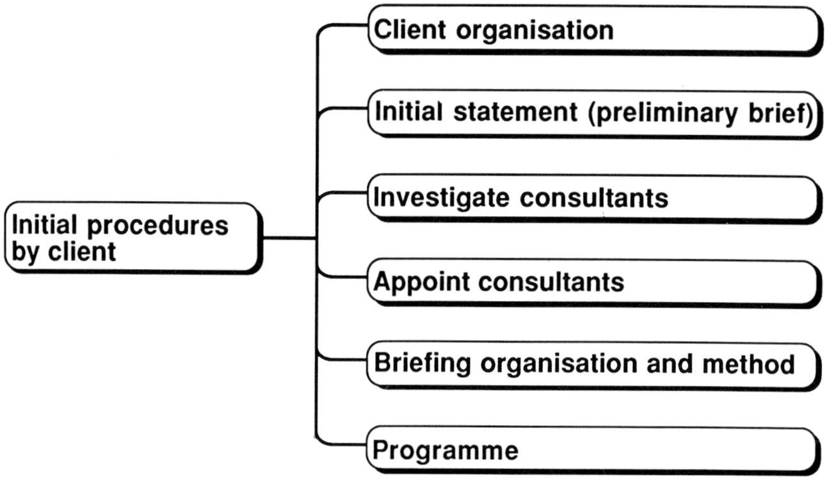

Client organisation

Set up organisation for decision-making and for management of the project from the client side.

Consider the following:

— committee or working party.

— departmental representatives.

— liaison with briefing and design team particularly on a day-to-day basis.

Determine roles and responsibilities of all concerned including who will be responsible for initial statement:

— is there sufficient expertise within the client organisation to do the required work?

— if not, consider appointing a professional brief writer or approaching specialists appropriate to this task.

Initial statement (preliminary brief)

This statement should be based on information and ideas used to arrive at the decision to proceed. It may be prepared by the client, someone within the client organisation or a professional brief writer.

Steps listed under 1.9 can be used as a checklist for the kind of information that should be included.

Prepare a written preliminary document: a statement of aims and requirements including all available relevant information. Describe:

— the nature of the client body and the implications of that fact.

— why a building is needed.

— what objectives should be met by the proposed building, setting out priorities.

Investigate consultants

Determine what consultants will be required at this stage and whether they should be appointed for developing the brief only or for briefing and design:

— professional brief writer and/or briefing specialist.
— architect.
— surveyor: for obtaining accurate site information or when adapting/converting existing building.
— quantity surveyor: for cost estimates.
— structural, mechanical and electrical engineers.
— other specialists: landscape architect, interior designer.

Investigate suitable firms and ascertain position with regard to services provided, fees, contracts etc. Consider, amongst other things:

— experience of architects and other consultants in dealing with similar building types/projects.
— personalities: close working relationship and confidence between all concerned is important.

For summarised guidance on services offered, fees charged etc. by the main groups of consultants see Appendix A.4.
The type and size of project, as well as, amongst other things, the aesthetic qualities envisaged will influence the choice of architect and the decision on what other consultants/specialists are required.

Appoint consultants

Approach selected firms and discuss terms. Appoint the following:

— architect: to prepare brief only; or for complete project; or something in between.
— other consultants required now; further appointments may have to be made at a later stage.

Consult architect for his recommendations regarding the most suitable consultants.

Formal agreement should include definitions of limits of responsibility, precise scope of services to be provided, time implications, details of fees and expenses etc. Standard forms may be used; exchange of letters may be adequate.

Briefing organisation and method

Establish formal organisation for briefing and design process: committee, steering group etc. Identify likely participants and define:

— relationship to client organisation.
— a single client instruction route. This is particularly important if the client is a public authority or a government department, or in the case of a joint use project with more than one client.
— responsibilities and procedures, for example administration and control.
— role to be played in process by users and/or user organisations.

Decide on briefing methods:

— communication: regular meetings, circulation of documents etc.
— documentation, for example recording of data and decisions for easy retrieval and reference.
— techniques: surveys, use of computer etc.

An outline of some briefing methods and techniques is given in Appendix A.5; for more detailed information see Appendix A.1.a: Jones[1], Palmer[2], Preiser[3] and Sanoff[4].

Use Section 2 as a checklist of steps to be taken/tasks to be done. A simple linear sequence will not, however, be suitable for drawing up a programme since there is bound to be overlapping. Techniques are available to help in the preparation of charts that relate overlapping steps to time. See Fig. 1.5.

A quantity surveyor and an accountant will be best suited to give advice on building economics and financial implications. For outline information see Appendix A.4.

Programme

Identify and schedule briefing and design work:

— list tasks to be done and decisions to be made.

— assign responsibilities: who will be involved with each task and when.

— estimate financial and other resources needed.

Determine realistic timetable. Consider:

— key target dates set by external circumstances: expiry of lease on existing premises etc.

— dates for building commencement and completion.

— effect of seasons on building operations.

— scope of project and quality of work required.

— availability of manpower.

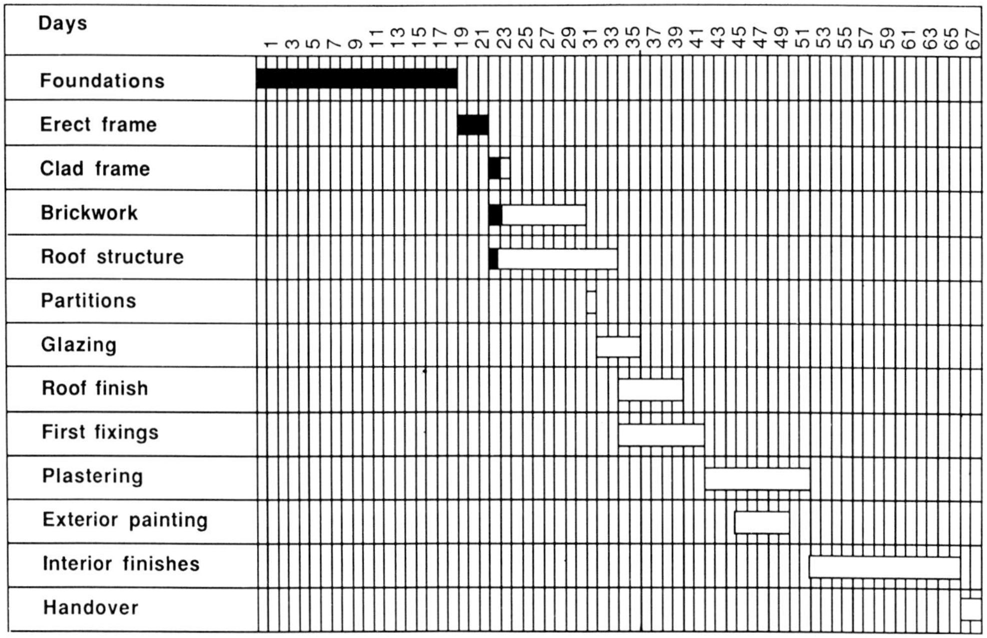

A.

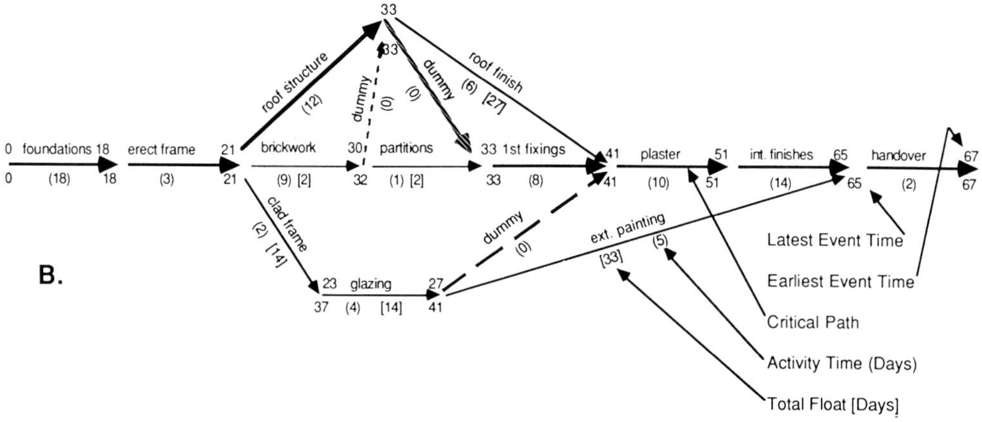

B.

Fig. 1.5 *A. A simple bar chart showing estimated duration of sequential steps or activities in relation to a time scale. Dependencies between the activities are not indicated in such a chart. This means that should one activity be delayed it is not immediately apparent how this will affect subsequent events. B. A critical path method (CPM) chart in which interconnecting arrows form a network diagram with the time of each activity shown below each arrow (in curved brackets). This is a sophisticated method used for charting time overlaps and activity interdependencies amongst other things, and from which the critical path – the sequence of interdependent activities which establishes the shortest possible time in which a project can be completed – is determined.*

— cash flow over time.
— financial implications of timing, for example, income on investment versus interest paid on loan.

1.9 General data and objectives

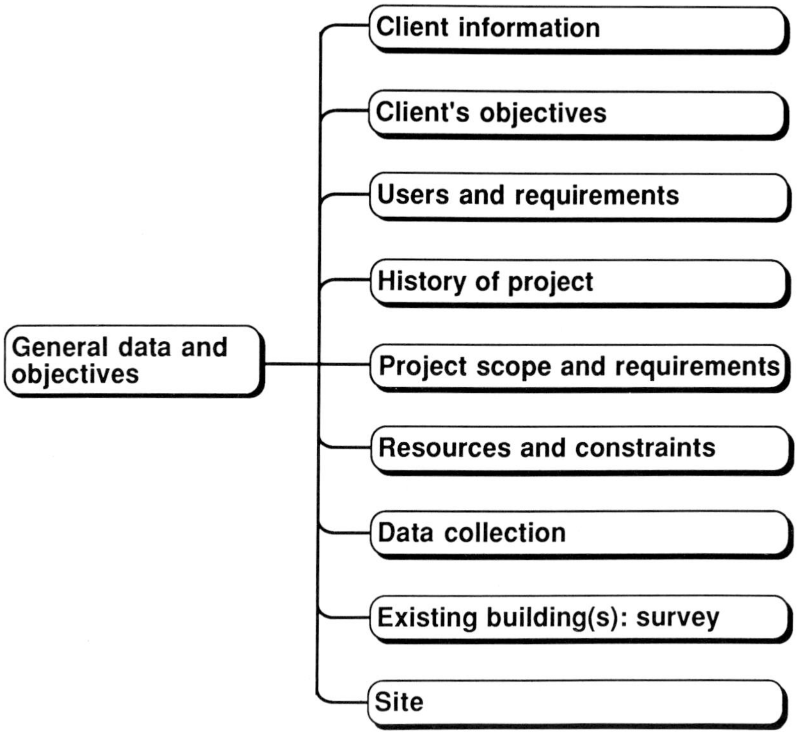

Although addressed to the architect the following should be used by the client, and whoever assists him, as a guideline to the information required in the 'Initial statement' (see p.16). Read together with 2.6.

Client information

Evaluate preliminary client statement. Check that all information on the nature and character of the client enterprise/body is available:
— what they do, how they do it: public authority, joint venture, private concern or other.
— whom they employ or collaborate with.
— involvement with outside services.
— corporate priorities and the likelihood of change.

Client's objectives

Ensure that all information regarding the client's overriding objectives and priorities – both short and long term – is available:

— financial return required or service to the community (social, cultural, educational).
— image to be projected.
— planned or predicted growth and likelihood of change.

Users and requirements

Method(s) used will vary with circumstances and building type. For a broad description of survey methods see Appendix A.5.

Establish who the potential users are if not the client. If possible take steps to contact the different kinds of users. Decide how user requirements are to be communicated/determined, for example:

— direct involvement/consultation: through union or elected representatives.
— and/or through questionnaire/survey.
— and/or through building studies.

History of project

It may be necessary to contact any other architect involved in accordance with RIBA code of conduct.
If possible/relevant go through client records and documents for information directly related to proposed project. Avoid duplicating work already done, for example, data collection.

Check whether any work has previously been undertaken:

— feasibility or other.
— have any other consultants been involved? Has their work been paid for?
— have any decisions already been made?
— has data already been collected?

Project scope and requirements

Who decides what will depend upon circumstances. The architect and/or professional brief writer must, however, ensure that the client and users are aware of the available options, and that the necessary decisions are made and understood by all.
See Appendix A.1.a: Alexander[5] which is a useful tool for all involved in the briefing and design process: a variety of options at various levels/scales are listed and described.

Determine the scope, limitations and basic requirements of the proposed project:

— demand for the type of facility envisaged.
— proposed size; future expansion; phasing? If maximum predicted space is built immediately can present surplus be sub-let?
— degree of flexibility/adaptability required, i.e. the likely use of the building over a period of time.
— character envisaged.
— interface with outside world, for example, free or controlled access.
— requirements for space and equipment; relationships between component parts, individuals etc.; standards for accommodation – environmental, finishes etc.
— other criteria, for example, energy conservation.

Resources and constraints

Ensure that all necessary information on available resources and possible constraints is either included in the initial statement or, alternatively, obtained from the client. Consider particularly:

— budget (cost limit): what is included in the cost of building, equipment and furniture, landscaping, consultants' fees?
— whether the effects of inflation have been taken into account.
— recommended and mandatory standards, statutory requirements, regulations and restrictions affecting the project. Draw up a list for reference purposes.
— other resources that can be used (expertise, manpower) and imposed constraints (cash flow, time limits).
— how the resources and constraints relate to the requirements and objectives.

For detailed information on the building regulations in the UK see Appendix A.1.a: Elder[6]; Speaight[7] is a useful reference covering the law of property and land and building regulations amongst other things.

Data collection

Organise and analyse data presently available. Consider:

— relevance, relationships, priorities.
— what information still needs to be obtained and/or confirmed? For what purpose?
— the form in which it is required, by when it will be needed and who will carry out the various tasks. How will this affect the programme?
— the primary information sources for the different kinds of data needed: client, user groups, publications.

Gather data in relation to stated needs/objectives and in time to be useful; confine initial surveys (user requirements, site) to bare essentials, and to data that are readily available and immediately useful. Balance the penalty of insufficient information against the cost of obtaining it. Store data in a flexible way so that new information can be added readily.
Different techniques may be needed for obtaining different types of data: for summaries of the main methods see Appendix A.5.

Existing building(s): survey

Where applicable, survey/appraise existing building(s): premises presently occupied to be altered/extended or new premises to be converted.

— measure up and prepare survey drawings.
— investigate construction, materials, elements, finishes, services.
— prepare report on all defects including cause and recommended method of correction.

In premises presently occupied, how is client accommodated now? This is useful as basis for comparison even when new building is being planned.
Determine:

— how the building has been used through the period of occupation.
— the deficiencies and advantages in terms of the various users' needs.
— running costs, for example, maintenance, operation and changes.

Specific guidance on finding new premises is not given here. Specialist help may be required for the survey and report: to open up and examine foundations and structure; to trace services; to investigate rot, woodworm.
For outline of approach to evaluation of existing buildings see Appendix A.5.

Site

The same basic technique is followed for both site selection and site survey/analysis. Appendix A.2 sets out the requirements in broad outline.
The survey and analysis is a very important part of the brief investigation and development. Data gathering can, however, be expensive and time-consuming and the survey must be well planned. It is generally advisable to employ the services of a qualified surveyor.

Where applicable, investigate site. If client owns specific site:
— visit and inspect.
— check if survey is available; if not, arrange for survey to be prepared.

If site is not fixed:
— investigate alternatives; determine appropriateness for proposed development.
— will owner sell? Is sale price reasonable: how does it compare with valuation by local authority? Are there any legal problems?
— make proposal based on analysis of potential sites.

SECTION TWO
OFFICES

Introduction

2.1 General

Definitions of what constitutes an office are becoming increasingly blurred as the range of activities which can be described collectively as 'work' proliferates. The growth of the application of technology to traditional office functions has furthered the confusion to the point where the lines between offices, factories, laboratories, studios and even homes and cars can be difficult to distinguish. In parallel with this, the proportion of the population involved in office occupations is shifting; the industrial revolution moved the emphasis from agriculture, and similarly this second revolution is reflected by a decline in primary manufacturing. As a direct consequence large numbers of buildings whose original function is no longer viable are being converted to offices; offices catering for occupations and using equipment which could not have been envisaged when the building was designed.

The new technologies have created many jobs which did not exist previously; jobs directly concerned with the production and development of computer hardware and software, and the application of them to commercial activities. However, it is not these jobs which have caused the need to reconsider approaches to office design, but rather it is the spread of technology to existing office work.

In the not very distant past an office consisted simply of a room, or a series of rooms, where people worked at desks or spoke on telephones. Additional space would be needed for reception areas, meetings, and to store all the bits of paper which emanated from these activities.

What then constitutes and defines the high-technology office? There are many items of complex equipment where the only provision necessary in terms of the building is a 13 amp socket and, although there may be other considerations such as heat loads, ergonomics and lighting on which relevant information will be found in this guide, essentially they require very little that differs from the traditional office.

The developments which radically altered the requirements placed upon the office environment began with computerisation. Early computers were large, cumbersome and very susceptible to environmental change. The people who operated them were specialists, working in spaces more akin to laboratories than offices. Now the situation has changed; although machine rooms housing mainframe computers are often needed, they are linked directly to terminals within normal office space. In addition, personal computers, often interlinked, sit on desks alongside word-processors, modems, telephones and facsimile machines. The loadings placed on the services of a building by this plethora of equipment, and the frequency of change to the equipment and its interconnections, are in part what puts it within the scope of this book; but it is mainly the fact that high-technology equipment is now commonly used in normal office space, not by specialists, but by all manner of workers as a tool to assist their function. This guide sets out to assist in the process of designing for high technology, to aid the anticipation of future changes and allow for them in the design, and to design for the needs and comfort of the people operating all this equipment.

2.2 Types of client

Although many individual businesses still manage without technological assistance, there is probably no area of commercial activity where examples of its use cannot be found. Categorising the typical characteristics of different types of client therefore involves a broad simplification from which individual circumstances will almost certainly vary. However, the following designation provides a working classification which, although specific clients may fall under more than one heading, will still be useful in discussing different types of project.

Corporate

Large organisations probably involved in a number of areas of business. Characterised by a multitude of departments at the same plane in the hierarchy with different functions and requirements, interrelating in a variety of ways. Relatively low rate of change, but changes when they do occur may be major with far-reaching consequences for the building. Client contact will probably be through someone whose role is in facility or project management; a professional client, in other words.

Medium size, manufacturing industry

Sales, marketing, financial and general administrative functions supporting manufacturing base. Narrower, more easily defined range of operations than corporations. Not traditionally users of innovative technology; change may be *ad hoc* (though not necessarily ineffective for that). Relatively stable organisation. Client contact may be professional as above, or more likely someone who normally fulfils some other role and consequently does not necessarily have any experience of being a 'client'.

Medium size, service industry

Broad designation covering wide range of activities from advertising through publishing, professional consultancies, banking etc. Often high-profile image-conscious organisations who may as a result be used to being involved in the design process; but equally may be similar to the above.

Small, entrepreneurial

Again covering a wide range of activities and may be related to a manufacturing operation. Characterised by an *ad hoc* response to change in the past; major developments involving expansion often causing the need to employ consultants. Commonly this would be the first time such a move has been made, and, perhaps more significant, the first time the organisation had studied its needs and requirements in depth. The client contact is likely to be the head of the company.

Developer

In the past, developers have tended to put up nondescript buildings apparently in the hope that their very lack of character or quality would cater for every manner of function. Although there is still evidence of this thinking, there are also more promising signs with interesting buildings, often designed for more specific requirements, appearing. As it seems probable that this trend will continue, and as the demand for highly serviced office space grows, the instances of speculative buildings fulfilling the need for high-technology offices will increase. In these cases the roles fulfilled by client and consultants are well understood; what is new is designing in sufficient and appropriate flexibility to suit the specific market at which the building is aimed.

2.3 Types of office

Offices can now be found housed in a very wide variety of buildings, from one room of a house through converted industrial, agricultural, domestic or religious buildings to purpose-built blocks. The range of possible activities and building types is probably best illustrated by listing a few specific examples:

- an accountant with part-time assistance operating out of one room of his or her house. Equipment might include one personal computer, a word-processor and a photocopier.
- a small group of designers working in a converted warehouse providing shared facilities such as meeting space, reception etc. Equipment might include two personal computers with draughting software linked to a plotter and printer, a word-processor and a large photocopier.
- a medium-sized firm of advertising agents based in a former large town house. Equipment might include personal computers used for accounts and word-processing, and sophisticated audio-visual presentation space.
- a medium-sized firm of insurance underwriters occupying one floor of a speculative office block. Equipment might include a mainframe computer

housed in a separate machine room and linked to terminals at each workstation.

— a large firm of stockbrokers moving into purpose-built offices able to accommodate the vast quantities of cables linking the mainframe computer with terminals at the desks, alongside mini and personal computers, information screens etc.

2.4 Scope of guide

The major problems associated with high-technology equipment in office – comfort of the users, providing for flexibility, coping with the quantity of cabling and dealing with the heat-gains – are more or less common to all types of offices; with the degree of difficulty caused by the problems being dependent on the size of the office and the complexity of interlinking of equipment required. The emphasis of this *Guide* is on the larger, sophisticated installation to ensure that all aspects are covered; much of the information will, however, be appropriate for any office building.

Inception and initial brief

See Appendix A.1.a: 'Plan of Work', Stage A in *Architect's Job Book*.

The object of this phase is to establish enough information about the client's and users' overall requirements to:

— allow the *feasibility* of the project to be assessed.
— set the broad *framework* within which the design team is to work.

The standard sequence of actions, starting with problem definition (1.6), should be followed initially. The steps described in 2.5 and 2.6 are supplementary and pertain specifically to offices and high-technology offices.

2.5 Initial procedures by client

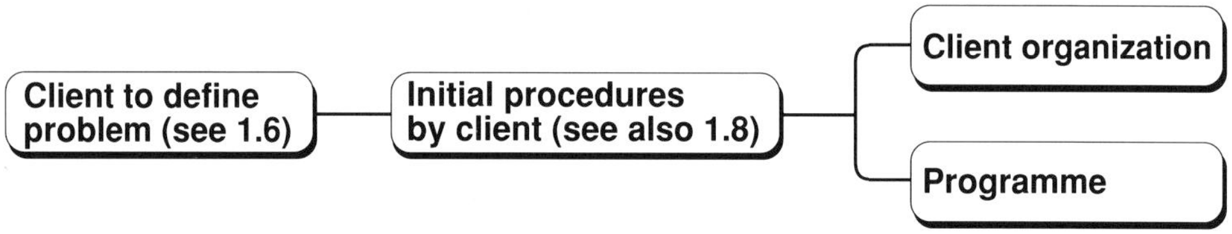

Client organisation

The client may be small, medium or large with a complex organisation and administrative network or a relatively simple hierarchy. Whatever size or form, the client must define (and the designer verify):

— *who* from the client's organisation will be involved in the project.
— what their *functions* and *responsibilities* will be.

According to the nature and scale of the project this may be best fulfilled by one individual, or by a co-ordinated structure of individuals and groups with varying responsibilities throughout the course of the project. However, to achieve a satisfactory answer to the client's needs, a considerable amount of time and effort has to be devoted to the process of understanding and information gathering necessary to the development of a suitable and comprehensive

The following procedures will need to be defined and the responsibility for them allocated to individuals or groups:

— Co-ordination of the process of gathering *information* to form the brief.
— Formulation and/or approval of *budgets*.
— Approval of *feasibility* schemes.
— Approval of *outline* designs.
— Approval of *detail* designs.

— Approval of alterations to scheme or budget after scheme approval has been given.

Programme

Ascertain whether the timespan for the project will be influenced or determined by:

— budgetary allowances.
— expansion plans.
— need for equipment or facility replacement or improvement.
— requirement to achieve a return on money invested.
— any other factor which might set specific deadlines.

brief. This is demanding on the client's time and will be most effectively achieved by a clearly defined hierarchy of individual and collective responsibilities.

In a commercial world, money invested in a building will need to be seen to be producing a return. This will remain true regardless of whether the building is being developed as an investment for letting or is for the client's own occupation; and regardless of whether the money is borrowed with interest to be repaid or not. The impact on programming will depend on individual circumstances, but may dictate that an accelerated programme with attendant additional costs makes economic sense.

2.6 General data and objectives

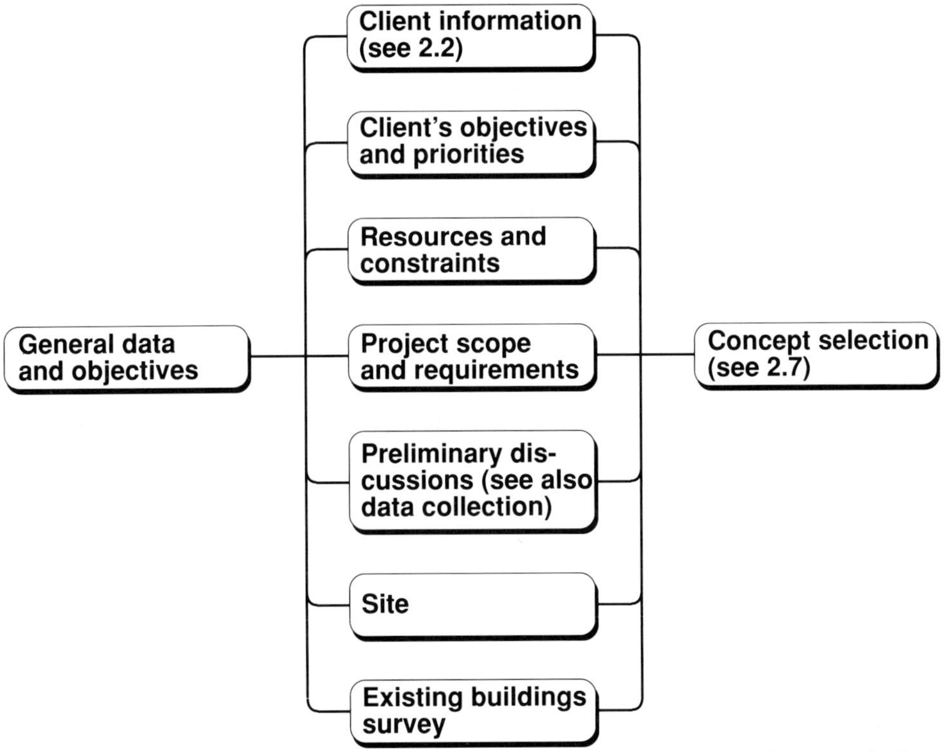

While Section 2 provides specific information and guidance for the design of high-technology offices, Section 1 offers guidance on the initial procedure basic to all design projects and should be referred to when considering general data and objectives.

Client's objectives and priorities

The client to define prime objectives in the following terms:

— why a *new* facility or change in an *existing* facility is required.
— what *function*(s) the new facility will fulfil.
— how it should *integrate* with existing facilities, both in physical terms and in terms of the corporate image.

In large or otherwise complex organisations it will be important to establish what the various users feel about their requirements; and to determine whether they will have any involvement in the briefing process.

Where a development is being considered as a financial investment for letting, maximising lettable space and attractiveness to potential tenants will be prime objectives.

At this stage cost limits should be defined in broad terms, either as £($)*x*-per m^2 or 'not to exceed £($)*x*. For more detailed information on cost planning see 2.15.

See also 1.5 and 'Existing building survey', this section. For more detailed information see *Planning Applications and Appeal*[16].

Resources and constraints

Discuss and/or determine:

— limits of expenditure and the basis for computing *costs*.
— what, if any, outline *approval/consents* must be obtained and, if so, who will be responsible for doing this.
— the implications of the project on current work situation and employees, and vice versa; particularly where the conversion or alteration of an existing installation is involved.

For a summary of briefing methods, including questionnaires, surveys etc., and for an outline of approach to evaluation of existing buildings, see Appendix A.5.

For large projects with a number of variations the task of scheduling requirements will be simpler if a proforma is devised to tabulate the information; frequently such proformas can be re-used on subsequent projects. For an example see Fig. 2.12, Section 2.22.1.

Project scope and requirements

The client/briefing committee must define the general scope of functions to be covered and in broad terms the range and amount of technological equipment which will be installed.

Prepare a schedule covering each department listing:

— *functions* to be accommodated.
— *numbers of staff* defined by broad job description (i.e. managerial, professional, secretarial etc.).
— *relationships* between individuals, groups and departments.
— use of technological *equipment* for each job function.
— anticipated *growth* in staff numbers and in the use of equipment.

Preliminary discussions

Once objectives have been defined, all interested parties identified and contacted, and basic data gathered, arrange meeting of all concerned with briefing process to:

— determine what further exploration should be undertaken.
— establish what specific functions and facilities should be provided for.

Site

If a site is not already owned or identified, establish parameters by which potential locations should be judged:

— *existing* building for conversion, or *new* building.
— *size* in broad areas.
— *location* in relation to suppliers, transport, customers and staff (existing and/or potential).

If more than one site appears suitable, the architects could be asked to prepare feasibility studies to help an informed decision be made.

Existing building(s): survey

If the project is conversion of, or addition to, an existing building, conduct a survey to establish suitability and condition. Where large or complex projects are concerned, the survey will need to be very thorough and detailed to establish the feasibility.

Note that even where speculative buildings are apparently finished to a high stndard, major works including the replacement of newly installed items may be justified in the long term.

The main sections of this guide are written on the assumption that a new building is being purpose designed. This approach has been adopted to facilitate the rational consideration of all required matters. However, many office projects will

entail the refurbishment of existing buildings, whether they be speculative offices or structures originally intended for some other, quite different, function.
The following section addresses the processes involved when dealing with existing buildings. As each project will be unique, it takes the form of a feasibility checklist itemising all the main aspects which may need investigation. By working through the list a design strategy to suit individual requirements will be evolved.

Developers will judge capital cost a high priority; the user, however, will regard lifetime costings to be important and should include maintenance and energy usage in the calculations.
When the existing installation is judged to be sub-standard, or when the proposed refurbishment will represent an enhancement of a leased building, the landlord should be approached with a view to reflecting this in the terms of agreement.

Location
Assess the suitability of the location, taking into account:
— *communications,* accessibility to public and private transport.
— availability of suitably skilled *staff,* if new required.
— *vehicle access* for staff, visitors and goods.
— *parking;* capacity, security, relationship to building.

See also 2.12.

See also 2.9.

Size
Establish available space and estimate suitability for proposed use.

See 2.7 for guidance on initial assessment of space requirements. Estimates of suitability will also need to take into account distribution of space and its effect on usage.

Regulations
Determine whether any specific *regulations, listing* or *scheduling* affect the building or any part of it.

See also Appendix A.5. In the UK, consent for altering use involves obtaining planning permission from the local planning authority. Application is usually made in two stages. The first, or outline, application should be made as early as possible.

Access
Assess the *size* and *suitability* of entrance lobbies, reception area and circulation routes. Estimate the impact of modifying if necessary.

See also 2.8.

External finishes
Note:
— any *remedial work* required.
— implications of materials and finishes on *future maintenance* requirements.
— any facilities for *window cleaning.*

Structure
Note:
— *type.*
— *soundness.*
— *non-structural* internal divisions.
— complexity involved in making *modifications* to structural elements.
— implications for forming *new service routes* through structural elements.

Planning
Determine all items which may have implications for internal planning:
— *clear space* between external walls.
— *column grid.*
— *mullion grid.*
— structural *floor* to *soffit height.*

See also 2.14.

— finished *floor* to underside of *suspended ceiling height.*
— clear space in *ceiling void.*
— positions of any *fixed elements:* WCs, staircases, lifts, service ducts etc.

Facilities

See also 2.9.

Note provision of lavatories, kitchens etc. and assess adequacy for proposed use in terms of:
— *size* and *quantity.*
— standard of *finish.*

Estimate impact on services, drainage, etc. of providing additional facilities if necessary.

Arrange checks on existing lift systems to determine:
— age and *condition.*
— any *defects.*
— *adequacy* of provision for proposed use (including any goods lifts and possible fire service requirements).

Electrical system

Power

See also 2.10.

Establish:
— location of main *switchroom.*
— capacity of incoming *mains cable.*
— available space for *additional switchgear.*
— *capacity* of: main risers, sub-distribution panels and local ducting for small power, telephones and co-axial cables.

Lighting

See also 2.23 and 2.30.

Establish:
— *switching* arrangement of existing lighting.
— *reliability* of existing switchstart gear.
— existing *levels*, and check against requirements.
— incidence of *glare* and consider possible remedies.
— *integration* with ceiling system.
— that *acoustic integrity* of ceiling is not compromised by fittings.
— integration with proposed *planning grid.*

See also 2.11 and 2.24.
Background noise in office space not exceeding 35–40 dB would be ideal; 40–45 dB may be acceptable. Note that some types of noise, while not high, may be very disturbing.
See also 2.23.
High noise levels in plant rooms can have implications for maintenance; if they exceed limits laid down in local, or company, regulations, working time whilst plant is operational may be severely restricted.

Emergency and security systems

Note type and distribution of existing emergency systems and planning, including:
— *escape routes.*
— *compartmentation* of building against fire.
— *detection* systems.
— system *zoning.*
— breakglass and alarm bell positions.
— *fire-fighting provision:* sprinklers, foam distribution, extinguishers etc.

Establish existing *security systems,* including lock types and suiting, monitoring facilities, intruder alarms and lighting (particularly external).
Assess implications of existing provision against current scheme options.

Environmental services
Acoustics
Measure noise levels in *occupiable space* and, if unacceptably high, determine cause.
Measure noise levels inside and outside *plant rooms.*

Daylight
Determine daylight levels at various appropriate positions in the building and assess whether:

See also 2.23.

— *supplementary artificial lighting* will be necessary for a significant proportion of the year.
— *solar gain* and/or *glare* will need to be controlled.

Air-conditioning and ventilation systems
Ascertain *design parameters* of existing system, including assumed occupancy levels, activity, lighting and ventilation levels. Compare with proposed use parameters.
Arrange survey of installation to establish:

Where existing parameters do not match proposed, it may be possible to re-balance the system by increasing the capacity in some areas at the expense of others. However, note that with some systems, resultant increased fan speeds may cause unacceptable noise levels.
See also 2.10.

— *type*, *age* and *condition.*
— availability of *spares* for maintenance.
— positions of fresh air and exhaust *grills* (assess implications for current planning proposals).
— *access* requirements for maintenance (particularly note filter positions and sizes).
— *control systems* (local or central; if zoned, assess implications).
— *heat discharge:* are any environmental problems caused? could heat be recovered?
— likely *failure rates* of units; assess implications for building maintenance.

See also 2.11.

Internal finishes
When demountable partitions are installed, check:

See also 2.28.

— *compatibility* of *dimensions* with proposed planning grid.
— availability for *additional requirements* and/or future maintenance.
— *durability* and *aesthetic* suitability of finishes.
— *sound attenuation* achieved between adjacent spaces.

Where suspended ceilings are installed, check:

— *compatibility* with proposed planning grid.
— access to *void* where required.
— *structural stability* and ability to accommodate proposed partition fixing.
— standard of *finish* and *aesthetic suitability.*
— *acoustic* qualities.
— *integration* with *lighting* (existing or proposed).

Sound attenuation of 30–35 dB would be acceptable for most uses; where higher levels of concentration or confidentiality are required, or where greater notes are likely to be generated, 45 dB may be necessary.
If existing ceiling tiles are unsuitable, consider re-using the suspension system with new tiles.
Acoustic properties may be enhanced by the addition of a sound-absorbent quilt over the tiles.
See also 2.27.

See also 2.29.

Where floor finishes are laid, check:

— *suitability* for proposed functions.
— *condition* and degree of wear.
— *durability* and *aesthetic suitability* of finishes.
— if unsuitable, ease and means of *removal.*

2.7 Concept selection

See Fig. 2.1 for a broad outline of various fundamental ways in which offices may be arranged.
Initial rough estimate of floor area required may be based on 9.3–11.6 m^2 (11–14 yd^2) per person for office space, with this forming approximately 80 per cent of the gross floor area.
Alternatively, calculate initial estimates using the examples provided in Fig. 2.2 as a guide.

The development of the *brief* is usually in progressive steps, in an increasing degree of detail. It is useful if this process is integrated simultaneously with the development of the building *design* so that there is interaction with the early design work. This will not only help to identify problems but will also lead to the testing of initial thoughts and the questioning of any preconceived ideas.
Consider the various *basic* strategic design concepts that are possible. Keep in mind in particular:

— stated *objectives* and overriding *priorities* (for example: security, programme requirements, outside awareness, public image).
— constraints (site, cost etc.).
— differentiation between '*public* space' (i.e. areas visited by people not employed by the client) and *secure* space (if applicable).
— the *interaction* required between departments, areas and individuals for the performance of their jobs.
— electrical and mechanical *service* requirements and the need for *access* to allow change and development.
— *flexibility* required and allowance for *growth.*
— *energy* consumption/conservation.
— natural vs artificial *lighting* and *ventilation.*
— *sizes* of offices required in broad terms, i.e. large, open-plan areas; medium-sized spaces to accommodate groups; cellular offices and likely proportion of each.
— range of *floor depths* which will accommodate spaces required.
— effect of different *core locations.*
— likely *shape/form* of building (slab, tower, medium-rise, courtyard etc.).

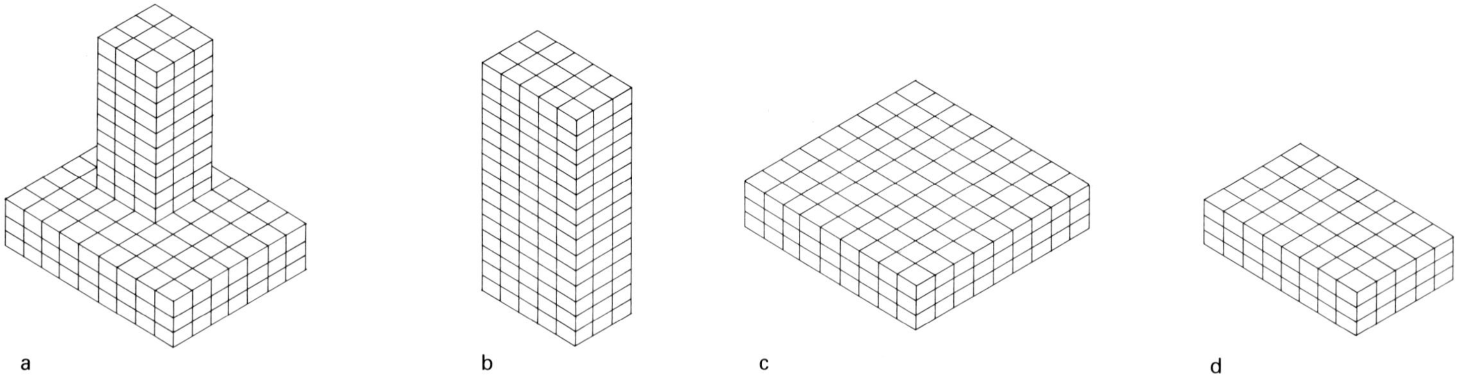

Fig. 2.1 *Some basic design concepts – there are many further options available and, except where the site places particularly severe restrictions on possibilities, no one solution should be considered definitive at this stage.*
a. Podium accommodating spaces with frequent visitor access (reception, conference facilities etc.) and large volume spaces (dealing rooms etc.) with office areas in tower.
b. High-rise block.
c. Low-rise deep-plan; outside awareness can be increased by the introduction of courtyards or light wells.
d. Low-rise, medium depth.

Example 1: Local office of a multi-national corporation with a high proportion of professional staff, relatively generous space standards and a high degree of support facilities. Total staff: 360.

Action		*Accumulating area per person*	*Accumulating total area*
1	Sum of workstations	10 m^2	3,600 m^2
2	Add 10% for circulation within	10 + 10% =	
	departments	11 m^2	3,960 m^2
3	Add space for departmental facilities	11 + 2 (say)	
	(meeting rooms etc.)	13 m^2	4,680 m^2
4	Add 15% for interdepartmental	13 + 15% =	
	circulation	15	5,400 m^2
5	Add area for support facilities – filing,	15 + 3.2 (say)	6,552 m^2
	vending etc.	18.2 m^2	
6	Add area for special facilities:		
	Cafeteria	18.2 + 1.3 (say)	
		19.5 m^2	7,020 m^2
	Machine rooms	19.5 + 75 (say)	
		20.25 m^2	7,290 m^2
	Net useable area (NUA):		7,290 m^2
	Gross outside area (GOA) (NUA + 18–20% for cores, outside walls, columns etc.)	24.3 m^2	8,750 m^2

Example 2: Medium-sized firm of commodity brokers requiring a densely populated dealing room, a small amount of back-up facilities, cellular offices and administration space. Total staff: 50

Action		*Accumulating area per person*		*Accumulating total area*	
		(m^2)	(yd^2)	(m^2)	(yd^2)
1	Sum of workstations	6	7.2	300	360
2	Add 10% for circulation within	6 + 10%	7.2 + 10%		
	departments	= 6.6	= 7.9	330	395
3	Add space for departmental facilities	6.6 + 1	7.9 + 1.2		
	(meeting rooms etc.)	= 7.6	= 9.1	380	455
4	Add 15% for interdepartmental	7.6 + 15%	9.1 + 15%		
	circulation	= 8.74	= 10.5	437	525
5	Add area for support facilities	8.74 + 2.5	10.5 + 3		
	– filing, vending etc.	= 11.24	= 13.5	562	675
6	Add area for special facilities:				
	Cafeteria	none			
	Machine rooms	11.24 + 1.76	13.5 + 2.1		
		= 13	= 15.6	650	780
	Net useable area (NUA):			650	780
	Gross outside area (GOA) (NUA + 18–20% for cores, outside walls, columns etc.)	15.6	18.7	780	935

Fig 2.2 *Examples of initial space requirement calculations.*

2.8 Primary functions to be accommodated

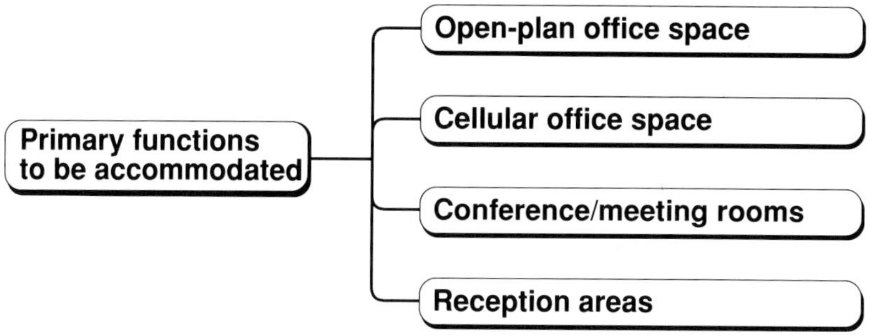

Open-plan areas

Recommended standards are given in Fig. 2.3; these are sufficient for initial planning and budgetary requirements but should be checked against studies of specific job functions during the scheme design stage.

Ascertain which *functions* (if any) are to be accommodated within open-plan office space. Establish maximum numbers of *staff* to be accommodated within any one area, and determine *space* standards for each function type, including allowances for local and main circulation.

Cellular office space

Establish which *functions* (managerial, professional, secretarial etc.) are to be accommodated within cellular offices along with a broad understanding of their relationship requirements with other areas.
Determine *space* standards using the information in Fig. 2.3 as a basis.

Fig. 2.3 *Typical space requirements of individual office functions*

Function	*Space requirement*	
	m^2	yd^2
Senior manager	25	30
Manager	18	22
Private office	12	14
Shared room/open plan	8–10	9–12
Secretarial	9	11
Administration	5–9	6–11
Dealer	5–10	6–12

Figures include local access around individual workstations.

Conference/meeting rooms

Recommended standards are given in Fig. 2.4.

Consider what facilities for meetings are required, and whether needs are best met by:
— areas within *open-plan* spaces.
— designated *rooms*.
— lecture theatre-type formats.
— or any combination.
— dimensions of special equipment.

Establish *capacities* for each, and consequently *areas* required.

Fig. 2.4 *A. Typical space requirements for meeting spaces.*

Type of space	*Number of persons*	*Typical space required per person* m²	yd²
Provision at the workplace			
1 Meeting at desk	2–3	2–2.75	2.4–3.3
2 Meeting area	4		
Provision for a group of workplaces			
3 Meeting area	6–8	1.5–2.25	1.8–2.7
Provision for all members of staff			
4 Interview room	2–3	1.5–2	1.8–2.4
5 Meeting room	8–12	1.5–2	1.8–2.4
6 Rest area	12–15	2.25–4	2.7–4.8
7 Board room	16–24	1.5–2	1.8–2.4
8 Conference room	15 and over	1.5–2	1.8–2.4
9 Lecture room	50–100	1–1.5	1.2–1.8

B. Typical meeting space provision for different types of office.

	Headquarters accommodation for an engineering organisation 1200 staff	*Manufacturing administrative organisation 400 staff*	*Headquarters accommodation for a clerical organisation 1400 staff*	*Consultancy organisation 80 staff*
Meeting area at workplace	1 per 15 office staff	1 per 40 office staff	1 per 18 office staff	1 per 16 office staff
Meeting area serving a group of workplaces	1 per 10 office staff	1 per 12 office staff	1 per 26 office staff	1 per 20 office staff
Meeting rooms 6–8 persons	1 per 80 office staff	1 per 45 office staff	1 per 55 office staff	None
Lounge/rest areas	1 per 280 office staff	1 per 80 office staff	1 per 400 office staff	None
Meeting rooms 12–16 persons	1 per 120 office staff	None	1 per 280 office staff	None
Meeting rooms 16–20 persons	None	1 per 60 office staff	1 per 230 office staff	1 per 80 office staff
Conference room 22–28 persons	1 per 1200 office staff	1 per 200 office staff	1 per 1400 office staff	None
Lecture room 100–150 persons	1 per 1200 office staff	None	None	None

Reception areas

Establish in general terms the requirements for receptions and entrances, determining in particular:

— whether usage will be primarily by staff, or staff and visitors.
— likely *traffic* flows, including anticipated peaks.
— position of reception *desk* in relationship to entrance hall.
— whether reception will be used as a *waiting* area.
— *security* requirements (see 2.11).
— the degree to which the *image* presented will be an important factor.
— other facilities/items to be provided: windbreaks (vestibule lobby); building directory; seating; display; notice boards; publicity material; vending machines; telephones; coat storage.

Related functions

High-technology offices frequently require associated activities to be located in close proximity to office space. For example:

— research and development laboratories.
— product maintenance workshops.
— spares storage for call-up by service engineers based in the office.
— product display facilities.
— training facilities.

Requirements will vary according to individual circumstances and specific functional needs investigated thoroughly, bearing in mind:

— relationship to office functions.
— access for materials, staff, visitors etc.
— floor loadings.
— impact on services (power supplies, cooling loads etc.).
— impact on adjacent spaces (noise, vibration, visual etc.).
— any specific additional service requirements (dedicated power supplies, chilled water, compressed air etc.).

Non-related functions

In certain cases entirely separate functions will need to be catered for. Examples would be city centre offices with ground floor shop or showroom units or community facilities incorporated within a development as a planning gain. The range of possibilities is too wide to be included in the scope of this book, and appropriate guidance should be sought according to requirements. It is important, however, to identify potential conflicts of interests between unrelated uses at an early stage to avoid problems later.

2.9 Secondary functions to be accommodated

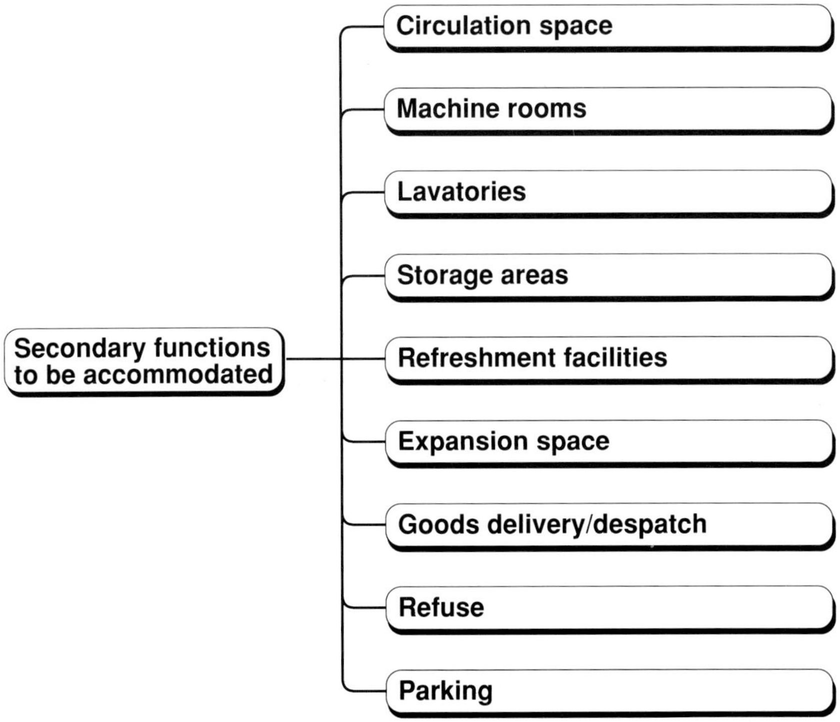

Circulation space

Establish the likely patterns of *movement* through the building, giving particular consideration to:

— the needs of *disabled* people.
— *vertical* circulation via stairs, lifts and/or escalators.
— *escape* routes.
— the movement of *staff and visitors* at peak times.
— the movement of *goods* in or out if applicable.

Note that if large conference facilities are a requirement then this will mean large numbers of people passing through circulation areas within a short space of time. See Appendix A.1.b: Goldsmith[4] and *New Metric Handbook*[1], chapter 6.

Machine rooms

Determine if any equipment is to be, or should be, located within designated rooms. In particular check on:

— *mainframe* computers.
— *communication* systems including telephones, telex and facsimile machines.
— *computer networking* system controllers.
— *word-processing* facilities.
— *photocopying* and associated processes, including document shredders.
— *security* systems.

For detailed information see 2.22.3.

Lavatories

See 2.22.4, also Appendix A.1.b: *New Metric Handbook*[1], chapter 38.

Determine:
— *numbers* – males and females – for whom provision must be made.
— *distribution and location,* for example within main circulation cores, adjacent to reception, adjacent to conference rooms and cafeteria.
— special requirements for *disabled* people.
— *area* to be allowed.

Storage areas

Determine requirements for storerooms:
— list *items* to be stored: furniture; stationery; cleaning equipment and materials; packing materials; spares stockholding. Note in particular any *hazardous* items, or any with *special* storage requirements (temperature, humidity etc.).
— establish *sizes and volumes* of material and equipment; determine *methods* of storage.

Plant rooms

Discuss with specialist consultants, manufacturers etc, at early stage. See 2.22.4.

Determine *need* for, and approximate *space* requirements of:
— gas meter; oil storage tank; LPG installation (usually outside the building).
— boilers and other space heating plant.
— ventilation and air treatment/cooling plant.
— electrical substation and emergency installation.
— water storage tanks.
— lift motor room(s).

Consider location of spaces:
— basement.
— ground level.
— roof.
— separate from main building.

Refreshment facilities

See 2.22.4
For detailed guidance see Appendix A.1.b: *New Metric Handbook*[1], and Lawson[2].
Information on local requirements should be obtained from the health department of the local authority.
In the UK see Food Hygiene (General) Regulations, 1970; local regulations in the USA.

Consider *need* for and *scale/type* of refreshment facilities:
— coffee bar/cafeteria/dining room/dining room used for entertaining clients/vending machines.
— *form* of service: waitress or counter.
— number of *seats* required.
— *how* service will be run, for example leased to an outside contractor.
— *hours of opening,* for example serving lunches only or breakfasts and evening meals as well.
— *location* in relation to other areas of the building.

Establish what ancillary facilities are required.
— kitchen and/or other *food preparation* facilities; washing-up area etc.
— *store(s)* for kitchen and/or vending machines.
— *access* for incoming food and outgoing refuse.
— *office* for manager if large-scale facilities are being provided.

Expansion space

Ascertain whether provision should be made at the outset for future expansion. If so, consider:

— whether to build it at this stage; in which case consider what the space is to be used for in the meantime: storage, sub-let offices etc.
— if it is not to be built at this stage, consider the impact when it is built on the facilities, services, lavatories, circulation and escape routes now being provided.

Goods delivery and despatch

Determine the needs for delivery and despatch of goods, materials etc. Consider:

— if requirements can be accommodated through *normal* entrances.
— whether a designated *goods lift* will be required.
— whether a *loading bay* will be necessary. If so determine whether it should be undercover or flush with the outside wall.

Refuse

Establish broad requirements for disposal of refuse, including:

— approximate quantities.
— frequency of removal.
— any special needs/problems (confidential waste material, noxious substances etc.).

Parking

Determine parking requirements (if any) for cars, vans, bicycles etc., including:

— entrance/exit.
— access to/from building.
— security.

For car parking allow 20–30 m^2 (24–36 yd^2) per space; for pedal and motor cycles 1.5 m^2 (1.8 yd^2per space.
For detailed information see Appendix A.1.b: *New Metric Handbook*[1], chapters 7 and 40.

2.10 Services concept

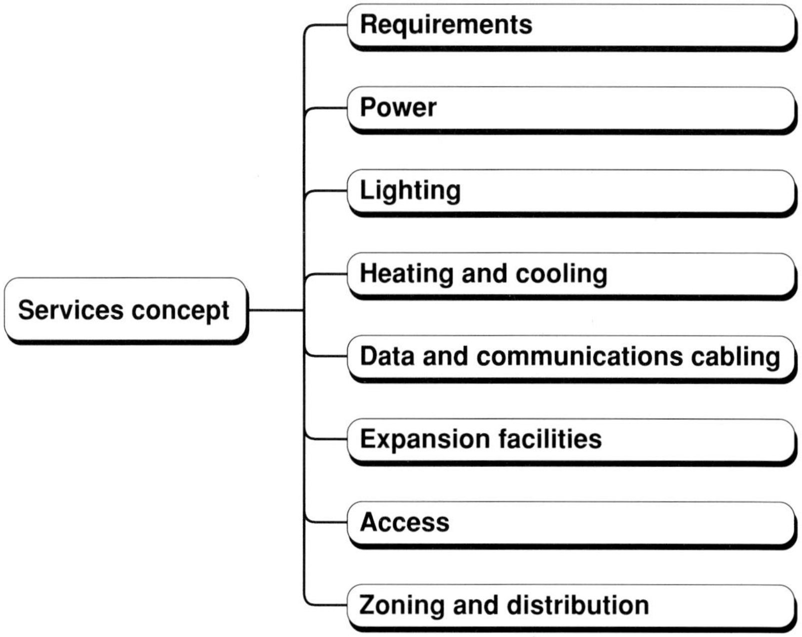

In high-technology offices it is essential that the development of the services design is concomitant with the development of the whole scheme. To this end, possible means of servicing the building should be investigated at an early stage to facilitate selection of an effective services concept. Begin to look at:

— *requirements* of all individual services (power, lighting, heating, cooling and data and communications cabling).
— *expansion* needs for the future.
— *access* requirements.
— *zoning* and *distribution*.

Requirements

Establish all service requirements, listing individual services by type and noting any specific characteristics which will have an impact on design solutions.

Power

Figure 2.5 gives loadings for typical areas; these are sufficient for early design stages but should be checked against specific information later. See also 2.24.

— Estimate overall *loading* expressed as W/m^2 (W/yd^2) and identify any areas of concentrated power requirements.
— Identify any equipment requiring clean, *dedicated* supplies.
— Identify any equipment requiring *three-phase* supplies.

Area	*Design load* W/m²	W/yd²
General offices	25	21
Copier rooms	175	146
Conference/meeting rooms	10	8
Word-processing areas	45	38
Mainframe computer rooms	550	460
Small machine rooms	350–550	293–460
Cable network distribution rooms	50–250	42–209
Lighting	10–15	8–13

Fig. 2.5 *Average electrical loadings of typical areas.*

Area	*Illumination level* (average at 900 mm [3 ft] above FFL) lux	ft-candles
General offices	320–550	30–50
Drawing offices	750	70
Conference rooms	550	50
Meeting rooms	320–550	30–50
Computer rooms	550	50
Corridors/staircases	150–200[a]	14–19
Entrance lobbies	150–200[a]	14–19
Reception desks	500	46
Storage areas	150	14
Cafeterias		
Dining areas	300	28
Servery	500	46
Kitchen	500	46
Exterior lighting		
Footpaths	30[a]	3
Parking areas	30–60[a]	3–6
Roads	30–60[a]	3–6
Road intersections	150[a]	14

[a] Illumination at floor level and not necessarily uniform.

Fig. 2.6 *Recommended illuminance levels for different tasks.*

Lighting

— Establish lighting *level* requirements, noting any specific requirements.
— Establish *control* requirements, including energy management control systems.
— Begin to investigate possible *solutions,* looking at daylight (including effects of building shape, orientation, depth and section on daylight levels), low-glare downlighting, uplighting and task lighting.

Figure 2.6 provides recommended levels of illuminance for typical functions for guidance. See also 2.23.

High usage of electronic equipment can produce large quantities of excess heat; to ensure a comfortable working environment, the design of the mechanical system (heating, ventilation and air-conditioning) must prevent local areas of heat build-up; and must achieve this without creating additional discomfort in the form of draughts. This can easily occur if such considerations are left until a later stage; resultant compromises frequently involve large volumes of air having to be forced through a restricted space at high velocity.

For further information on heating and air-conditioning see *Handbook of Fundamentals*[13], Martin and Oughton[14] and *New Metric Handbook*[1], chapter 41.

Heating and cooling

Commence preliminary investigations into the parameters which will govern the environmental design by:

- establishing *design temperatures,* periods of use and indirect heat gains (equipment, solar, lighting, people etc.).
- identifying any equipment which may require *local* cooling.
- establishing if *control* is to be global, or global with local override.
- determining likely *form*(s) of heating, cooling, ventilation and control.

Typical approaches to system design include:

- conditioned air circulated through a raised floor and extracted at high level, either through grills or through the light fittings.
- conditioned air ducted through the ceiling void with the void used as a plenum for extract.
- perimeter fan-coil units with extract at high or low level.
- perimeter circulating water heating with ducted fresh air input and extract.

Control of systems may be:

- manual (global, zoned or individual area).
- timer, set to working pattern.
- sensor, responding to temperature change, and, in sophisticated systems, the presence of staff.
- a combination, often with limited manual override allowing a certain extent of individual control over comfort conditions but protecting the principle of energy conservation.

See also 2.24 and 2.32.

Data and communications cabling

Establish data and communications cabling requirements, including:

- outlet/interface *distribution,* i.e. the pattern of outlets to suit possible furniture planning options.
- vertical and horizontal *routing.*
- *cable* types, sizes, separation requirements and bending radii.
- *compatibility* and capacity for *integration* with partition, ceiling and furniture systems.

Expansion facilities

Determine allowances to be made for expansion:

- where a future *extension* of the building is planned; allowing for the connection and integration of new services.
- *supplementing* or extending the services within the curtilage of the existing proposal.

Access

Establish access requirements for all services to allow:

- maintenance and repair.
- renewal or expansion.

Zoning and distribution

Determine zoned distribution concepts covering primary and secondary service routes and terminations. Zoning should take into account:

— origination and termination *positions*.
— physical *separation* of individual services where necessary or desired.
— *space* required, and space for cross-over of routes.
— *integration* with building elements.
— *access* requirements.

Routing possibilities to be looked at should include:

— *outside* the main envelope of the building.
— through ducts located in service *cores*.
— through ducts attached to structural *columns*.
— through *exposed* ducts.
— through a *ceiling void* created by a suspended ceiling with drops to serve local needs.
— by means of *raised-access flooring*.
— through trunking set into the floor *screed* (either fully or partially accessible).
— around the *perimeter*.
— via *fin walls* (non-structural nib walls, full height or not, used to sub-divide space and to carry services).
— a combination of any of these.

Selection of the most suitable option often involves comparing dissimilar factors; judgements will have to be made assessing individual circumstances.

Where possible, access positions should be away from work areas to avoid disruption or increased maintenance costs caused by having to do repair work outside normal working hours.

Assessing which possibility, or combination of possibilities, will best suit the requirements is a complex business involving many factors (lighting, flexibility, capital costs against maintenance costs, degree of disruption caused by future alterations etc.) However, in a building housing a high level of sophisticated technology this is probably the single most important aspect which will determine its success or failure; and great care must be taken to ensure that the most appropriate concept is finally selected.

2.11 General considerations

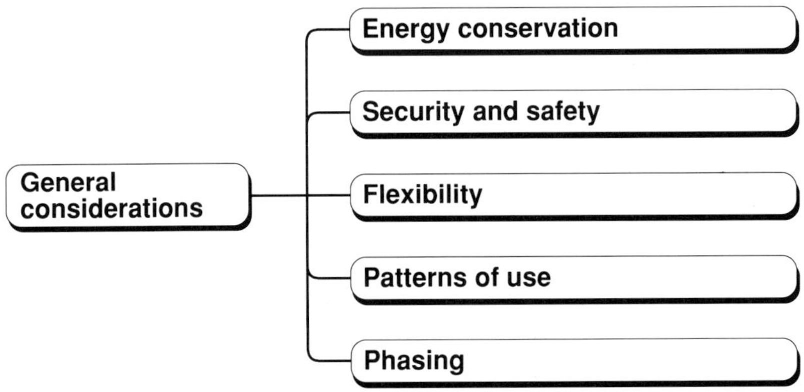

Energy conservation

Consider energy requirements and possible conservation:

— what *fuel*(s) will be used.
— *solar energy* and *solar gain*.
— *heat recovery* from light fittings and electronic equipment.
— lighting *levels; efficiency* of fittings and distribution; forms of switching.
— could building be connected into a *district heating system?*
— could waste be *incinerated* to generate heat?

See Appendix A.1.b: 'Energy Primer'[3]

Discuss with local fire department and police. See Appendix A.1.b: 'Thinking About Fire'[5] and 'Security in Buildings'[6]

Security and safety

Ascertain broad requirements with regard to:

- number and position of exits, fire escapes and fire escape routes.
- fire alarms; fire-fighting installation and/or equipment.
- control of access at entrances.
- control of access to specific areas of the building.
- the possible need to avoid spaces or accessible voids where an object or person could be concealed without detection.
- additional measures which may be necessary in certain areas of the building: rooms enclosed from slab to soffit; special locks to doors and/or windows; avoidance of visual access to rooms; additional acoustic insulation.
- central control and monitoring of the status of access positions via CCTV, card locks, cypher locks and/or magnetic contacts on doors and windows.
- intruder alarm systems.
- measures to combat vandalism, terrorism or industrial espionage.

It is not, generally speaking, realistic to consider providing total flexibility – the cost of services and the structure (designed to allow any facility to be repositioned anywhere) to do this would be extremely high. It is, therefore, important to decide what degree of flexibility is really essential.

Flexibility

Determine the extent of planning for flexibility/adaptability and growth required:

- to meet the *estimated needs* of the next 7–10 years.
- to allow, as far as possible, for *future changes* in technology and other probable changes.

Consider:

- *modular planning* and construction allowing freedom to use any part of the building for almost any purpose; as opposed to fixed function spaces.
- provision of *expansion space* at the outset.
- effect on *structure* and the capacity and accessibility of the *service distribution system*.

Pattern or use

Ascertain operating hours each day and number of days each week. Estimate any implications for:

- *energy conservation* forecasts.
- anticipated *lifespan* of building elements.

Phasing

If building contract is to be undertaken or completed in stages, consider:

- *priorities* for each element/section.
- method of *planning* to permit building to remain in use; or to be part-occupied ahead of final completion.

2.12 Site

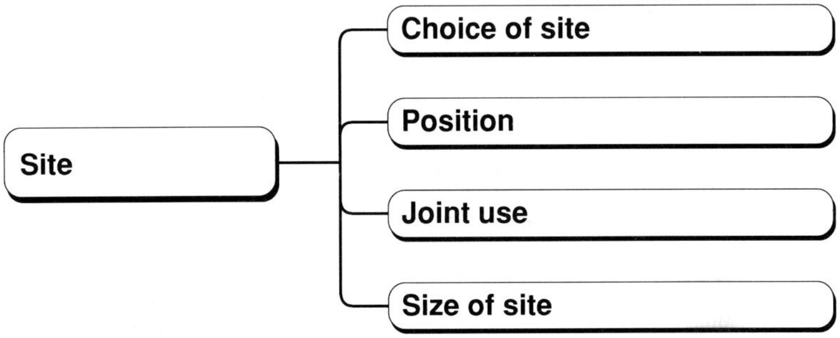

Choice of site

If site has already been chosen check that:

— client has ascertained that it is *suitable.*
— *alternatives* have been investigated.
— general *survey* and feasibility study have been undertaken.
— outline *planning approval* has been obtained.

If site has not yet been selected, investigate possible alternatives.

See Appendix A.2 for information on analysing chosen site or evaluating possible sites.
When considering cost of site keep the following in mind in addition to initial outlay:

- rates and taxes.
- effect of topography, soil conditions etc. on building and landscaping costs.
- possible cost of providing certain services on site.

Position

Check/ensure that the site is suited to client's needs in terms of:

— its *accessibility* for staff, potential staff, clients and suppliers.
— its *shape* (for example to allow correct orientation) and proximity to sources of noise or other disturbance.

Joint use

If joint use, part of a complex of buildings or shared occupancy, check that the office can be so sited that:

— it will be clearly and easily *identified* by visitors.
— there is no *conflict* with other uses.

Establish relationship to other buildings where appropriate, for example as a part of a manufacturing location.

Size of site

Establish that the site is large enough for:

— estimated *accommodation.*
— future *expansion, parking* and *landscaping* if required.

Feasibility

See Appendix A.1.a: 'Plan of Work', Stage B in *Architect's Job Book*.

This phase is concerned with a study and analysis of the data collected in the initial brief in order to reach a decision on the feasibility of the project. If feasibility has already been established before the architect is appointed, this stage should be used to check the client's assessment and conclusions, and to ensure that no factors have been omitted.

The depth of analysis and design sufficient to prove feasibility may vary considerably. The factors included here are only the basic essentials; where a more thorough study is required, the more detailed information given under 'Outline proposals/scheme design' (p.63) should be used.

2.13 Appointments: architects/consultants

A design team containing people experienced in dealing with high-technology offices can contribute to smooth running of the project. Approach relevant professional bodies for advice.

If it has not already been done, the architect and other consultants selected for the design phase should be formally appointed.

Agree to:

— clear definitions of *roles* and *responsibilities* of all concerned.
— *services* to be provided by each member of the design team.
— channels and methods of *communication*.
— scale of *charges*.

Figure 2.7 provides an example of the sort of roles and responsibilities which may need to be fulfilled by representatives of the client and by consultants.

Role	*Responsibility*
Client	
Project manager[a]	Co-ordination of input of information from departments and individuals for the development of the brief. Monitoring progress of scheme and cost plan and reporting to board/management/staff etc.
Consultants	
Architect/designer	Overall responsibility for the development of the brief and scheme, co-ordinating the input from other consultants, monitoring progress and reporting to the client.
Quantity surveyor	Preliminary cost advice on design and construction approaches, estimating costs of alternative schemes, cost planning, advising on contractual methods, preparing bills of quantities, financial management during construction and preparing final accounts.
Electrical engineer[b]	Design of lighting, power and cable distribution systems.
Mechanical engineer	Design of air-conditioning and mechanical systems.
Structural engineer	Structural design and calculations.

Fig. 2.7 *Typical roles and responsibilities of the design team.*

Notes

[a] Many large organisations will employ professional project managers for whom it is a full-time role. Sometimes they will be able to call on other in-house specialists in electrical or mechanical engineering, data cabling etc.

[b] For complex schemes other consultant specialists in areas such as lighting, acoustics, communications, data cabling etc. may be required.

For detailed information see Appendix A.4.

2.14 Preliminary planning

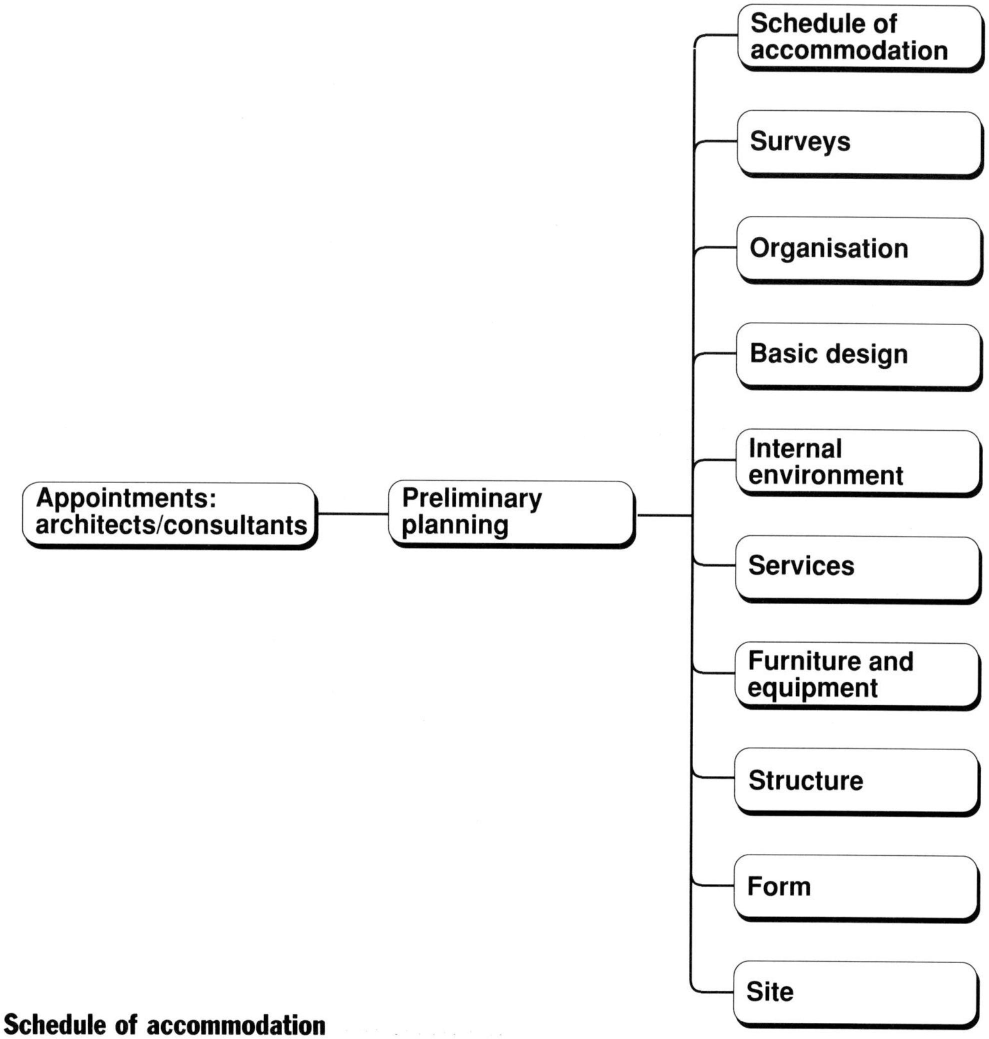

Schedule of accommodation

For basic information on floor areas see 2.22.1–4.

An outline schedule of accommodation will have been drawn up during the previous stage (see p.36). Now:

— *check* schedule, compare with known similar examples.

— determine *floor areas* for each of the individual spaces.

Surveys

For list of references see Appendix A.1.b. Useful sources include AJ 'Annual Review' (including bibliography) and AJ 'Guide to Information Sources'; also 'Architectural Periodicals Index' (RIBA).

Identify sources of information:

— survey current *literature* specifically relevant to project.

— prepare a *list of references* as a working document.

— investigate/visit *related projects:* pre-plan – know what to look for and why; carefully select buildings to visit (ideally good examples of reasonably comparable type and size).

— research *users'* attitudes and feelings towards needs and requirements.

Organisation

Confirm the pattern of organisation and work which will apply to the new building. Prepare:

— *flowcharts* of identifiable tasks which will be performed within the building.
— interaction/relationship *matrix*.

See Appendix A.5 for outline information on interaction matrices etc.

Basic design

Work out approximate form of building. Prepare several alternatives. Consider:

— *building regulations* and other special legislation affecting siting, design and construction.
— vertical or horizontal *organisation*: if vertical, which areas on same level(s) as main entrance and goods entrance?
— ratio of *perimeter* to gross *floor area*.
— ratio of *gross* to *net* floor area.
— integration of *planning grid* (taking into account possible ceiling, lighting, partition and furniture layouts) with *structural grid* and *fenestration*.
— position of *columns* relative to outside walls, circulation routes etc.
— *depth* of building and relationship to positions of *cores*.
— zoning of *services* distribution (see also internal environment and services below).
— *security* requirements: supervision of entrances, areas needing physical, visual and/or acoustic separation etc.
— *circulation* of staff, visitors and materials – entrances, corridors, vertical circulation etc – for greatest possible economy of effort.
— external *access*: for staff and visitors arriving on foot, by bicycle, car or public transport; position of areas needing direct vehicular access for deliveries.
— *noise*: position of noisy equipment, for example computer printout, telex; circulation, for example stairways, entrances to cafeteria or conference rooms; external sources, for example traffic, railways.
— *orientation*: in terms of heat gain and loss; view; external noise sources; prevailing winds (for example windows and entrances).
— *fenestration*: general percentages in different facades. How will this affect ventilation, daylight, heat gain and loss, construction, furniture layouts and appearance? Consider, for example, effect of different patterns of fenestration on possible furniture layouts, taking into account outside awareness, avoidance of glare and reflection on VDU screens etc. (see also internal environment below).
— *flexibility* and *phasing*: degree of modular planning (see also internal environment, services and structure below); position of areas to be added or spaces to be extended, in the future.
— *relationship* with adjoining facilities.

See Fig. 2.8A.
For basic information on space and activity relationships see 21.22.1–4.
There should be no premature bias towards one single solution. Alternative solutions should, at this stage, be kept diagrammatic.
Care must be taken with windows, which should be carefully located and designed: obtain maximum effect from them, but keep glass areas to a minimum to conserve energy.

Fig. 2.8 Grids

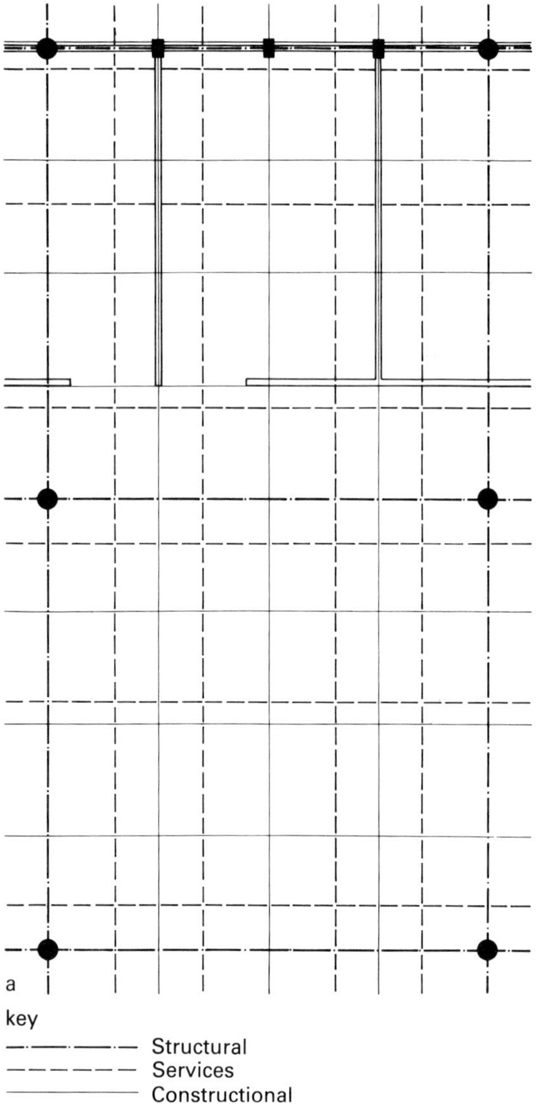

a. Example of integration of structural, service and constructional grids. Final selection of modules should be assessed against detailed knowledge of usage to ensure, for example, that the service grid suits possible furniture layouts and maintenance requirements.

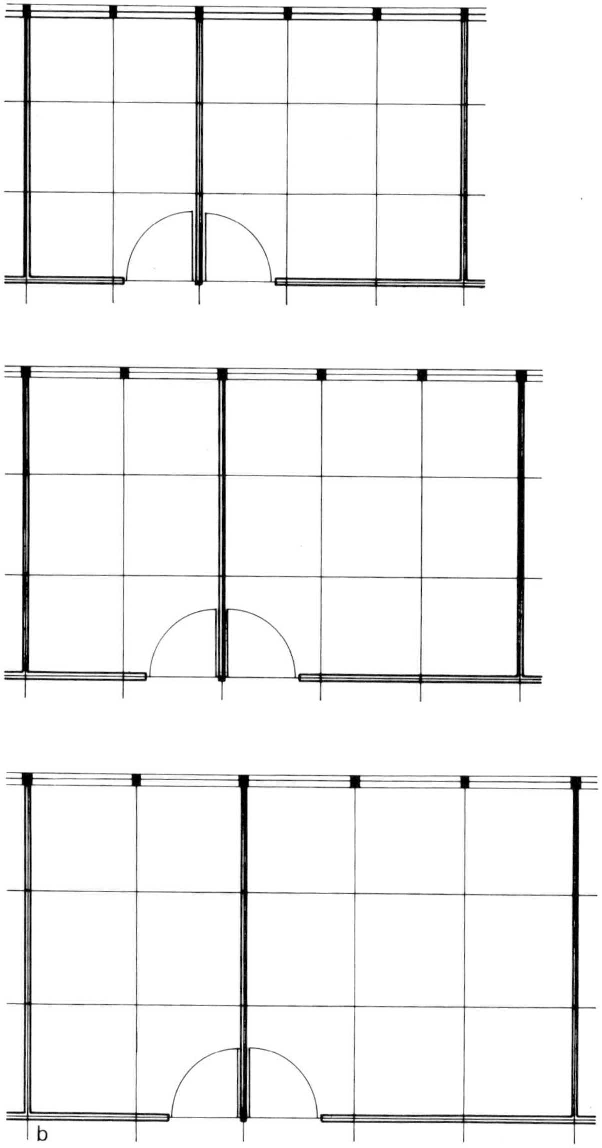

1.200 (4 ft) Mullion spacing giving smallest office size of 8.64 m^2 (96 ft^2) with larger offices by 4.32 m^2 (48 ft^2) increments.

1.350 (4 ft 6 in) Mullion spacing giving smallest office size of 10,965 m^2 ($121\frac{1}{2}$ ft^2) with larger offices by 5.48 m^2 ($60\frac{3}{4}$ ft^2) increments.

1.500 (5 ft) Mullion spacing giving smallest office size of 13.5 m^2 (150 ft^2) with larger offices by 6.75 m^2 (75 ft^2) increments.

b. Effect of different constructional grid modules as determined by mullion spacing on room sizes. The examples assume a proportion of 3 : 2.

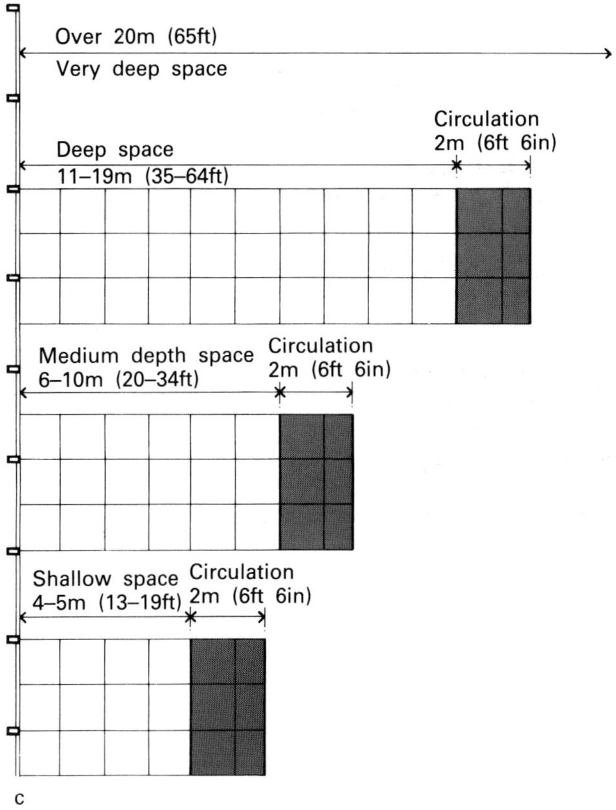

c. Four basic depths of space. In practice, depths should be tested against possible uses (various combinations of cellular and open space) as certain depths will be found to be impracticable to utilise economically.

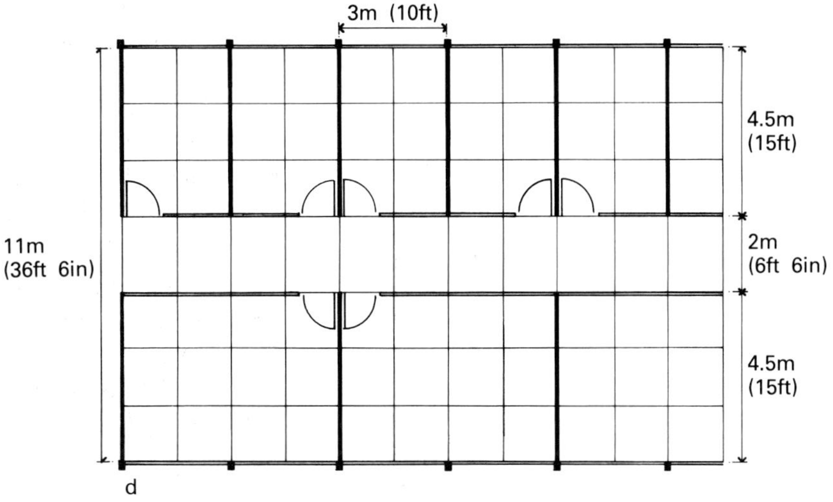

d. Shallow floors maximise use of daylight and outside awareness, and can permit natural ventilation where this is desirable. Assuming a mullion spacing of 1.500 m (5 ft) and a room proportion of 3 : 2, then a minimum shell depth of 11 m (36 ft 6 in) results.

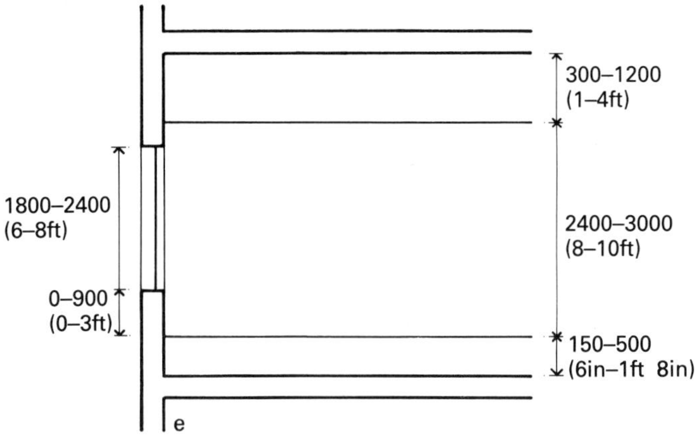

e. Storey heights should be considered at an early stage to ensure sufficient space for the zoning of services in floor and ceiling voids, suitable floor to ceiling heights and window sill and head heights.

Internal environment

Consult appropriate specialists, manufacturers and suppliers.
See also 2.23.

Consider broad requirements for:

— *air-conditioning*: heating, cooling, ventilation, humidification, dehumidification, filtering and washing; also space requirements for plant, trunking etc.
— if no air-conditioning: mechanical *ventilation* with heating in winter. What will be done to ensure there is no overheating during hot summer months?
— lighting.
— *acoustic control*: double glazing, insulation or absorbent ceilings, floor finishes, orientation, layout etc.

Determine:

— *zones* for air-conditioning, heating etc.; consider effect of fenestration.
— whether *smoking* will be prohibited in parts of the building.
— special requirements for *electronic equipment* (e.g. specific items of equipment needing additional local cooling or extract).
— the degree of *flexibility/adaptability* required (see also 2.23).
— the degree to which *atmospheric* and *comfort* conditions must be suitable for both equipment and users (e.g. where equipment is particularly sensitive to changes in temperature or humidity, or requires a dust-free atmosphere).
— the degree to which internal *energy* will be *recycled*, for example waste heat recovery.

Investigate alternatives which will be most appropriate for:

— each of the *layouts* selected.
— the different types of *spaces*.
— the *structural systems* under consideration.

Services

Ensure that adequate supply and disposal services will be available:

— *water, gas* and *electricity* supply: will new incoming mains have to be laid? Will a transformer be required? If so, how much space will be needed?
— *waste disposal*: how much waste accumulates weekly? How will it be collected, stored and removed?

Consider:

Discuss with local authorities/supply boards etc. The location of plant rooms and main distribution runs (vertical and horizontal) must be considered together with the structure at an early stage if services are to be satisfactorily integrated.
For more detailed information see 2.23.

— *communication systems* (internal and external telephones, teleprinters, data networks etc.), including floor space and other requirements; location, power, air-conditioning etc.
— *protection systems* (for example fire and security) and effect on design.
— *integration* and *distribution* of services: position of distribution boards, terminal boxes and plant rooms to keep runs to a minimum; compatibility with structural systems.
— *flexibility*, for example wiring – power, telephone and data cables etc.
— *access* requirements to facilitate change or maintenance.

At this stage consider requirements in broad terms to identify possible areas of conflict or special needs (for example, data cable systems which may be subject to frequent change and modification, and therefore require easy access with minimum disruption).
For more detailed information see 2.24.

Furniture and equipment

Ascertain what fixed and loose furniture and equipment must be included. Investigate:

— *workplace requirements* for each job function, including worktop area and arrangement, storage, service needs (power, telephone, data etc.), pinboard, shelving etc.
— *dimensions* and *weights* of equipment.
— *costs*.
— *flexibility* to allow for future changes.

The furniture and equipment to be used can have a significant influence on planning, structure and cost. Consult manufacturers/suppliers.
See also 2.25 and 2.27.

Structure

Investigate structural possibilities for the various layouts. Consider:

— column *grid*: this is a crucial decision to ensure economic use of space and maximum adaptability; must be worked out in terms of structural design economics, fenestration modules, lighting layouts, mechanical and electrical service layouts, ceiling, partition and raised flooring modules if applicable, cellular room dimensions and furniture dimensions and possible arrangements.
— *floor loadings*; for example, are heavy items to be restricted to particular areas?
— *height* of buildings and storey heights: preferred floor to ceiling height(s) plus ceiling and/or floor voids where required. Keep air circulation in mind.
— *distribution* of *services*: flat slab with suspended ceiling; raised floor; exposed services etc.

Fig. 2.8B shows effect of typical structural grids on layout options.
See also 2.22 and 2.25.

Recommended minimum ceiling heights are 2.4 m (8 ft) for office space and 2.5 m for computer areas.

Form

Develop the massing of the various layouts (probable building shape) and relate to site and adjacent buildings. Consider:

— whether requirements of *internal spaces*, form/volume and relationships have been taken into account.
— suitability for *function* and *image* to be projected.
— suitabililty for *expansion* either vertically or horizontally.
— suitability for either *air-conditioning* or natural/mechanical *ventilation*.
— suitability for natural *lighting* and/or electric lighting.
— *heat loss and gain*: a form with a low surface : volume ratio will perform better.
— town *planning regulations* and local guidance.
— *cost*: ratio of net useable space to gross outside area.

Net useable area (NUA) is defined as the space available for use or change of use, i.e. excluding cores, service areas, reception, columns and the external wall thickness. Gross outside area (GOA) is measured to the outside perimeter of the building, excluding any external columns (for example, where curtain walling is positioned inside an expressed structure).
The ratio between the two is a rough measure of the efficiency of the design; for guidance NUA should constitute between 75 and 82 per cent of the GOA.
For more details see 2.22.

Site

Check that each of the layouts fits the site. Keep in mind:

— adequate *access* for staff, visitors and deliveries.
— future *expansion*.
— *visibility* of the building where it is to act as an ‘advertisement’ for the client.
— *outdoor requirements* where applicable: car and bicycle parking, links to other buildings, landscaping.

For car parking allow 20–30 m^2 (24–36 yd^2) per space; for pedal and motor cycles 1.5 m^2 (1.8 yd^2) per space.
For detailed information see Appendix A.1.b: *New Metric Handbook*[1], chapters 7 and 40.

2.15 Cost planning

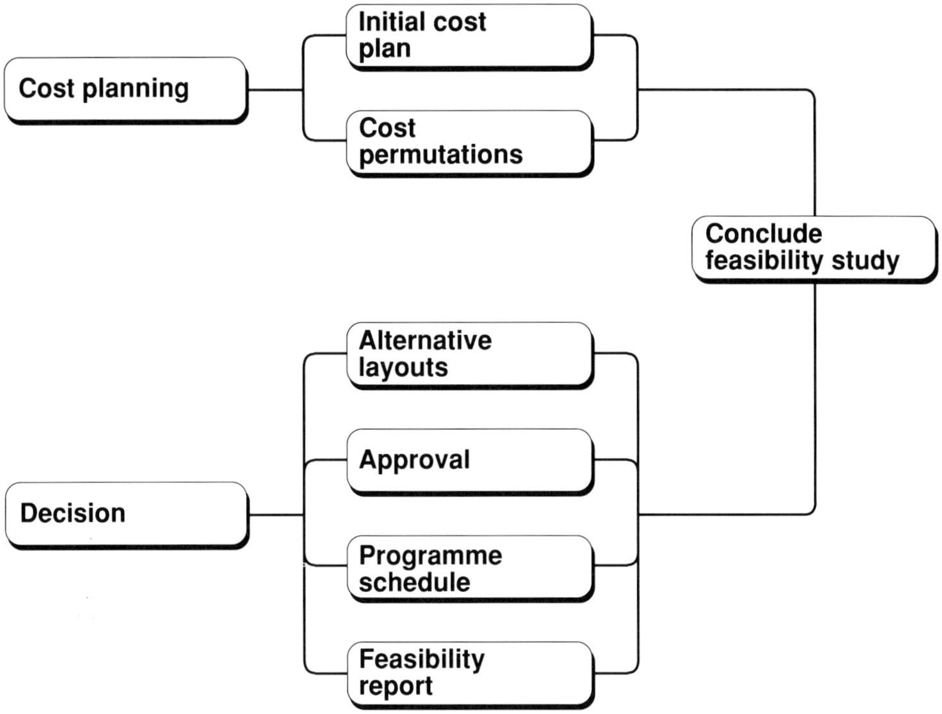

This function is very necessary, not only for the client's peace of mind, but also to provide a *framework* of parameters within which the design team can work.

Cost planning not only provides a *total budget* but will also divide it into as many *sub-sections* as the project requires (for an example, see Fig. 2.9). In this way, cost limits can be allocated to each main element and the team can, through constant updates of the information, remain within the guidelines.

Cost planning can also allow the *distribution* of building costs to be determined at an early stage by giving a greater or lesser *priority* to certain elements. For example, it may be decided that the accessibility of cabling through the provision of a raised floor is of overriding importance whilst the external appearance is less so; the balance of the distribution of costs can reflect this. Consequently, the cost plan should be looked upon as a tool to ensure the most effective use of financial resources.

To achieve a sensible cost plan a chartered quantity surveyor should be appointed, either by the client directly or by the lead consultant (usually the architect), at the inception of the project.

Achieving an even balance in the distribution of costs is not always the most effective use of money available; building to a standard of £x/m^2 may produce a functional but mundane result, whereas spending to a standard of £$x - y$/m^2 on some aspects and £ + z/m^2 on others could produce something equally functional but much more interesting.

For more details on the economics of office buildings see Appendix A.1.b: *Planning Office Space*[15], section 4, and 'Development Economics: Offices'[23].

1 Substructure
2 Structural frame
3 Upper floors
4 Stairs
5 Roof
6 External cladding
7 Windows and doors
8 Internal walls and partitions
9 Internal doors
10 Internal finishes (floor, wall and ceiling)
11 Fittings
12 Sanitary installation
13 Electrical installation
14 Mechanical installation
15 Drainage
16 External works
17 Other

18 TOTAL Building works ____________

19 Professional fees ____________

20 Sub-total ____________

21 Contingency and design reserve ____________

22 TOTAL ____________

23 Exclusions ____________

Fig. 2.9 *Cost planning typical elemental breakdown and expenditure. Note: each of the headings could be further split into sub-sections depending on the size, detail etc. of the estimate required.*

The surveyor will need the following information at this stage:

- overall budget cost or £/m^2 (\$/yd^2) where known.
- location of site.
- proposed shape, size and height of building.
- access to the site.
- restrictions on working on the site (specific hours, noise etc.).
- finishes and materials proposed.
- service installation details (e.g. air-conditioned or not).
- final use of building: resale, letting or client's own use.
- diversion of existing services or demolition of buildings where applicable.
- degree of concern about maintenance and energy costs.

Initial cost plan

With the above information, the surveyor should draw up an initial cost plan based on approximate square metre prices and experience and knowledge of similar buildings.

As this initial figure invariably becomes a yardstick by which all future fluctuations will be judged, it is very important that:
— the above information is as detailed as is possible at this stage.
— the appointed quantity surveyor is familiar with this type of building; and preferably also with the work of the designer.

Cost permutations

Development of the initial cost plan in greater detail is a continuous process through the scheme and detail design stages. This is usually achieved by quantifying all the different elements of the building and applying rates to them; in later stages element costs can be replaced by tender figures as these become known.
In this manner the cost plan can, with ever-increasing degrees of veracity, become the means of monitoring and controlling costs from initial budgets through to management of expenditure on site.

Once the initial cost plan has been established, the financial implications of alternative approaches can be examined sensibly. For example:
— comparison with costings for alternative layouts.
— variations produced by different construction methods (e.g. steel or concrete frame, alternative cladding materials, flat or pitched roof).
— life-cycle costings for alternative materials combining capital costs with maintenance costs during the life of the building (e.g. aluminium windows versus timber, asphalt roof versus built-up felt).
— energy consumption (alternative fuels, double or single glazing etc.).
— return on investment (e.g. enhanced standard of finishes and services can increase rental or resale value).

2.16 Conclude feasibility study

Alternative layouts

On the basis of foregoing studies and comparative analysis:
— select *best alternative* solution to building layout.
— prepare *final proposal* based on several alternatives.

Approval

Obtain approval of development in principle from local authority.

Programme schedule

Prepare revised programme schedule. Determine:
— *earliest* and *latest* dates for starts and completions for each aspect of work.
— *resource implications* affecting programme, for example finance.

Feasibility report

Prepare report on feasibility of project, including proposals, in terms of:
— client's *stated requirements*.
— *site* limitations.
— complete *financial implications*, making clear relative allocation of costs to building fabric, services, furniture and fittings, equipment, landscaping, professional fees etc.
— *structure*, *services* etc.

Note any modifications that should be made to the brief.

Decision

Submit report for consideration to client. On the basis of the information given, and the conclusions drawn, the client must decide:

— to *proceed with scheme design, detailed design and obtaining tenders,* or;
— to *modify requirements* and reassess feasibility, or;
— to *abandon* the project.

Detailed brief

See Appendix A.1.a: 'Plan of Work', Stage C in *Architect's Job Book*.

This phase is concerned with setting out a detailed brief covering all the major features with which those involved in the project must be concerned. It represents amplification of and addition to the broad issues discussed in the primary brief. In form it is usually written and diagrammatic and it emerges as a result of periods of extended talks with the client, the design team and the client's staff.
Further design work may start before the completion of a full brief, and certain studies under 'Outline proposals/scheme design' (2.21) may need to be made before the detailed brief can be substantially finalised. Obviously this brief will require review and, inevitably, amendment and revision as the work progresses.

2.17 Client responsibilities

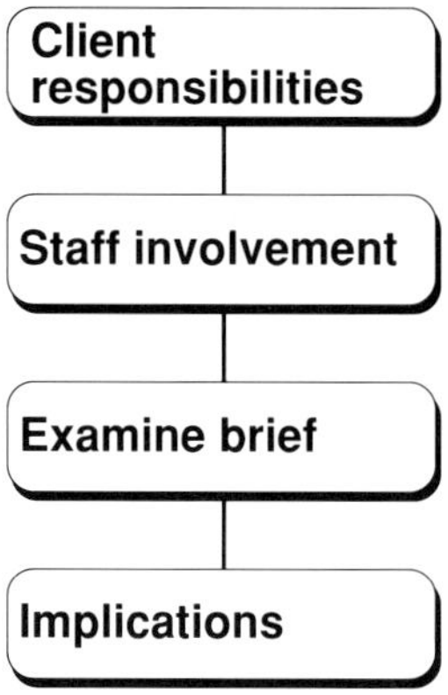

Properly approached, the development of a detailed brief provides an ideal opportunity to question many existing patterns of working and organisational structures. Frequently these have developed as an *ad hoc* response to some restriction imposed by existing facilities, or for reasons which are now outdated. In addition, the introduction of new facilities and/or technology may open up new possibilities for change.

During the course of the development of the detailed brief, the client should review:
- existing management *structures* and *hierarchies*.
- *departmental* structures and divisions.
- workflow *patterns* and *responsibilities*.
- suitability of existing *equipment*.

The client must make a decision based on the economic realities of all the options available, which, in addition to the project under consideration, may include:
- deferring or abandoning expansion plans if increased returns do not warrant capital expenditure.
- extending current workspace.
- making more efficient use of current workspace.
- renting alternative space requiring little or no modification.
- moving to a less expensive area (particularly one which attracts financial incentives such as government grants, rate relief etc.).

2.18 Staff involvement

Moving to new premises or making extensive alterations to existing ones causes major upheaval and can lead to a great deal of uncertainty amongst staff. To prevent the spread of misinformation by rumour, it is vital that procedures for communication are established at the earliest possible stage. Particular measures which will assist the spread of information include:
- appointing a member of staff to *liaise* between the project team and members of staff.
- informing everyone of the *appointment* of the *consultant*(s) and of their roles.
- describing the *objectives* of the project, and the methods of collecting data which will be adopted.
- advising everyone of the proposed *location* and probable *timetable* as soon as possible.
- devising a programme of *presentations* and *visits* at various stages throughout the project.

The frequency and format of presentations will depend on the size of the project and the organisation. Figure 2.10 gives a typical programme for a medium to large organisation and project.

Phase	*Presentation*	*Aim*	*Means*
Briefing	Client project committee	Understanding design concept	Sketches, photographs and visits to similar schemes
Completion of scheme design	All personnel	Explanation of site and design approach	Plans, perspectives, photographs
Completion of building shell design	All personnel	Description of building concept	Plans, perspectives, model
Sketch interior scheme	Group heads	Briefing on internal environment	Discussion of final design concept and sketch layouts
Layout	Group and section heads, top management	Briefing on alternative furniture systems	Discussion groups, conducted visits
Mock-up	Cross-section of personnel	Refinement of workplace design	Conducted visits evaluation questionnaire

Fig. 2.10 *Typical programme of presentations during the development of a medium to large project.*

Whether information is transmitted via a brochure, exhibition or meeting will depend on the size of the organisation and on the scale of effect of the changes. Where the effects of the proposed move will be major (involving moving house, for example) it is important not to forget the implications for spouses/partners/families.

Where a new site is involved, additional information about the location should be provided for staff. If the new site is close to the existing building, little change will be involved; where a move of some distance is proposed, it would be advisable to provide information on:

— the general *area*.
— *housing*.
— *assistance* being offered.
— *schools*.
— local *amenities*.
— *transport*.

Establish means of receiving and co-ordinating feedback and discuss response with client.

2.19 Examine brief

The various specialists (including manufacturers or suppliers of specialised equipment) must be asked to consider the implications of the up-to-date brief as it affects their particular responsibilities.

Be sure to:

— check that *all items* listed under initial brief and feasibility have been considered.
— list any *outstanding* items about which decisions have yet to be reached or research initiated.
— examine *basic changes* in *requirements* for their effect on previous feasibility judgements (Note: *costs*).

2.20 Implications

Consider implications of the detailed brief with regard to:

— *previous decisions*.
— *contracting methods*.
— the project *programme* as a whole.

Revise the programme if necessary; advise the client and other relevant persons/bodies of any changes.

Outline proposals/scheme design

This phase determines the general approach to layout, design and construction, which is developed to the point where one definite scheme (together with cost analysis) is produced and agreed upon by all the consultants and put forward as a recommended solution to the client. This phase may well have been reached by the end of the feasibility period, and may therefore be the confirmation of an already fairly detailed solution but incorporate any modification found necessary while preparing the feasibility study and detailed brief.

If the feasibility phase was bypassed, the factors outlined in that phase should be consulted for a broad appreciation of the size of the problem and as a quick check on the feasibility of the client's more detailed requirements now available.

See Appendix A.1.a: 'Plan of Work', Stages C and D (with the exception of part 2 'Architect's management function') in *Architect's Job Book*.

2.21 Detailed information

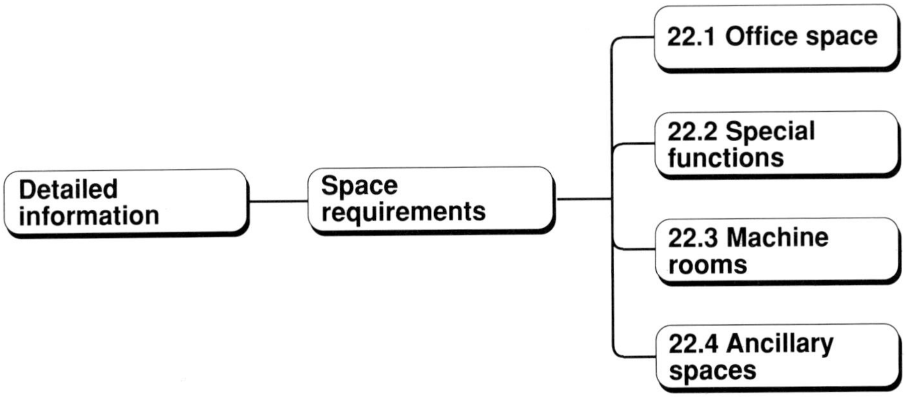

Studies undertaken in broad terms only at an earlier stage must now be carried out in detail:

— *site studies.*
— survey of *user requirements.*
— evaluation of *similar projects* etc.

2.22 Space requirements

Assess floor area and design requirements for individual spaces:
- office areas.
- special functions, for example conference rooms, meeting rooms, dealing rooms.
- machine rooms.
- ancillary spaces.

For each space list:
- nature of activity performed there.
- relationships to other spaces/functions.
- number of staff to be accommodated, and individual functions.
- equipment to be used.
- furniture and fittings.
- special requirements, for example additional security.
- requirements for services, lighting, heating, acoustics etc.
- provision for flexibility/adaptability and for expansion.

Sections 2.22.1–4 give basic requirements for each individual type of space. To save undue repetition certain detailed information which may only be required during the following phase (Detail design) is included in these sections.
Basic information is given on each space considered. This is followed in each case by layout/design considerations with accompanying detail/technical information in the margin.
Note: standards must be seen as flexible guidelines to be adapted according to the type of office and individual needs.

2.22.1 Office space

Space standards

Many organisations have developed space standards allocated to each individual grade or staff function within the company. These will have been developed after consideration of all or some of the following factors:
- *status*: in hierarchical organisations allocation of space will, broadly speaking, increase in line with position within the company.
- *requirement*: arising from studies of functional needs.
- *protection* of employee needs.

Approximate estimates of the floor area required may be based on 9.3–11.6 m^2 (11–14 yd^2) per person for office space; with this forming approximately 80 per cent of the gross floor area. For more accurate estimates see below and Fig. 2.11.

Fig. 2.11 *Typical space standards for various office functions. Areas given include local access around workplaces. The figures are suitable for initial calculations and assessment of space requirements, but should be checked against empirical data for individual circumstances at a later stage.*

Type of space	*Function*	*Area per person*	
		m^2	yd^2
Private office	Senior manager/director	20–30	24–36
Private office	Manager/department head	15–20	18–24
Private office	Manager/professional	10–15	12–18
Small group room	Professional	10	12
Large group room	Professional	9	11
Open plan	Professional	9	11
Open plan	Secretarial/administration	9	11
Open plan	Clerical	7–9	8–11
Group room/open plan	Dealer	6–9	7–11

In more enlightened organisations the use of space standards as an expression of status is becoming less of a determining factor, as it is recognised that space requirements do not necessarily increase with seniority, and indeed might, in certain instances, decrease. Although the desire for outward manifestation of status is often strong, the cost-effectiveness of satisfying this through space allocation should be open to question.

The *value* of space standards will depend on:

— how accurately they reflect the *functional needs* of individual jobs.
— the *precision* with which it is possible to meet them in the scheme.

The *limitations* affecting their use include:

— possible problems accommodating them within the *physical constraints* of the scheme. For example, standards which have been developed by an organisation which has traditionally occupied deep-plan buildings may prove impossible to achieve if it is decided to locate a section or department in what was once a grand town house.
— problems occurring when standards have not been revised to take account of *changes* in working practices. This can often happen when technology has been introduced in an *ad hoc* fashion resulting in desks which previously accommodated paper, a telephone and a calculator now failing to cope with VDU, keyboard, working files, manuals etc.

With these limitations understood, space standards are essential to the general planning of space. Figure 2.11 gives typical requirements for different functions; this may be used as a basis for establishing specific needs where definitive standards do not exist.

In all cases, however, it should be remembered that standards are most useful for:

— *initial* determination, planning and allocation of space.
— as a *check* against later, detailed studies.

In order to develop detailed studies of requirements it is necessary to begin from first principles, starting with the *people* who will be occupying and using the environment, and looking closely at the *roles* and activities they must undertake followed by the *facilities* which will meet their requirements.

Data collection

Information may be obtained by:

— *questionnaire.*
— *interview.*
— a mixture of *both.*

Questionnaires are very useful for eliciting simple factual information from a wide range of people, but may end up as a description of existing facilities rather than of future needs.

Interviews are a much better means of establishing a real understanding of activities and needs; and can in addition be followed up at a later date in more depth. They are, however, usually selective and can be biased.

For an example of a typical questionnaire see Fig. 2.12. For more information on data gathering, analysis and presentation, see Appendix A.1.b: Duffy *et al.*[15].

Fig. 2.12 *Typical questionnaire used to gather information about relationships and individual/group/department needs.*

PROJECT:

DEPARTMENT: SECTION:

NAME: JOB TITLE:
JOB DESCRIPTION:
REPORTING TO: SUPERVISING:

VISITORS: INTERNAL:
EXTERNAL:

MEETINGS: AT DESK:
ELSEWHERE:

FURNITURE:

Desk(s):

Chairs: Desk:
Visitors:

Storage: Filing:
Drawers:
Shelving

Other:

Screens:

EQUIPMENT:

Telephone:
Typewriter:
Calculator:
Task light:
Monitor:
Keyboard:
Printer:
Modem:

NOTES:

Whatever methods are used, information on the following will be required:

— *numbers* of staff, identified according to grades, groups and departments.
— patterns and means of *contact* between *individuals*.
— patterns and means of *contact* between *groups*.
— patterns and means of *contact* between *departments*.
— patterns and means of *contact* with *visitors*.
— use of *equipment* by individuals and groups.
— need for *meetings* and style (formal/informal, size, frequency, use of technology, need for privacy etc.).
— *methods* of working.
— *management style* and degree of formality.
— *furniture* requirements (desk(s) sizes and heights, storage, chair(s), screening).
— ancillary requirements (pinboards, whiteboards, projection facilities, flipcharts etc.).
— anticipated *changes* in staff numbers, equipment and methods of working.

The use of interviews will also allow other, less classifiable, information to be gleaned; such as an individual's own understanding of their role, the importance of informal social relationships, expectations and/or fears regarding the changes about to take place etc. Factors such as these can be difficult to define, analyse or represent; but can be decisive in determining the success or failure of the project.

Analysis

The information-gathering process can generate vast amounts of data, and reducing this to an easily understood tabulation of numbers, areas, needs and relationships can be laborious. Computer programs are available which can speed the task, but judgements will still have to be made to give a weighting to relationships according to a perceived priority, and to weed out trivial information.

Presentation

Presentation in fact forms part of the analysis process, for to understand the large amounts of information generated it is necessary to reduce it to some form of tabular or graphical representation.

Visual presentation usually takes the form of bubble diagrams; by using a variety of connecting lines these can demonstrate the relative importance of interaction and the form(s) that it takes (e.g. face-to-face communication, telephone or terminal link). By developing the diagrams in greater and greater detail they can be made to form the basis of the space planning.

See Fig. 2.13 for an example of a typical bubble diagram.

Fig. 2.13 *Typical example of a bubble diagram. More sophisticated models can be developed using colour to define relationships; showing, for example, physical adjacency (and separation) needs, relative importance of relationships, communication links etc.*

Key

1 Reception
2 Conference suite
3 Marketing
4 Finance
5 Production control
6 Directors' offices/boardroom
7 Cafeteria

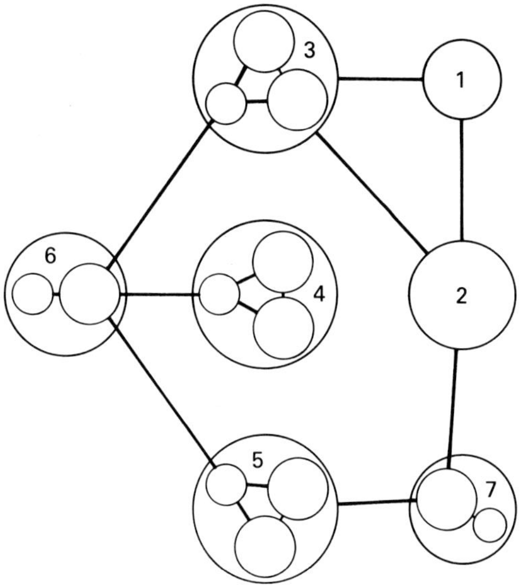

People

The test of the success of a project will be its ability to assist the users to perform their jobs with greater satisfaction, efficiency, comfort, safety or pleasure; preferably all five. It is therefore essential that the designer achieves an understanding of their needs. Although management will often feel that they know all that will be necessary to brief the designer, in practice it would be wise for the designer to insist on meeting representatives of all grades of staff. In very small organisations it should be possible to meet and interview everyone; in larger ones it will be necessary to classify functions and obtain information from a representative sample.

Planning

Means of escape

In the UK, statutory requirements covering means of escape are contained within *The Building Regulations 1985 Mandatory rules for means of escape in case of fire;* in the USA the *National Fire Codes 1979* produced by the National Fire Protection Association as enacted into local regulations.

Satisfying the regulations providing for means of escape will be a critical determining factor in finalising the internal layout. Regulations in the United Kingdom are summarised as follows:

— maximum travel distances where escape is possible in only *one* direction is *12.2 m*; on ground and first floors it may be 30.5 m if all offices have opening windows with a minimum opening of 840 × 535 mm wide, the lower level of opening lights is not more than 3.8 m above the exterior ground level or 915 mm above the internal floor level and the ground beneath windows is free of obstructions for a distance 1830 mm from the building.

— maximum travel distance where escape is possible in *two* directions is 45m; no part of an office should be more than 12.2 m from the exit door unless an alternative exit door exists.

— maximum distance between *two adjacent exits* from a storey is *61 m*.

— buildings with *floors more than 18.3 m above ground level* require at least *one fire-fighting stair* which must: have direct access to open air at ground level, have openable windows at each landing level, have permanent ventilation at the top of the enclosure of 5 per cent of enclosed area minimum, have a protected and ventilated lobby at each floor and be continuous throughout the building.

Minimum *staircase widths* are:

— *single staircase*, gross floor area *less than 230 m²*: 765 mm.
— *single staircase*, gross floor area *more than 230 m²*: 1070 mm.
— *two staircases* with only one floor above ground level, gross area *less than* 1860 m²: 1070 mm.
— *two staircases* with only one floor above ground level, for each *additional* 280 m² add 152 mm.

The precise relationship between circulation routes, core positions and the plan shape of the building can have very definite consequences for the types of accommodation which can be provided; affecting the areas which can be utilised as cellular offices, group rooms and open-plan space, as well as the qualities of the spaces. Figure 2.14 shows the implications of typical approaches.

Layout

With escape routes defined, *develop layout* options by *refining existing information* and investigating in increasing detail several aspects simultaneously:

— develop bubble diagrams into *building overlays* by refining space requirements for each function.

See Fig. 2.15 for an example of how bubble diagrams can be developed into space-planning drawings.

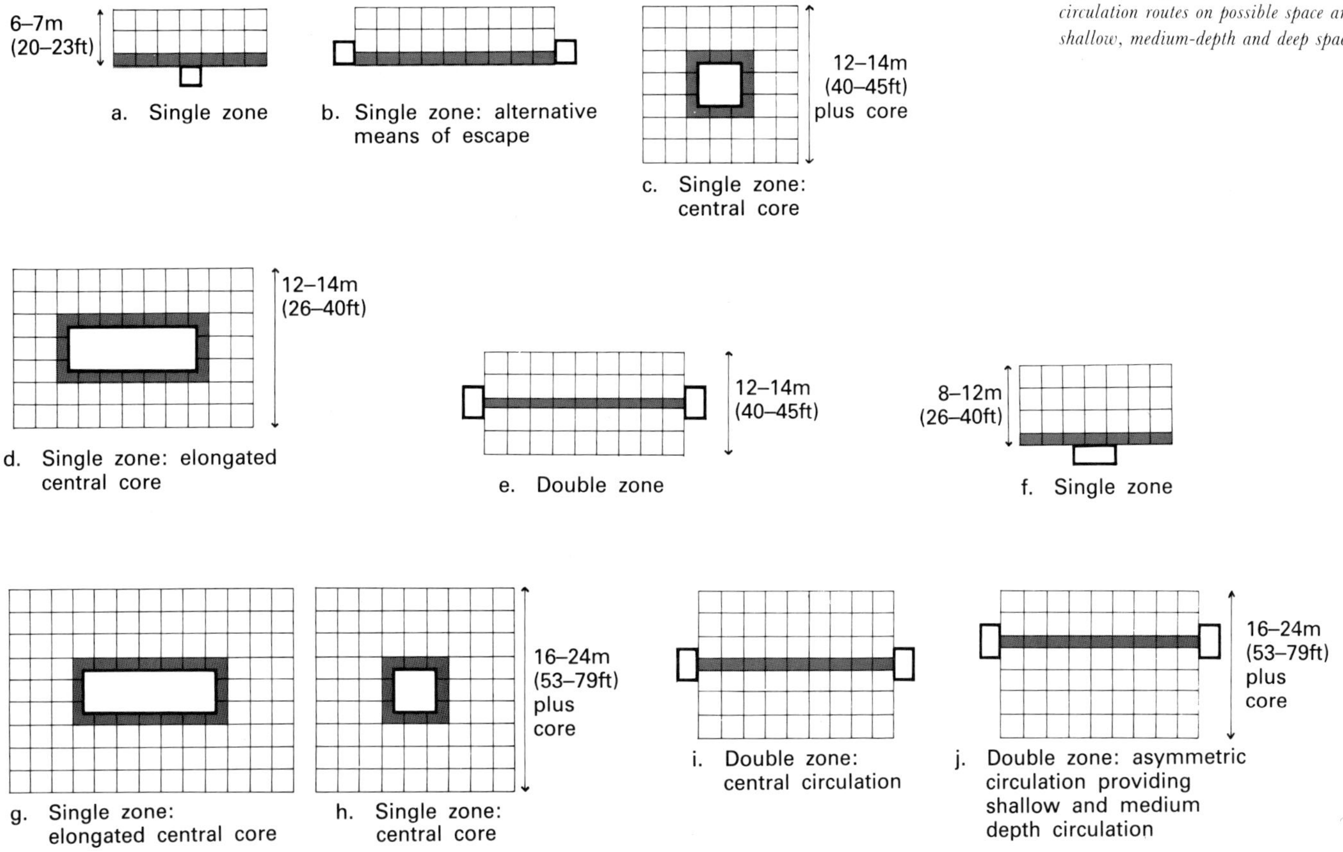

Fig. 2.14 *Effect of plan form, core positions and circulation routes on possible space arrangements for shallow, medium-depth and deep space.*

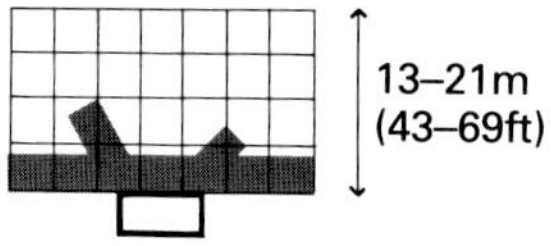

k Single zone

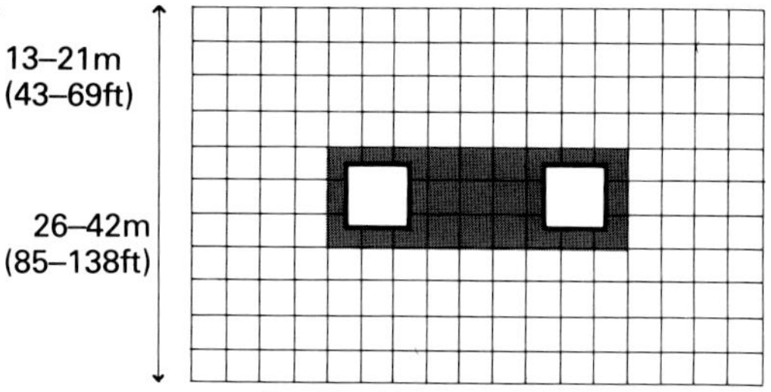

l Double zone: split core

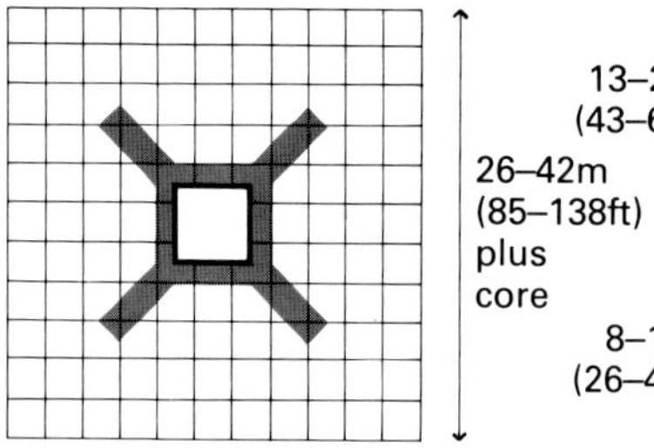

m Single zone: central core

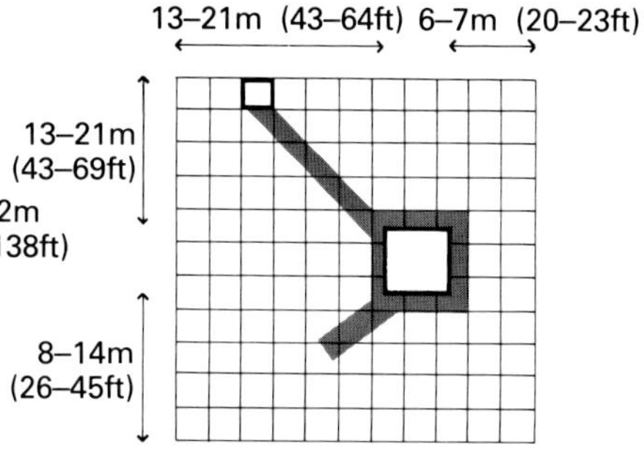

n Single zone: asymmetric core creating a mixture of deep, medium and shallow space

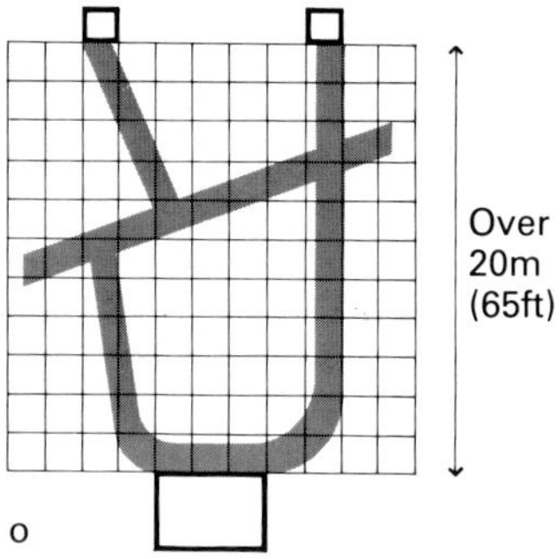

o

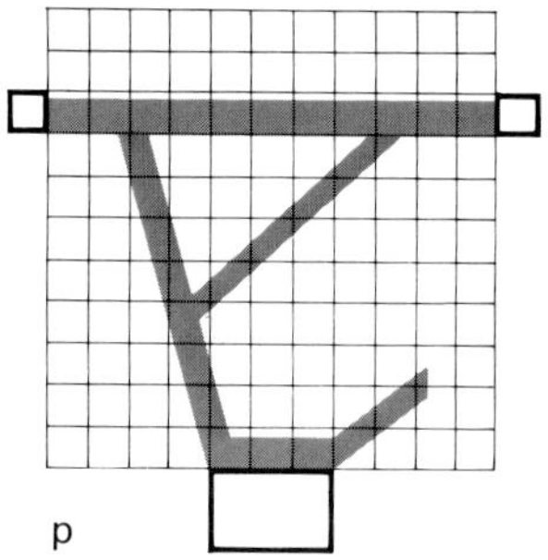

p

The choices available for locating circulation in very deep space are so wide that circulation ceases to be a significant factor in the preliminary zoning of space.

- establish all *circulation routes*: primary, secondary (linking groups to primary) and tertiary (within groups). Also determine widths (e.g. primary: 2000 mm (6 ft 6 in), secondary: 1500 mm (5 ft) tertiary: 750 mm (2 ft 6 in).
- confirm all *desk requirements* and sizes (see below).
- confirm all *storage requirements*: individual and shared (see below).
- investigate *furniture system* options in depth.

Ideally the layout should be a reflection of the *patterns* of *work-flow, communications* and *interaction*.

Although dimensions of different systems are broadly similar, each embodies assumptions about the functions they will satisfy and will allow different approaches to planning. Thus where a concept has been developed with one particular system in mind, a different system may require a completely fresh concept.

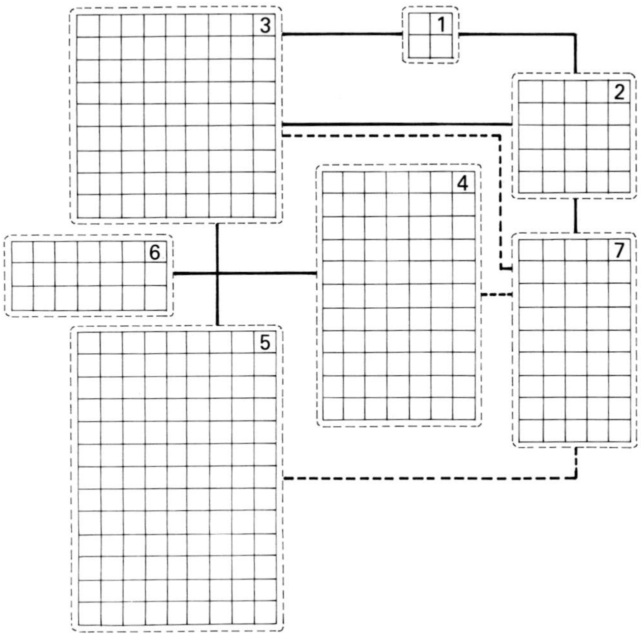

Key

1 Reception
2 Conference suite
3 Marketing
4 Finance
5 Production control
6 Directors' offices/boardroom
7 Cafeteria

Fig. 2.15 *a. The development of the bubble diagram shown in Fig. 2.12 into spatial representation by allocating areas to the various departments.*

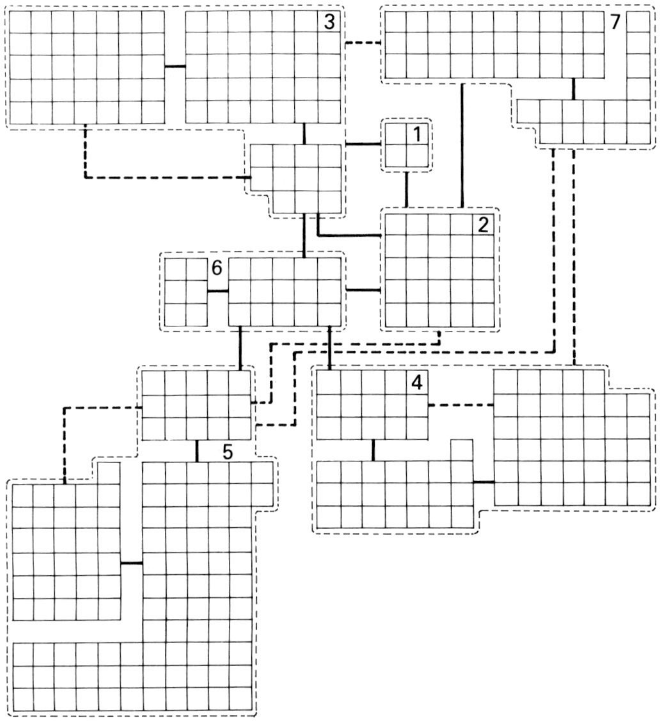

Key

1 Reception
2 Conference suite
3 Marketing
4 Finance
5 Production control
6 Directors' offices/boardroom
7 Cafeteria

b. The bubble diagram taken one stage further by identifying individual groupings within departments. Further development along these lines will produce the beginnings of a scheme.

As the planning is developed, certain *rules* will be fixed which establish the integrity of the scheme. For example, rules may be established governing the specific relationship of workstations to the services grid, or to the windows; or concerning the use of different heights of screens, or how planting is used. To assist with the continued effectiveness of the scheme such rules should be noted and passed to the client in a suitable form after completion.

Fig. 2.16 *Dimensions of typical desks and areas required for activities.*

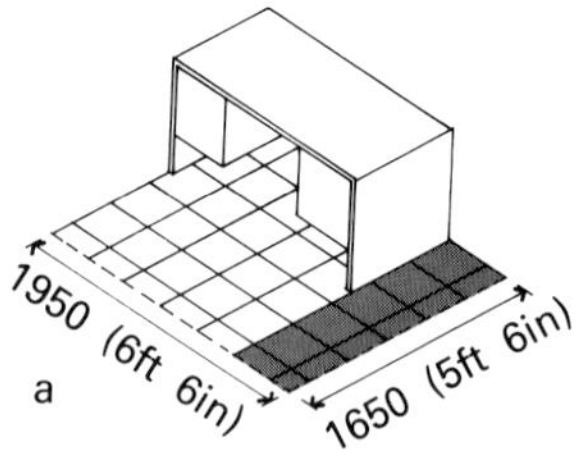

a

a Task characteristics: Clerical activities processing paper with minimal need for filing and material storage at the workstation. Furniture requirements: Desk 1500 × 750 mm (5 ft × 2 ft 6 in) with one or two pedestals. Area 3.2 m² (36 ft²).

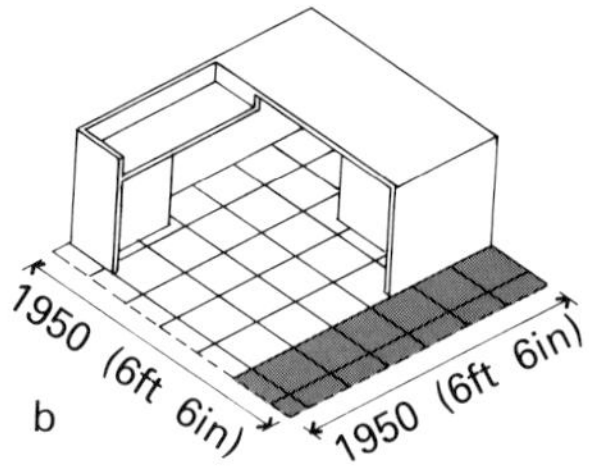

b

b Task characteristics: Secretarial activities involving typing, routine paperwork and telephoning; small amount of file and material storage at the workstation. Furniture requirements: Desk 1500 × 750 mm (5 ft × 2 ft 6 in) with 1150 × 450 mm (3 ft 6 in × 1 ft 6 in) extension and two pedestals. Area 3.8 m² (42 ft²).

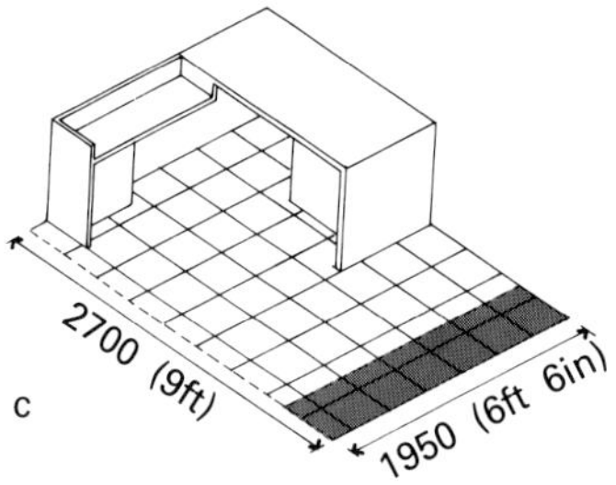

c

c Task characteristics: As b with the additional need for discussions at the workstation. Furniture requirements: As b with an additional guest chair. Area 5.3 m² (58 ft²).

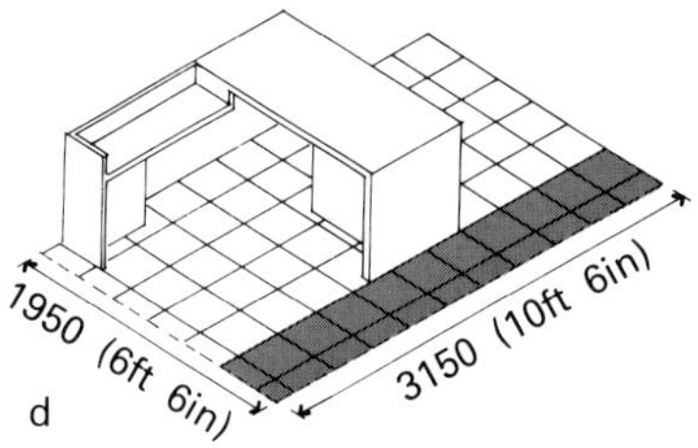

d

d Task characteristics: As c with greater need for discussions and meetings at the workstation. Furniture requirements: As b with additional 2 guest chairs. Area 6.1 m² (68 ft²).

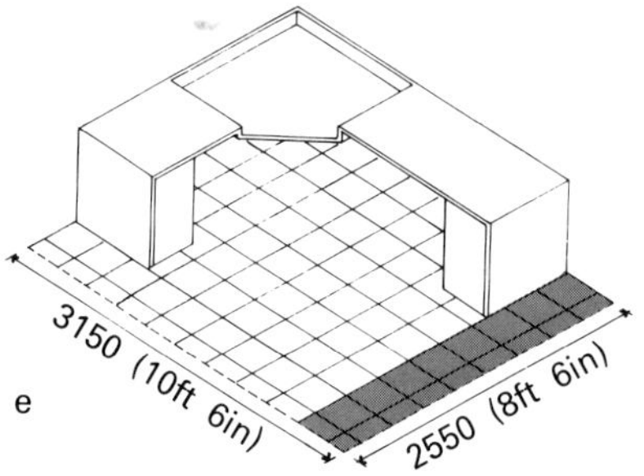

e

e Task characteristics: Entering data to terminal with frequent use of reference material. Limited amount of storage required at workstation; screening may be necessary to aid concentration. Furniture requirements: Angled worksurface 1200 × 1200 mm (4 ft × 4 ft), 1500 × 750 mm (5 ft × 2 ft 6 in) desk with 900 × 750 mm (3 × 2 ft 6 in) extension, two pedestals. Area 8 m² (89 ft²).

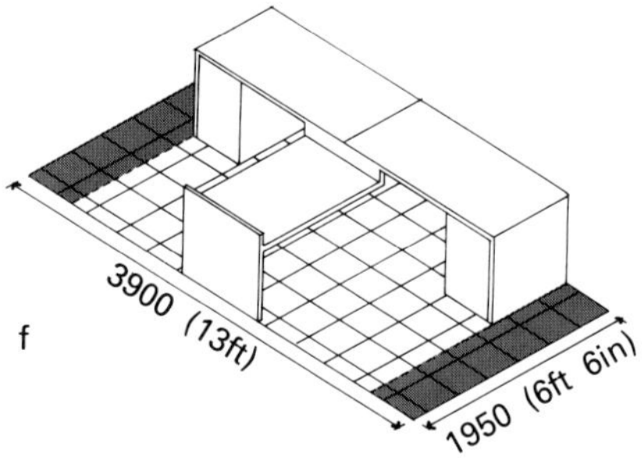

f

f Task characteristics: Data processing with shared equipment; frequent use of reference material. Limited amount of storage required at workstation; screening may be necessary to aid concentration. Area 7.6 m² (85 ft²).

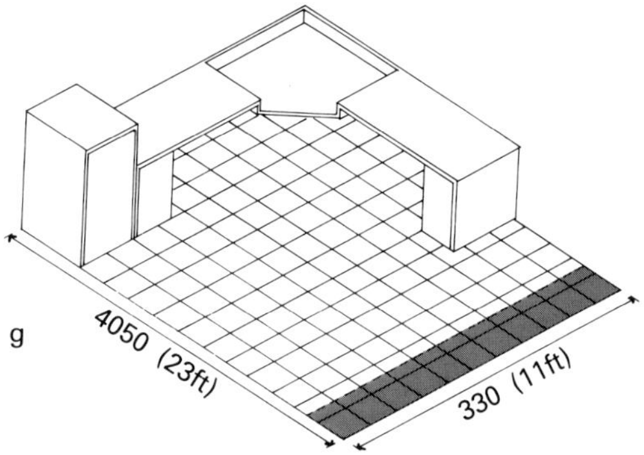

g

g. Task characteristics: Administrative/managerial activities involving limited conferencing facilities at desk, frequent but not prolonged use of electronic equipment and reference material. Extensive storage required at workstation and screening probably necessary to provide balance between need for privacy and ability to see and communicate with colleagues directly. Furniture requirements: Angled worksurface 1200 × 1200 mm (4 ft × 4 ft), 2 no. 1500 × 750 mm (5 ft × 2 ft 6 in) desks with 2 pedestals, additional filing/storage and shelving on screens where provided. Area 13.4 m² (253 ft²).

Desks

Desk area dimensions and activity requirements are given in Fig. 2.16. The information given is typical and should be checked wherever possible against actual circumstances; it can, however be used:

— to check the *suitability* of furniture ranges.
— for *schematic* design purposes.
— to produce basic layouts for *interpretation* by furniture suppliers.

See also 2.33.

The increasing complexity of systems makes it difficult for designers to have sufficient knowledge in depth to be able to fully exploit a system, particularly at a stage when three or more systems may be under consideration. They should, however, ensure that they have sufficient understanding to be satisfied that the interpretation presented is the best possible with that system.

Screens

Identify need for screens on the plan to provide:

— visual and acoustic *privacy*.
— *display* space.
— *definition* of separate functions.
— routes for *services* (for example, from a perimeter distribution system).
— *visual breaks* to large spaces.

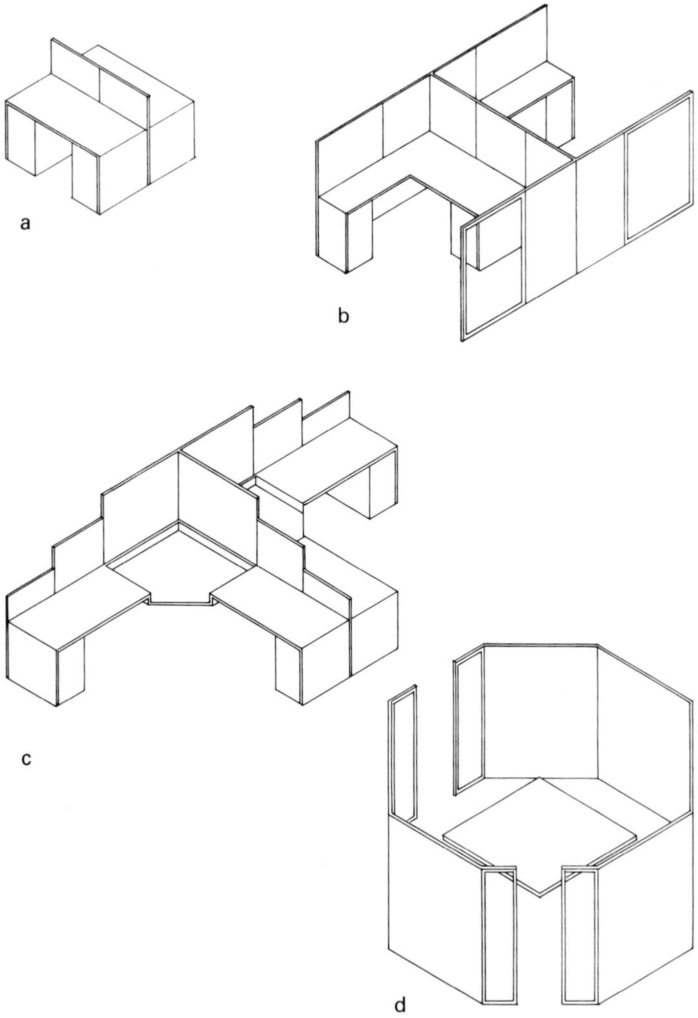

Fig. 2.17 *Examples of using screens to provide privacy for workplaces.*

a 1200 mm (4 ft) high screens separating two desks to give privacy when seated without restricting view when standing.

b 1500 mm (5 ft) high solid and glazed screens providing a degree of privacy to large workstations.

c 1000, 1200 and 1500 mm (3 ft 4 in, 4 ft and 5 ft) screens providing graded separation to avoid an over-restricted view when standing.

d 1800 mm (6 ft) high solid and glazed screens providing privacy to a meeting area within open space.

Where there is a danger of screening creating a maze-like appearance, consider varying heights and/or finishes, or using alternative means of screening (e.g. planting or using shared facilities such as filing or meeting areas to break up the space).

Storage

Common dimensions of stored items are given in Fig. 2.18. Check that these figures reflect client's requirements.
See also 2.33.

Ensure that all forms of storage requirement are identified, including:

— *individual needs*: filing, computer printout (burst and unburst), books, discs, pens, personal etc.
— *group storage*: filing, stationery, books, magnetic tapes, discs, coats etc.
— *central storage:* archives, stationery, spares etc.

Fig. 2.18 *Sizes of commonly stored items (all dimensions are given first in millimetres, with figures in brackets being inches).*

Item	*Dimensions*
Printer paper	380 × 280 (15 × 11)
	380 × 230 (15 × 9)
	330 × 280 (13 × 11)
	280 × 230 (11 × 9)
Conventional paper	
Letter	280 × 220 (11 × $8^1/_2$)
Legal	360 × 220 (14 × $8^1/_2$)
A4	297 × 210 ($11^5/_8$ × $8^1/_4$)
A5	210 × 148 ($8^1/_4$ × $5^3/_4$)
Magnetic tape reels	180, 200, 270, 380, (7, 8, $10^1/_2$, 15) diameter
Floppy discs	80, 130, 200 (3, 5, 8) diameter
Winchester discs	140, 200, 360 ($5^1/_2$, 8, 14) diameter
Disc packs	250, 380 (10, 15) diameter, 25, 75, 100 (1, 3, 4) thick
Microfiche sheets	150 × 100 (6 × 4)

Common sizes of storage systems and space for access are shown in Fig. 2.19.

Determine best form of provision for each type of storage required:

— filing systems.
— high cupboards.
— screen or partition hung high-level cupboards.
— open shelves.
— low cupboards.
— pedestals (mobile or fixed).

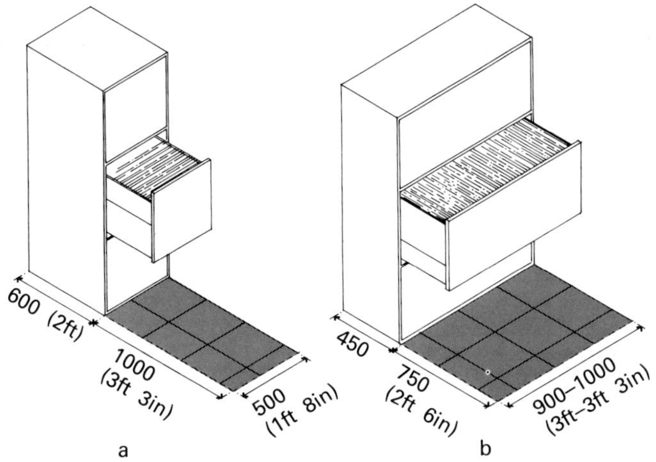

Fig. 2.19 *Common dimensions of storage units and space for access.*

a Standard drawer filing cabinet.

b Lateral filing cabinet.

2.22.2 Special functions

This section covers the particular requirements of dealing rooms, meeting spaces and cafeterias. In addition to providing guidance on space planning, it also covers services, lighting, finishes etc. where specific needs differ from the requirements relating to general office areas covered in the sections (2.27–2.35) on detail design.

Dealing rooms

Typically, dealing rooms are very large spaces characterised by high occupancy density, noise and frenetic activity. This form owes much to the market place traditions and origins of dealing; it is sometimes argued that modern technology will make such spaces redundant and that in the future dealing rooms will operate out of more usually proportioned through highly serviced office spaces. Against this are the feelings of the dealers themselves, who want to be able to sense the level of activity in other parts of the room, and prefer to have the reassurance of eye contact and hand signal communication to confirm the information on the screen. The designer of dealing rooms has to provide for not only the extreme demands made on the space by the equipment, but also for the difficult requirements of the people working in it.

Space planning

Dealers work in groups of varying numbers, which are subject to change. Members of each group (usually referred to as a 'desk') work in close proximity to each other, and need visual and aural proximity to other groups. Establish:

— size and composition of each desk.
— relationships between desks.
— allowance to be made for expansion.

Spacing between desks will be dependent on the acoustic properties of the space; the aim being for sound to travel clearly over certain distances then fade into background. In an acoustically neutral environment the spacing between desks should be approximately 1.5 m (5 ft).

Four people working at a square or cruciform desk arrangement is considered ideal; though frequently larger groupings have to be accommodated for reasons of density or function. Densities are usually high: approximately 3.75 m^2 (40 ft^2) per person.

Whilst determining space-planning options take account of:

— administrative support functions: adjacent but isolated acoustically from main space.
— toilet facilities: adjacent and ensure ample provision; no-one likes wasting time in a queue, but dealers can provide particularly strong financial arguments in their favour.
— possible future alterations in planning and sizes of groups.

Desks

See Fig. 2.20 for diagrammatic representation of a typical workstation.
For more information on the detail design of desks see 2.33.

In the past, desks have often been purpose made and tailored to incorporate all the equipment. It is now recognised that this approach does not provide sufficient flexibility for the frequent changes required when spaces and arrangements are altered, or when items are replaced. Usually desks are either:

— proprietary systems.
— purpose made, adopting a loose-fit approach to the incorporation of equipment.
— modified standard office furniture ranges.

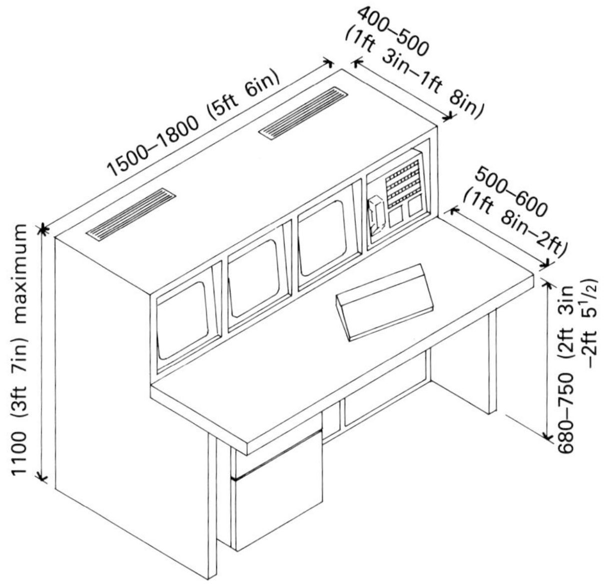

Fig. 2.20 *Diagrammatic representation of a typical dealing workstation. Actual dimensions will vary according to the number of screens installed, though it is usually desirable to keep the overall width to a minimum; in some instances the pedestal is omitted to aid this. Ideally the worksurface height should be adjustable, but this desire can conflict with the need to avoid excessive overall height.*

Facilities to be incorporated might include:

— VDUs up to six (though usually two or three) per workstation, depending on the market, often of different shapes and sizes (sometimes additional shared screens will also be a requirement, either to serve a desk or an area of the room).
— dealer board: telephone switchboard with up to 50 outside lines and 20 direct lines.
— telephone handsets: one or two.
— personal computer and keyboard.

Careful selection of handsets, in conjunction with the user, is needed; they need to be robust and should be capable of being comfortably cradled against the shoulder, leaving both hands free.

— squawk boxes (telephone loudspeakers): up to six.
— calculator and task light.

In addition, space will be required for directories and dealing tickets, and mobile storage with one or two file drawers.

Squawk boxes should be located as near as possible to ear level to allow minimum volume.

Electrics/cabling

The very high service requirements of dealing rooms (up to four times that of a normal office) mean that almost invariably a raised floor will be necessary. Selection of the raised floor system should progress concurrently with the development of the underfloor services layout; particular points to be noted include:

— the location of service outlets should not constrain furniture layouts.
— voids will need to be deeper than usual, perhaps 300–500 mm (12–20 in).
— frequent access will be required: allow sufficient space to avoid problems caused by congestion and consider the effect of floor panel module.

Data cables and power will run from junction boxes under the floor to the desk positions, usually then being run within the desk to serve each workstation. Power requirements will include:

— clean supplies to data equipment: ensure that these are separate from other sources to prevent misuse.
— normal ring supplies to serve personal equipment (calculators etc.) on the desk, and for cleaners' sockets.

Cable access within the desks should be simple to facilitate alterations; ensure that this can be achieved without moving furniture and without having to thread wiring (use lay-in trays).

Allow 120 W/m^2 (100 W/yd^2)until specific loadings are determined.
See also 2.24 and 2.32.

Standard 600 × 600 (2 ft × 2 ft) panels will normally allow sufficient access without having to move furniture and equipment.

Lighting

Fluorescent lighting can cause problems with screen scanning rate, causing apparent flicker. Test effects using a mock-up installation, or consider uplighting combined with desk-mounted task lighting.

Illuminance should usually be 500 lux (46 ft-candles) at desk level; but care will be needed to prevent glare and reflections.
See also 2.30.

Mechanical design

Temperature changes are often rapid because the quantity of equipment in use can vary. Consider:

— openable windows (not often feasible, particularly in large spaces).
— individual controllable outlets mounted within the desk.

In addition to providing for personal comfort, the system will need to remove excess heat created by the equipment. Often this will involve direct cooling by either:

— chilled water circulation within the desk connected to manifolds in the floor void.

See also 2.31.

— air circulation, either ducted from under the floor or by using the floor void as a plenum, passing through a grill in the top of the desk and rising to ceiling-mounted extract grills.

Additional fans and/or pumps may be required under the floor; consider the implications for service layout and for access.

Meeting spaces

The term 'meeting' can cover a very broad spectrum of activities, including:

— informal discussions around a desk (or casually instigated over a cup of coffee).
— group discussions around a table.
— formal meetings or presentations.
— gatherings of the entire staff.
— interviews.
— conferences, training sessions, lectures, seminars etc.
— trades union, or other staff meetings.

Characteristics of meeting types are shown in tabulated form in Fig. 2.21.

Many of these functions overlap in their requirements; consequently this section begins by considering provisions according to the location and method of satisfying the need, rather than by specific functions. Types of meeting space are categorised as those occurring at the workstation, meeting areas within normal working space (i.e. those defined by furniture and other flexible elements), and specific, dedicated facilities (i.e. those defined by fixed, 'permanent' elements).

Fig. 2.21 *Characteristics of meeting types.*

Type of space	Usage	Provision, furniture and equipment	Location
Provision at the workplace			
1 Meeting at desk	Short discussions, briefing subordinates, personal interviews	1 or 2 visitors' chairs at workstation	Screened if in open-plan space
2 Meeting area Working discussions amongst staff or with visitors	Table, chairs, pinboard, whiteboard		
Provision for a group of workplaces			
2 Meeting area	Working sessions within group or personnel from outside. May last several hours	Table, chairs, screening, flipcharts, pinboard, whiteboard. Possible location for group notices	Within group area adjacent to primary circulation to limit disturbance

Fig. 2.21 *Characteristics of meeting types (cont.)*

Type of space	*Usage*	*Provision, furniture and equipment*	*Location*
Provision for all members of staff			
4 Interview room	Interviewing personnel or sales representatives. Discussions with members of public. Short periods of use up to 3/4 hour	Aural and visual privacy required	Good access from main reception and departments with major usage. May require adjacent waiting area if used frequently
5 Meeting room	Meetings with outside visitors or internal policy making and planning meetings. Duration 2–3 hours	Slides, overhead projector, flipcharts, dimmer lights, good ventilation. Storage for drinks and audiovisual equipment	Ease of access to all departments. Easily serviced with refreshments. Access for outside visitors without going through work areas. Coats storage adjacent
6 Rest area	Primarily for refreshment breaks, but also an area where general notices can be displayed. Used throughout the day for short periods	Vending machines, stand-up counters, low tables and easy chairs. Display board. Screening from work areas	Adjacent to WCs and rest room. Easily accessible to all personnel
7 Boardroom	Formal board meetings, signing of contracts. Management meetings. Business lunches and entertaining. 2–3 hour meetings	Formal layout. Audio-visual equipment. Good ventilation. Space and facilities for stenographer	Anteroom for coats and refreshments attached
8 Conference room	Presentations. Working discussions with outside visitors	Audio-visual equipment. Dimmer lights and black-out. Storage for equipment and furniture. Allow space for alternative layouts	Easy access for visitors
9 Lecture room	Large conferences, presentations, lectures and training sessions	Video display. Control room for audio-visual equipment	Adjacent area for audience to assemble before/ after meetings

Workstation meetings

Workstation meetings characteristically involve a small number of people and last for a relatively short period of time. Their functional requirements may be met by one of the following sets of facilities:

— simple addition of one or two visitors' chairs.
— desk extension (often three-quarter circular) designed for meetings with two or three chairs.
— additional table, either adjacent to desk or separate, with appropriate number of chairs.
— easy chairs and/or sofas and low table (occasionally used in cellular offices for senior management).

Care is needed in planning area meeting spaces to provide sufficient separation to prevent their use as a workstation, or as an extension to one person's workspace.

Area meeting spaces

Included in this category would be meeting spaces in open-plan areas and those utilising cellular offices without any major alterations (i.e. those which could be turned back to normal office use simply by a change of furniture). Meeting types would include briefings, group discussions and project working sessions involving up to eight people and possibly lasting several hours. If in open-plan areas, suitable acoustic screening will be required, and facilities might include:

— table and appropriate number of chairs.
— pinboard, whiteboard and flipchart display.

Such areas might form a focal point for a department or group, and consequently could be a useful location for the display of information relevant to that section.

Dedicated meeting spaces

Dedicated facilities will need to be provided where meetings require special equipment (projection, televideo conferencing etc.), a higher quality environment (for example, where presentations are made and there is a need to impress) or where greater privacy is required. Provision will vary considerably according to the particular needs of an organisation, but characteristics and facilities might include:

— locations to suit shared usage by different departments, but directly accessible from reception where visitors will attend.
— the ability to accommodate a variety of types of meeting: formal/informal, interviews, presentations, large/small (consider large spaces capable of sub-division by movable partitions).
— display facilities: whiteboards, flipcharts, pinboards, shelving.
— projection facilities: slide, film, video, overhead; either from within the room or outside (back or front).
— variable lighting: either separate switchable circuits or dimmers; consider switch positions in relation to projection control position.
— tele-conferencing facilities: see below.

Where occasional meetings of all staff will be a requirement, consider temporary use of another space (e.g. cafeteria) for that purpose, and determine the implications for that space.

Control of mechanical systems for meeting rooms should ideally be separate from other areas. For example, consider individual thermostats to cope with high heat concentrations, additional extract (especially if smoking is permitted) and control of fresh air input by sensors detecting CO_2 build-up.

Consult with manufacturers or specialist consultants to determine projection equipment requirements: screen dimensions, distance of lens from screen, projection room dimensions, control wiring etc.
See also Appendix A.1.b: *New Metric Handbook*[1], chapter 31.

Tele-conferencing

Tele-conferencing consists of remote linking of people via normal telephone transmissions (including satellites) for voice-only conferencing or video conferencing.

Voice tele-conferencing

Facilities can be provided at the workstation or within meeting rooms. Requires good acoustic privacy.

Video tele-conferencing

Requires a dedicated, specially equipped suite of rooms, usually consisting of conference room, equipment room and sound-lock entrance lobby. Facilities, characteristics and equipment required will include:

The design of video tele-conferencing facilities is a specialist task, and the advice of a communications consultant or specialist installer should be sought.

Equipment: cameras (directed at participants and display material), microphones, video display, electronic blackboard and facsimile machine for transmission of hard copy.

Furniture: seating and tables located to suit camera positions.

Acoustics: minimal ambient noise levels; consider sound isolation from adjacent spaces, all service runs through space (plumbing, ductwork etc.), air movement through diffuser grills, reverberation time, vibration (physical effects on equipment as well as sound impact).

See 2.27 and 2.28.

Lighting: should create relaxing atmosphere to help overcome the intimidating effect of cameras and equipment: glare-free general illumination in front of and above participants supplemented by directional incandescent lamps (controlled by dimmers) to enhance flesh tones.

Construction: sound-insulating walls extended to soffit, acoustic ceilings, all service penetrations sealed, solid-core doors with seals all round.

See also 2.27 and 2.28.

Finishes: dense-pile carpeting on underlay, fabric covering to walls, colouring to provide good contrast background for participants.

Wall finishes which will form the background to participants should have a reflectance value no greater than 40 per cent to provide good contrast. See also 2.29 and 2.34.

Meeting space size and allocation

Type, size and allocation of meeting spaces will vary considerably from organisation to organisation, depending on:

Space requirements for various sizes of meetings are shown in Fig. 2.22.

- size of organisation: the larger or more specialised will have a greater need, particularly in headquarters buildings.
- degree of bureaucracy: generally a complex hierarchical structure will require more formal meeting rooms; an informal structure will require more informal meeting areas.
- number of outside visitors, and need to keep them away from work areas (for example, a graphic design consultancy may work for a number of clients in related fields, and will need to meet them away from the studios).

Fig. 2.22 *Space requirements for various forms of meeting.*

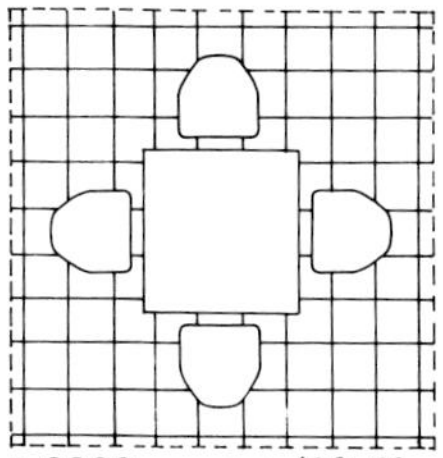

a 2900 square (9ft 6in sq)

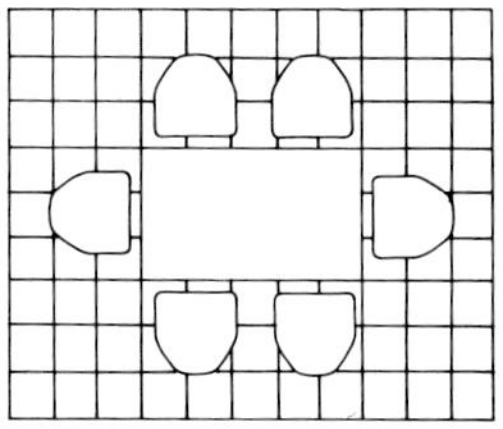

b 3300 × 2700 (11ft × 9ft)

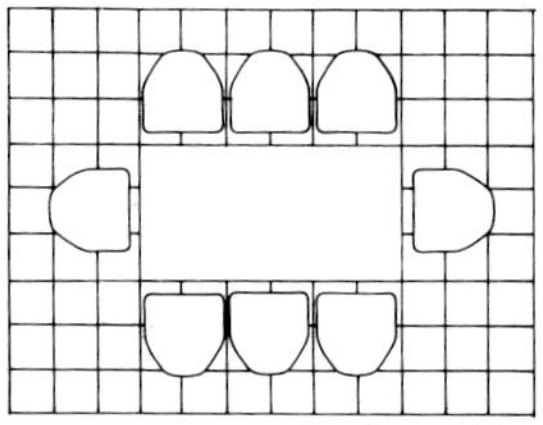

c 3600 × 2700 (12ft × 9ft)

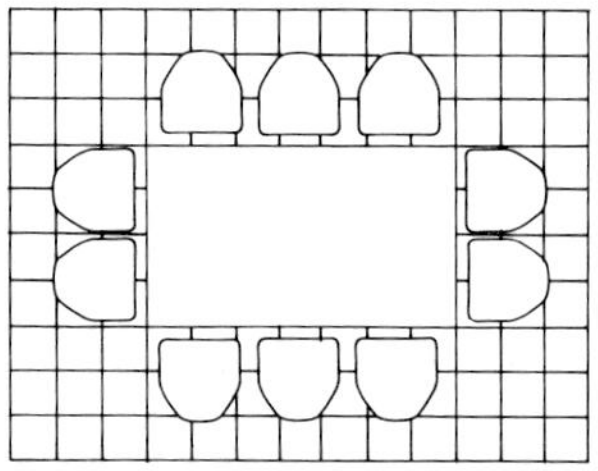

d 3900 × 3000 (13ft × 10ft)

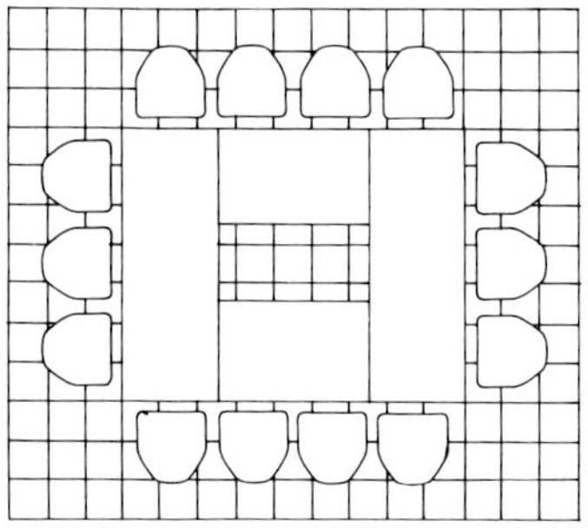

e 4500 × 3900 (13ft × 10ft)

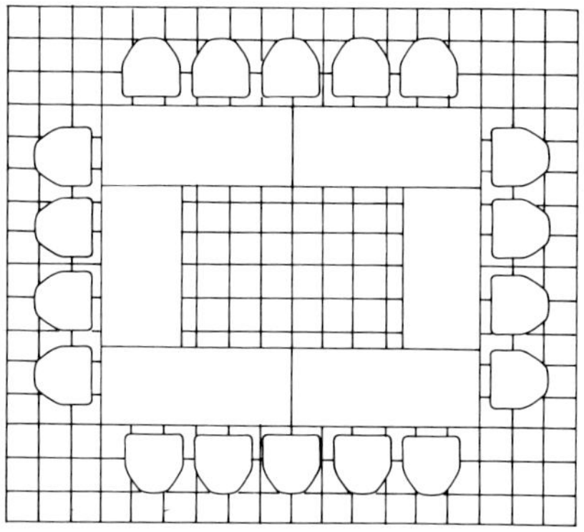

f 5400 × 4800 (17ft 6in × 16ft)

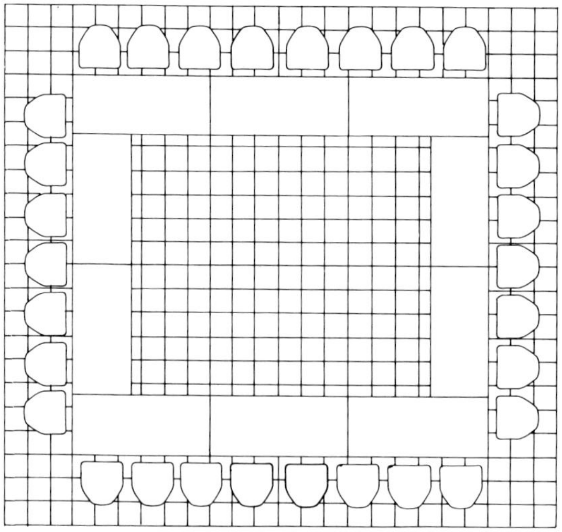

g 7200 × 6600 (23ft × 21ft 6in)

— type of work: project-orientated will have a greater meeting requirement than clerical/administrative functions.
— planning concept: cellular offices provide the facility for small, private meetings without separate, special provision necessarily having to be made.

Dining facilities

Provision of dining facilities within offices can vary across a very wide range, from none at all through domestic-scale kitchens to full cafeteria facilities catering for several hundred diners. Requirements in individual circumstances will depend on:

— numbers of staff likely to take meals.
— individual preferences (whether staff prefer a break away from the office, or prefer to bring a prepared lunch etc.).
— size of organisation and number of visitors.
— locally available alternatives (sandwich bars, cafes, restaurants etc. in a suitable price range).
— management attitudes to providing facilities and to subsidies.
— other reasons (e.g. where clients are entertained frequently, conferences organised, or where unusual hours are worked).

Where there is only a limited need this can be met within a small space containing perhaps a sink, refrigerator, kettle and/or coffee maker and perhaps a hotplate and a microwave oven. Consideration should also be given to providing table(s) and chairs in a space separate from work areas where lunch can be taken.

Where the demand is for more elaborate facilities, making provision will be more complicated with greater implications for the rest of the building; and the following guidelines relate to this situation.

For detailed information on catering facilities see Appendix A.1.b: Lawson[2] and *New Metric Handbook*[1], chapter 20.

Location

Determine location of cafeteria and kitchen, taking into account:

— outlook from dining area (upper floors may provide best views).
— access for people, equipment, goods and kitchen waste.
— ventilation – particularly kitchen extract.

Kitchens will be ideally positioned on the north-east (coolest) corner of the building.

Air-handling systems for kitchen areas should be designed to ensure that they are negatively pressured in relation to all adjacent spaces (including the dining area) to prevent the spread of odours.

Dining area

Determine circulation patterns, ensuring that there is no conflict between entry and exit points and that potential areas of congestion are avoided (tray and cutlery stands, drinking water fountains etc.).

Develop the scheme, taking into account:

— achieving maximum capacity without restricting circulation.
— the functional qualities of the finishes.
— providing a relaxed contrast to general office areas.

Space requirements for dining areas are shown in Fig. 2.23.

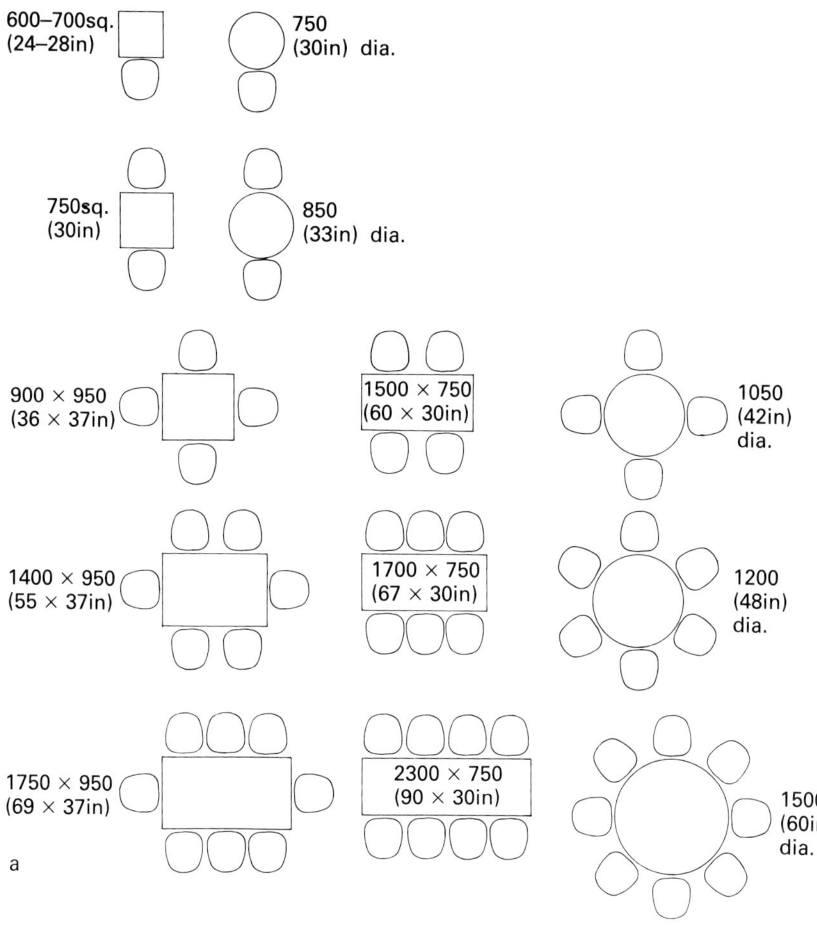

Fig. 2.23 *Space and furniture requirements for dining areas. a Examples of recommended table sizes for various numbers of persons.*
b Examples of different layouts for cafeteria tables.
c. Example of formal dining room layout.

Servery

The servery should be positioned close to the entrance but with sufficient space allowed to prevent congestion. Arrangements are usually in the form of either a single line, or separate counters offering different options. The latter takes up more space but can provide a quicker throughput of people; and particularly aids those only wishing to purchase one or two items. In either case consider:

- menu and price display.
- tray pick-up.
- counter design: either standard, complete units, or standard units positioned behind a purpose-designed screen incorporating a tray slide.
- methods of keeping food hot: bain-marie, heated counter top, infra-red lamps etc.
- sneeze-screens over food display areas.
- cash desk(s): usually the biggest bottleneck; open-plan counter arrangements can facilitate the deployment of a greater number of cash desks.

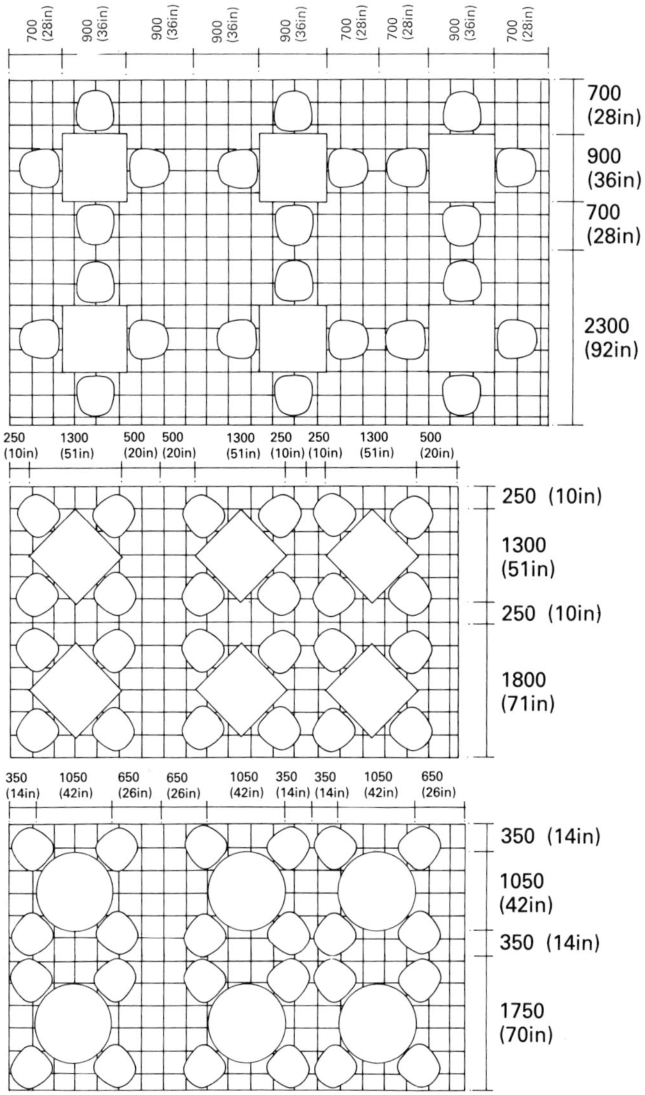

b

b Examples of different layouts for cafeteria tables.

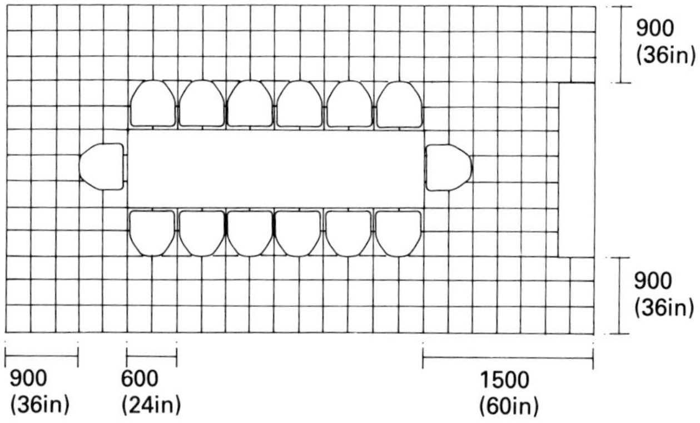

c

c Example of formal dining room layout.

Collection of dirty crockery

Determine means of clearing dirty crockery:

— trolley collection, requiring an aisle width of 1350 mm.
— self-clearance, requiring co-operation and either slots or a conveyor through to the dishwashing area.

Kitchen

Large-scale kitchens require the services of a specialist catering consultant. Facilities required may include various sinks, storage for utensils, equipment for mixing, chopping, weighing etc., tables, benches and various ovens, hotplates and grills. Determine the services required by the equipment, including:

— gas and electric loads, and whether three-phase supply will be necessary.
— drainage, incorporating grease traps where necessary.
— extract and ventilation, particularly over cooking, servery and dishwashing areas; establishing grease trap and fire damper provision.

Handwashing facilities entirely separate from preparation and dishwashing sinks will be necessary.

Finishes should be hygienic and able to withstand frequent cleaning, with construction being solid without any voids.

Great care is needed in the selection of floor finishes to ensure that they are non-slip, yet can be kept clean.

Dishwashing

Area required will depend on the size of the facility; dishwashing is usually by machine.

Ensure that sufficient space is allowed for dirty crockery, removing debris, loading the machine, unloading and sorting before return (usually back to the servery).

Staff

Separate lavatory and changing facilities may be required for kitchen staff. In large installations the catering manager may need an office within the kitchen area.

Types and volumes of storage required will depend on catering methods, but will normally include separate spaces for vegetables, dry goods, chilled storage and frozen storage.

Storage/delivery

Consider methods and requirements for delivery, including:

— access and turning space for vehicles.
— space for unloading, checking and weighing.
— storage spaces required adjacent to the kitchen (a goods lift may be necessary).

2.22.3 Machine rooms

In office areas, space requirements and planning standards can be identified because of accepted ergonomic data and because furniture generally conforms to similar dimensions whoever the manufacturer. The same situation does not apply to computer rooms; requirements are dictated by the particular equipment, which varies greatly from model to model, manufacturer to manufacturer and installation to installation. The designer must consult closely with the system installer/supplier to identify and cater for all requirements.

However, general guidance can be given on all aspects of machine room design except space requirements to aid sensible discussion. Subjects covered in this section include:

— electrical design and data cabling.
— mechanical design.
— lighting.
— finishes.

Operation of computer rooms is usually very intensive, often subject to 24 hour working, and the equipment is likely to require frequent modification, replacement or repair. Care is needed to ensure that all facilities can cope with rigorous requirements.

Where computer rooms do operate on a different time-scale to the rest of the building, separate electrical and mechanical systems will be required to facilitate energy management.

Electrical design and data cabling

Electrical

Electrical requirements will normally include:

— panels designed to cope with 24 hour operation at full load.
— distribution board(s) with a high degree of spare capacity (allow 25 per cent).
— radial supplies and clean earths (ensure that any other power supplies to the same area, such as cleaners' sockets, are on a different circuit).
— frequency meters to allow monitoring of variations where disc-drive equipment is installed.

Guidance is given in this section on aspects of particular relevance to machine rooms; 2.23, 2.31 and 2.32 should also be consulted.

Data cabling

Computers in machine rooms (often known as controllers) need to be connected to the building data cable system (known as a local area network, or LAN) via patch panels which allow connection patterns to be altered rather in the manner of old-fashioned telephone switchboards. Where possible they should be located in a room directly adjacent to the machine room; if this is not feasible they can be sited alongside the controllers.

Dimensions of patch panels will vary from installation to installation; essentially they consist of steel cabinets with lockable doors and cable entries top and bottom.

See Fig. 2.24 for a diagrammatic representation of a typical data cable network.
See also 2.24 for more information on data cable distribution systems.

Fig. 2.24 *a Diagrammatic representation of a typical data cable network. b Schematic representation of data cable network in a medium-rise building.*

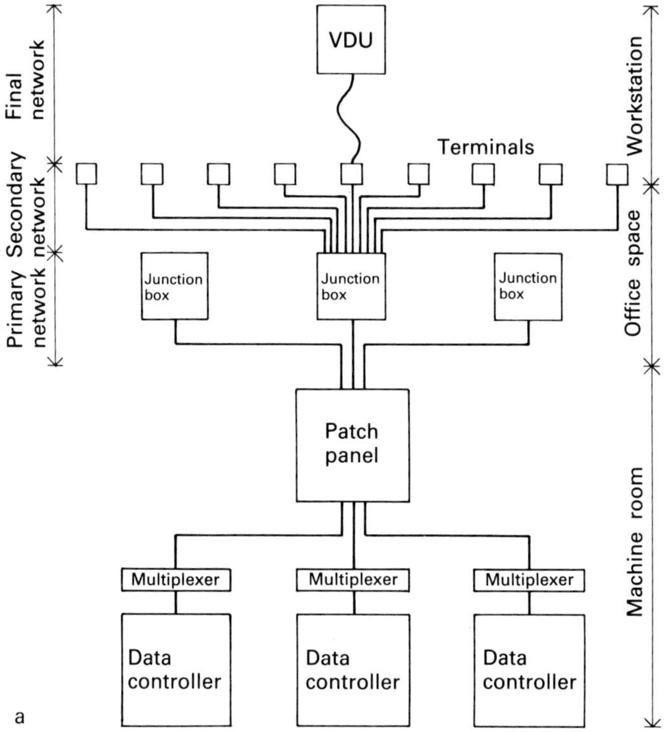

a

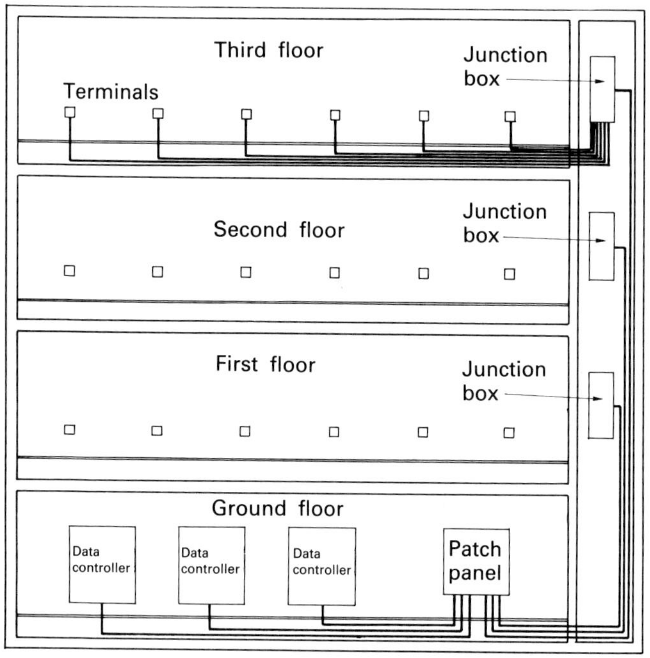

b

Inside is a series of sockets connected at the rear to multi-core cables, one set linked to the controllers, the other to junction boxes throughout the building. At the front, space is left for jumper cables to allow any one socket to be connected to another. The specification, manufacture and installation of patch panels is a specialist operation, but the building designer should be aware of their function within the data distribution system, and should establish:

— dimensions of particular boxes to be installed.
— cable space requirements and routes.
— access space requirements.
— expansion space to be allowed.

Mechanical design

The heat levels generated by equipment in computer rooms is often high, unevenly distributed and subject to change. If a ceiling distribution system is used, simply accommodating everything within the void, and on the ceiling, whilst leaving sufficient room for lighting, smoke detectors etc., will prove difficult. Consequently, distribution via a raised floor void is to be preferred where possible, and, as some equipment requires direct cooling with chilled water or conditioned air, will sometimes be essential.

If the floor void is to be used as a plenum for the supply of conditioned air, check that the flow is not restricted by other services.

In all cases ensure that:

— provision is made to prevent the formation of condensation should the system be shut down for a period of time.
— waste-water pipework is not routed through the space.
— the air distribution does not result in dust or fibres being introduced into the space.

Where routing water pipework through the space cannot be avoided, for example those carrying chilled water supplies, ensure that runs are away from equipment locations and consider the installation of leak detectors under the raised floor.

Where clean room conditions are required, air-conditioning filters should be to the standards laid down in US Federal Standard 209B.

Where equipment requires direct cooling by chilled water, consult manufacturers' specifications for information on:

— flow and return manifolds.
— valve arrangements, sensors, connections etc.
— flow rates, temperature and pressure drops.

Supply of chilled water should be separate from the main building supply, in the form of either a heat exchanger on the main chillers or independent chillers.

Lighting

See also 2.30.

The demands placed upon the lighting system in machine rooms are quite rigorous, and will often require variable levels to suit different situations including:

— normal, glare-free illumination with gooddddd distribution on vertical surfaces
  giving an average illuminance at desk level of 500–600 lux (46–56 ft-candles).
— lower lighting levels in certain areas to allow illuminated consoles to be seen.
— higher levels (800 lux, 75 ft-candles) as a task lighting for servicing.
— minimum levels for CCTV surveillance where applicable.

The colour rendition properties of the lamps should be considered carefully, particularly with regard to the needs of service engineers; colour characteristics other than white could make their task difficult.

In some cases screening against electromagnetic interference will be necessary in machine rooms; requirements might include: mesh installed over external glazing, metal foil or panels on the walls, all bonded to raised floor and ceiling supports. For general information on finishes see 2.34.

Finishes

Finishes in machine rooms should:

— not create dust.
— be light in colour (with a minimum reflectance value of 70 per cent) to aid illumination of vertical surfaces.
— be easily maintained with minimal disruption to operations.

2.22.4 Ancillary spaces

Entrance, reception and circulation

To determine requirements for lifts, estimate peak traffic flows and consult with alternative manufacturers to establish space, structural, power, waiting area and machine room needs.
The security function at the reception desk may also include monitoring electronic devices, CCTV screens etc.; equipment which may need to be built into the desk. Allow for cabling requirements, access for maintenance, ventilation etc.
Recommendations for entrance matting are that a minimum of 2 metres (6 ft 6 in) of grit-removing matting and 5 metres (16 ft 6 in) of sacrificial (i.e. readily replaced) dirt and moisture-removing matting should be provided before general floor finishes are reached.
Acoustics: noise generated in entrances should not penetrate to office areas or vice versa.
Lighting: 150 lux (14 ft-candles) scalar 1.2 m (4 ft) above floor level plus special for displays etc. as required.

The reception area may have to fulfil a number of functions; in determining the appropriate size, layout and form, consider the following:

— traffic flows for staff and visitors.
— relationship between entrance and main circulation, horizontal and vertical (lifts and waiting space, main stairs, corridors etc.); access to office areas, meeting rooms, lavatories etc.
— number of people likely to be waiting at any one time and type of seating.
— security requirements, including siting of desk to allow visual monitoring of movement of people in and out of building.
— image: in providing first impressions the reception can be an important advertisement for the company. Maintenance factors play a role in this; an area which is difficult to keep clean will not create a good impression.
— visibility from outside.
— entrance requirements (double, single or revolving doors, draught lobby etc.).
— display of company's activities for staff and/or visitors.
— signage: directory and/or directional.
— storage of staff and/or visitors' coats (consider problems of security of belongings; and of storing wet coats and umbrellas).
— telephone for visitors.

In addition to the main reception area, subsidiary receptions may be required at other entrances or on individual floors.

The reception desk itself may require considerable thought, as receptionists often have combined functions, including:

— greeting, signing in and directing visitors.
— security responsibilities.
— receiving and despatching materials, packages, post.
— switchboard duties.
— typing.

Assess the requirements for each function to be incorporated and determine whether they can be met by a proprietary item of furniture or purpose designed.

Photocopying/printing areas

Requirements will vary depending on the size of office and the nature of the work. In a small organisation a single machine may be located within general office space; larger companies may require separate, centrally located space accommodating related facilities. In any case, copiers can be a source of noise, heat, waste material and general untidiness, and these characteristics should be taken into account when siting facilities. Consider:

- combined location with related activities: foil preparation (for overhead projection); document shredders; stationery storage.
- storage for paper and materials.
- spillage onto floor when refilling machine.
- security: ensure that access to and from copier area is visible.

Location: related to users; balance convenience against nuisance.

Equipment: detailed information on space, power and other requirements should be obtained from manufacturers/suppliers.
Acoustics: ceiling and walls may need to be sound absorbent; for equipment located in open space consider acoustic screening.
Where ammonia printers are to be installed consult with manufacturers to determine special ventilation requirements etc.

Lavatories

Statutory requirements will vary from place to place. The following is a general guide to minimum provision:

Men:

WCs – one for up to 15 persons; two for 16–35; three for 36–65; four for 66–100.

urinals – nil up to six persons; one for 7–20; two for 21–45; three for 46–70; four for 71–100.

wash-basins – one for 1–5 persons; two for 16–30; three for 31–50; four for 51–75; five for 76–100.

Women:

WCs – one for up to 12 persons; two for 13–25; three for 26–40; four for 41–57; five for 58–77; six for 78–100.

wash-basins – one for up to 12 persons; two for 13–25; three for 26–40; four for 41–57; five for 58–77; six for 78–100.

In small offices shared accommodation may be permitted.
Locations: in or adjacent to core areas on each floor; adjacent to reception, cafeteria and conference areas. Consider special requirements for handicapped people.

In the UK, requirements for the provision of sanitary accommodation are given in the Offices, Shop and Railway Premises Act 1963. See also Appendix A.1.b: *New Metric Handbook*[1].
Finishes: hard-wearing, impervious and easy to clean; care must be taken with detailing.
Lighting: 150 lux (14 ft-candles) on the floor.

Vending areas

Vending machines are best grouped in designated space; establish need for hot and cold beverages, chilled water, cigarettes, sweets, change machines and perhaps a microwave oven. Consider also including staff information and notice boards within space.

Finishes and design maintenance factors and hygiene should be carefully considered; floor finishes should take spillage of drinks into account.
Consider also acoustic factors to reduce noise nuisance to adjacent areas.
Microwaves may require a 30 amp supply.
Lighting: 300–400 lux (28–37 ft-candles) on the floor.

In determining location(s), consider:

— allowing minimum movement through doors.
— relationship to office areas and meeting/conference rooms.
— balance between convenience and noise/disturbance factors.
— avoiding proximity to areas requiring confidentiality or high degree of concentration.

Storage areas

Fittings: cleaners, store may require sink with drainer for filling buckets etc.
Lighting: 150 lux (14 ft-candles) on floor.

Storerooms and/or cupboards may be required for stationery, materials, equipment, furniture, cleaning materials and general maintenance equipment (spare fluorescent tubes, access ladders etc.).
Location: generally close to delivery point; stationery store easily accessible from office space.

Plant rooms

Detailed information regarding equipment and requirements should be obtained from appropriate consultants and specialist manufacturers/suppliers.
Ventilation: must be adequate and care must be taken to ensure safe disposal of fumes (for example, from boiler or from batteries).
Acoustics: measures may be required to restrict noise transmittal to adjacent areas.
Lighting: 100–150 lux (9–14 ft-candles) on floor.

These may be required for air-conditioning or heating and ventilation; also electrical substation and emergency power supplies. Space requirements will depend on size of office, systems used, and requirements of various authorities involved.
Spaces should be grouped together and located to minimise length of service runs. Certain spaces (for example, electrical substation) will require direct access from the outside.

2.23 Environmental control

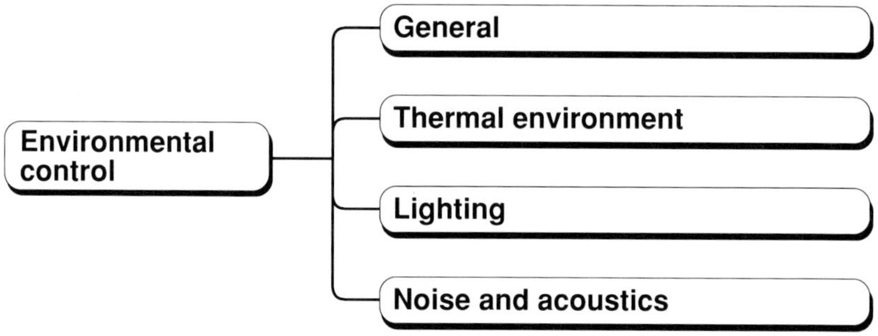

General

Close co-operation between all members of the design team is particularly important. See also 2.31 and Appendix A.1.b: Littler and Thomas[11], Markus and Morris[12]. *Handbook of Fundamentals*[13] and Martin and Oughton[14].

Develop and integrate environmental installation proposals to meet layout, constructional, statutory and economic requirements. Consider installation as a whole and no one aspect in isolation.

Thermal environment

Climate, amongst other things, will influence requirements which should, generally speaking, be as follows:
– in general office areas, circulation areas, meeting rooms, cafeteria etc. constant

Determine best and most suitable method of ensuring fairly *constant temperature* and *humidity* levels; also of ensuring that an adequate circulation of air, free of dust and impurities, is maintained.

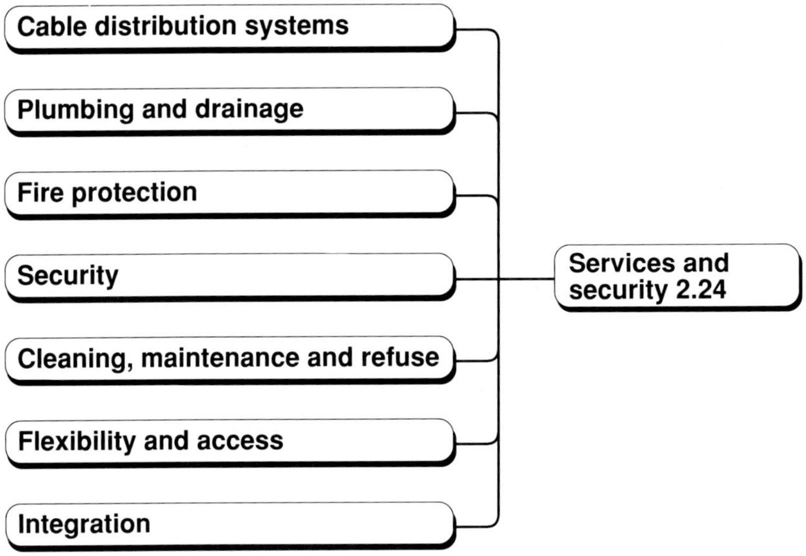

temperatures of 22°C ±4° (72°F ±5°) and relative humidity between 35 and 60 per cent. Temperatures in lavatories, staircases etc. may be lower at 19°C ±3° (66°F ±5°) with no need for humidity control. Machine rooms, data processing tape and paper stores may need higher temperatures at 24°C ±2° (75°F ±3°) and stringent humidity control at 50 per cent ±5. It will probably be necessary to maintain these conditions 24 hours a day.

– ventilation providing minimum circulation of 14 $m^3/h/m^2$ (22 $yd^3/h/yd^2$) and minimum fresh air input of 3 $m^3/h/m^2$ (5 $yd^3/h/yd^2$). For meeting and conference rooms these figures should be increased to circulation 35 $m^3/h/m^2$ (55 $yd^3/h/yd^2$); fresh air 20–30 m^3/h/person (31–47 yd^3/h/person). Machine rooms should be pressurised to prevent infiltration from outside.

For further information on air-conditioning systems see Appendix A.1.b: *Handbook of Fundamentals*[13]; Martin and Oughton[14] *New Metric Handbook*[1], chapter 41, and 'Space for Services'[24].

Certain areas may require separate air-conditioning units to provide the necessary level of filtration.

Consider:

— *full air-conditioning* most satisfactory; consider feasibility of using heat pump.
— *mechanical ventilation* if air-conditioning not feasible (for example, on economic grounds); consider heating and/or filtering air, and heat recovery.
— *zoning* of building for air-conditioning or warm-air systems.
— *extracting air* through air-handling luminaires.
— zoning of trunking routes to facilitate *access* for maintenance etc.
— *natural ventilation*: may be difficult to achieve; will influence building form.
— position of air outlets to ensure that there is no *draught* at workstations.
— *heating*: radiators and convectors will use valuable wall space: consider under-floor heating (electric or hot water). Is district heating available?

Establish detailed requirements for plant rooms. Consider:

— *location* of plant to minimise distribution losses and noise nuisance.
— *access* for maintenance.
— *sound insulation*.
— ease of providing natural air cooling.
— visual/environmental effects.
— service intake positions: gas, electric, water.
— possible future expansion needs.

Where cooling towers are to be installed, ensure that their siting will not cause condensation problems on adjacent buildings.

Lighting

Determine lighting requirements for each area of the building. Establish:

— the visual *tasks* to be provided for.
— the *shape* of each space in relation to sizes and position of windows etc.

For approximate levels of lighting required in office areas see Fig. 2.6 Section 2.10. Figure 2.25 shows additional data for individual areas. For detailed information see 2.30.

Discuss emergency lighting requirements with local fire officer.

The avoidance of glare and reflections on screens can be aided by the use of large-cell parabolic louvres with sharp light cut-off (⩾ 50°), low-brightness lenses or uplighting where the ceiling height is greater than 2.75 m (9 ft) (care needed to avoid bright spots or excessive energy consumption) and by ensuring that screens are arranged parallel to light sources (natural and artificial). The quality of light (quantity/level of light; control of glare both direct and indirect; shadows) is very important: great care must be taken in selecting luminaires and lenses and in deciding on their positions. Consider having mock-ups made with fittings at correct height to test and compare alternatives. Also compare fluorescent units for noise and radio frequency interference of ballast – VDU images can be affected. Windows to main computer rooms may need blinds or similar to reduce daylight levels; otherwise console or signal lamps may not be visible.

Fig. 2.25 *Lighting characteristics suitable for areas within offices. For recommended levels of illuminance see Section 2.10, Fig. 2.6. For further information see 2.30.*

Area	*Colour appearance of lamps*	*Reference letters of available lamps (see Fig. 2.28)*	*Notes*
General offices	Intermediate or warm	CDEFHIKL	Minimise reflections on desk tops and screens by suitable luminaire location and selection; consider indirect and task lighting
Drawing offices	Cool, intermediate or warm	ACDEFHIKL	Where colour rendering is important use A, D or E. Note boards may be at any angle, consider task lighting.
Conference rooms	Intermediate or warm	DEFQ	Consider use of different lighting systems on separate circuits to suit alternative functions. Dimming on at least one circuit may be necessary
Meeting rooms	Intermediate or warm	CDEFGHILQ	Consider display lighting on one wall for presentations. Dimming on main circuit may be necessary
Computer rooms	Intermediate or warm	DEFHIKL	Avoid veiling reflections on monitors. Ensure internally lit signal lamps will be visible. Provide task lighting for maintenance
Dealing rooms	Intermediate or warm	CDEFHIKL	Avoid potential problems with screen flicker by testing a mock-up installation
Corridors/staircases/ entrance lobbies	Intemediate or warm	CDEFHIKL	Ensure even illumination throughout, particularly on stair treads. Avoid glare, taking angle of view up and down stairs into account
Reception desks	Intermediate or warm	CDEFHIKLPQ	Consider lighting for effect, display and security
Cafeterias, dining areas	Intermediate or warm	DEFHIJQ	Consider separate circuits to allow for different functions; also display lighting
Servery	Intermediate or warm	DEFHIJQ	Heat lamps may also be required
Kitchen	Intermediate or warm	DEFHIQ	

— *levels* of lighting required overall (ambient) and for tasks.
— *natural lighting*: orientation, shape, sizes, sill and head heights of glazed areas to avoid glare, uneven light, reflections, and unwanted solar gain and heat loss.

Develop artificial lighting scheme, taking into account:
— *distribution pattern* to allow flexibility of office layouts.
— *co-ordination* with ceiling and furniture layouts; possible need to rotate fittings through 90° to suit new furniture arrangements.
— *type* of lighting: general overhead, uplighting, tasklighting or a combination.
— need to maximise *energy efficiency*.
— need to minimise direct and reflected *glare*, and veiling reflections at workstations, particularly where VDUs are to be used.
— *emergency* and *security* lighting requirements: generator or batteries; automatic changeover device; separate circuit(s) to light strategic routes, exits or areas; maintenance of minimum levels for CCTV cameras where applicable; sustained illuminated signs where required.
— means of *access* to luminaires for maintenance and cleaning.
— *controls*, switching patterns and sub-circuits to facilitate: energy conservation; limited operation out of normal hours; central and local control; security lighting; possible future sub-division of space; time controls; utilising natural light during daytime; shedding unnecessary loads during power failures.

Sophisticated control systems are now available. Options to be considered may include:
– central microcomputer co-ordinating data from occupancy sensors in individual spaces, time clock and daylight sensors and programmed to adjust lighting levels to suit. Systems such as these are able to offer a very high degree of energy management.
– simple time-switching with local override (for example, for people working after normal hours).
– dual or multi-circuit systems with programmed switch-off on one and local override (so that, for example, in an individual office half of the lights are automatically switched off periodically and will only be turned on again by the occupant if really necessary).
– zoning circuits so that areas adjacent to windows can use less artificial light when appropriate.
– local or automatic dimmer controls.

Noise and acoustics

Ensure that the following factors have been considered:
— *siting* (external sources of noise).
— *layout* of building to minimise nuisance from noisy areas and equipment: main traffic/circulation routes away from quiet areas.
— *insulation* of meeting and other sensitive areas both to prevent disturbance and to aid security.
— *sound reduction* value of external walls and fenestration – double glazing may be required.
— *finishes*: absorbent or insulating ceilings; flooring to reduce impact noise.

Acceptable maximum levels of background noise are roughly:
– general office areas – 40–50 dB.
– noisy areas (lobbies, cafeteria etc.) – 50–60 dB.

Although these are given as maximum figures it should be noted that it is possible for offices to be too quiet, in that nearby conversations will become distracting, and in some instances it becomes necessary to introduce background ('white') noise to mask this. Normally this is achieved either via the air-conditioning system, or electronically through loudspeakers.

For detailed information on acoustic control see 2.27–2.29; and for general data on sound see Appendix A.1.b: *New Handbook*[1], chapter 44.

2.24 Services and security

Cable distribution systems

General

The design of a properly considered and co-ordinated cable distribution system covering power, communications and data cabling is essential to the success of the scheme. A successful solution will provide for immediate needs, facilitate simple

See Appendix A.1.b: *IEE wiring regulations, 15th Edition/ (US) National Electrical Code*[19].
In the UK, cabling in furniture and free-standing screens should conform to BS 6396: 1983, *Requirements for electrical systems in office furniture*.

Fig. 2.26 *Examples of approaches to cable distribution networks.*

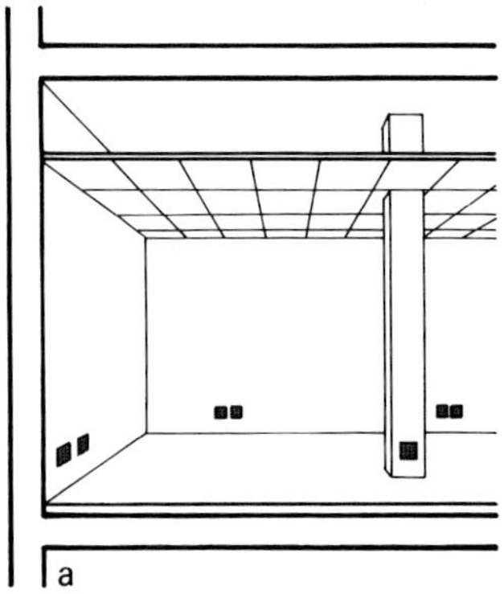

a Fixed wall and column systems are rarely used on their own now, being unable to provide the coverage and adaptability usually required. Alterations involve cutting new holes and chases and cause considerable disruption. However, as a means of providing permanent supply positions, such as cleaners' sockets, it can be effective.

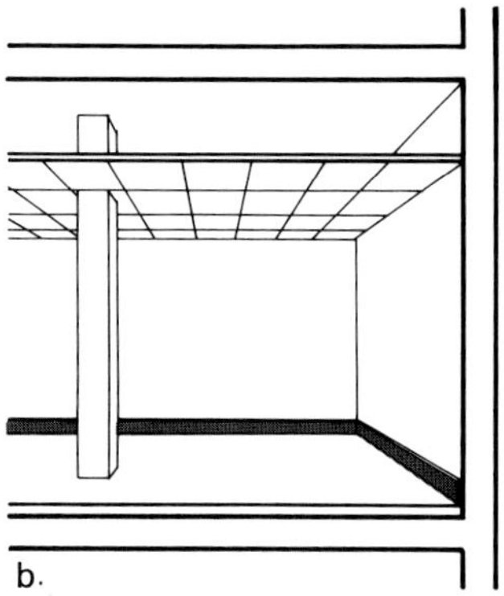

b Skirting trunking can be a cost-effective system in shallow space and does allow alterations to be easily accommodated. It can, however, only provide distribution to the perimeter unless used in conjunction with another system.

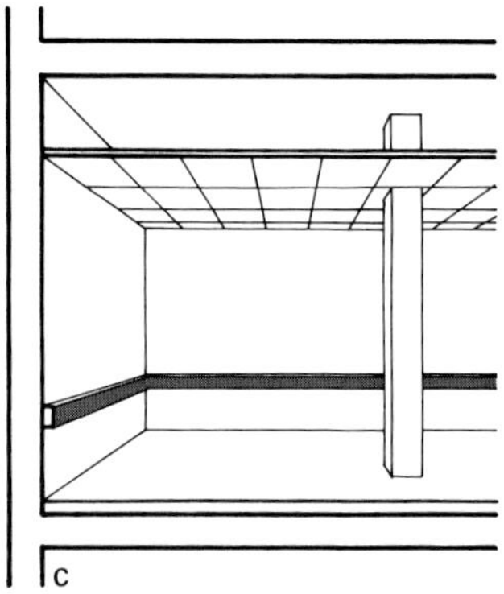

c Dado trunking shares the advantages and disadvantages of skirting trunking, but may be a suitable system where frequent access will be assisted by the convenient height.

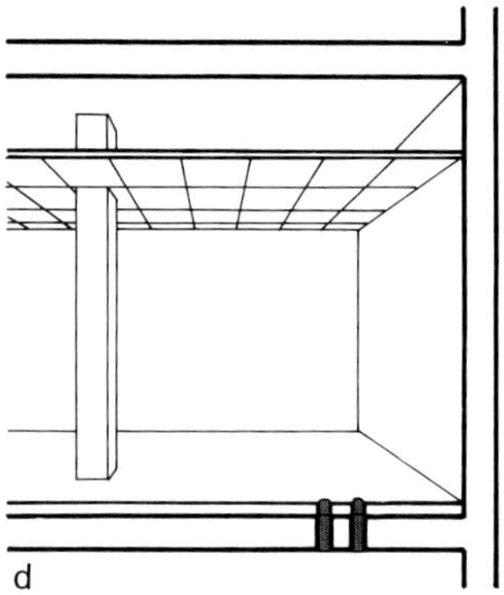

d Under-slab systems with the distribution networks located within the ceiling void of the floor below are very flexible, with outlet positions limited only by structural considerations. The disadvantages are that alterations cause disruption to two floors, any new holes formed must respect the structural design, and local fire regulations may severely restrict or even preclude its use.

alteration of the pattern of final distribution and allow access to the cable routes for maintenance, alteration or the addition of new services with minimal disruption to normal operations.

In evolving the cable distribution concept, take into account the following:

— optimum *intake positions* for electricity and telephones.

— possible need to *duplicate supplies* in large installations where continuity is vital.

— optimum *siting* for main distribution rooms such as electricity and telephone switchrooms, and central machine rooms as applicable.

— *primary distribution network* via ducting to local distribution points (generally one per floor).

Figure 2.26 illustrates various distribution concepts.

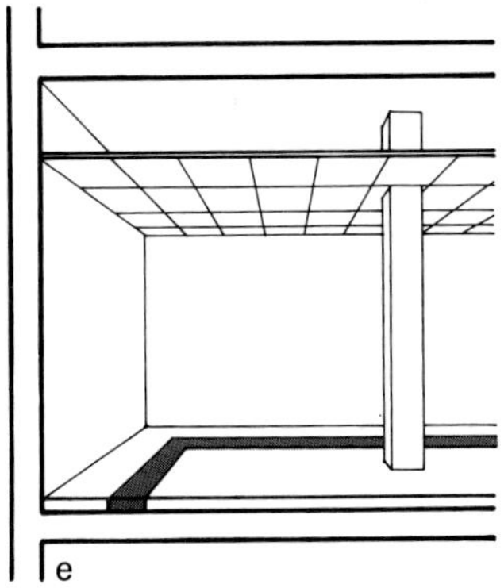

e

e Floor trunking systems are very commonly used and, provided that the distribution pattern is carefully determined, taking all possible furniture and office arrangements into account, can be extremely effective. The disadvantages are that existing systems may not have sufficient capacity for modern needs (and extending the capacity will be expensive and disruptive), and the annoyance (and carpet wear) caused where trunking runs coincide with castored chair positions or traffic routes.

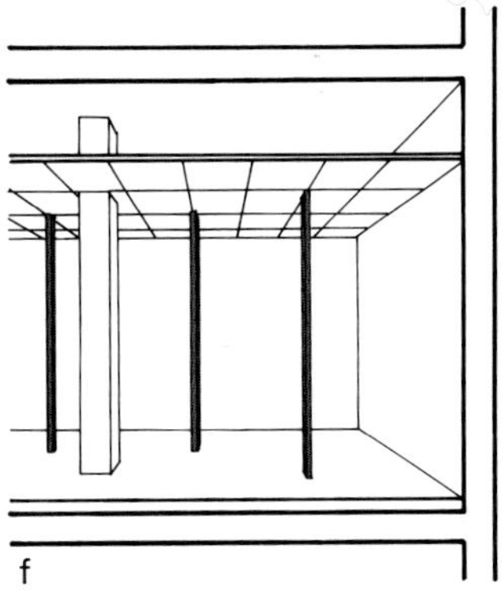

f

f Integrated ceiling systems incorporating cable trunking with final distribution to the workstation via 'power poles' provide an economical and adaptable solution. However, the cluttered appearance caused by the dominant effect of the cable drops on the interior is a problem that is rarely resolved successfully.

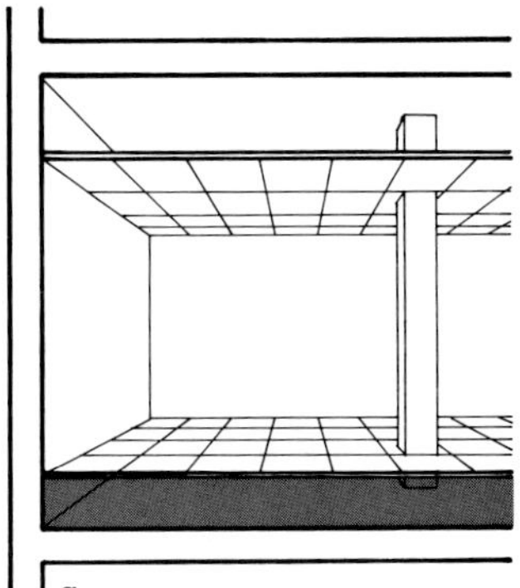

g

g Access flooring provides almost limitless flexibility and, although expensive, currently provides the most effective solution in areas requiring high levels of servicing. Its high cost can in some instances be offset by accommodating the a/c trunking in the floor void, omitting a suspended ceiling and using uplighters.

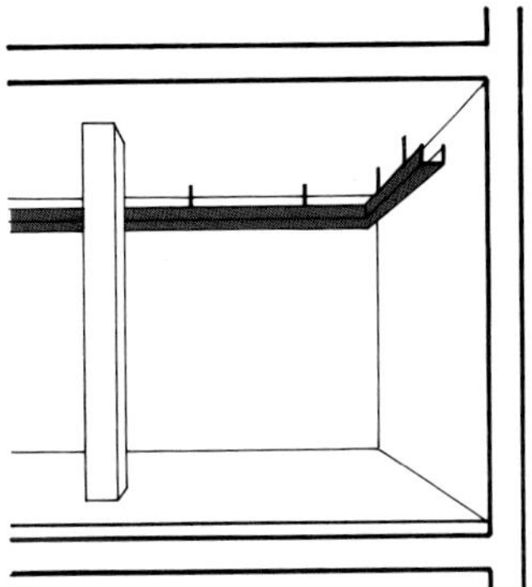

h

h In areas requiring only a low level of servicing, a very economical and adaptable solution can be provided by suspending a cable tray below the soffit with final distribution being simple flex drops to the workstation.

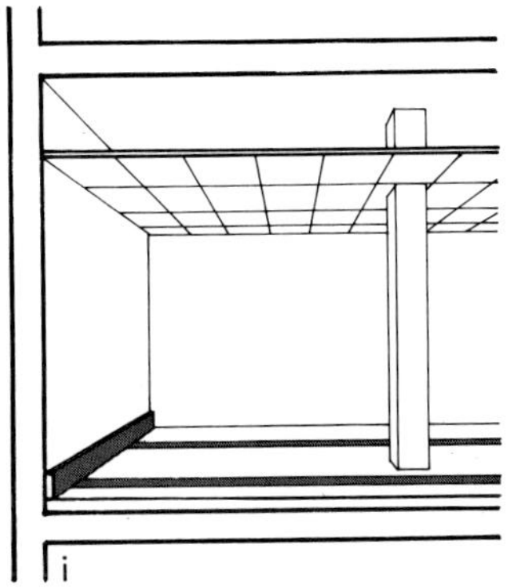

i

i Flat-wire cable accessed from perimeter supplies and run under carpet squares provides a very flexible and adaptable system. Although it requires special junction boxes, terminals and other components, alterations can be undertaken by in-house staff. If current concerns about interference and problems at cross-over points are overcome, it could gain much wider acceptance.

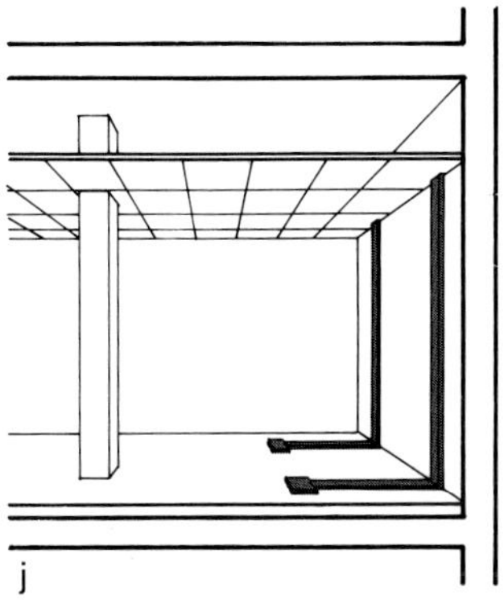

j

j In many schemes, particularly when existing buildings are being refitted, a combination of systems will provide the most effective solution. In the example shown, for instance, cables are routed through the ceiling void to perimeter drop positions (which could be concealed behind a feature capping), and thence via surface trunking on the floor to multi-outlet terminal boxes. Although apparently adhoc, such solutions can, with careful co-ordination with furniture arrangements, be extremely successful.

— *secondary network* via ducts, conduit, trunking or cable trays in ceiling void or floor screed; via raised floor; or via skirting, dado trunking or power poles dropped from the ceiling.
— *final distribution* to workstation positions.
— need to allow for *expansion* (25 per cent as a guide, but check against client's future plans and expectations).
— *compatibility* with partition and furniture layouts and systems; and other service routes and requirements.
— *consequences* of system for immediate surroundings, equipment and staff.

— *cables*: types, specifications (taking particular note of minimum bending radii), connectors and terminations.
— *flexibility*: ability to facilitate possible future change, modification or addition.

Power

Figure 2.27 shows typical equipment power requirements; consult with manufacturers for specific items.
For detailed information see Appendix A.1.b: *IEE wiring regulations, 15th Edition/US National Electrical Code* [9].

Confirm *design loads* for each area (Fig. 2.25, Section 2.10 provides data for guidance) and phasing requirements. Develop scheme in more detail, taking into account:
— need for *clean supplies* and/or individual radial circuits to any items of equipment.
— need for *gas detection sensors* at mains incoming position.
— any areas requiring *emergency power-off* buttons.
— power requirements at *workstations* and in *offices*.
— *special power requirements* for machine rooms, photocopiers etc.
— *ancillary power requirements* for telephones, facsimile machines, cleaning, external sockets, shaving outlets or macerators in lavatories, vending machines etc.
— *emergency power requirements* for lighting, fire alarms, public address, telephone, security and alarm systems, extract fans, lifts etc.

Fig. 2.27 *Typical equipment power loading requirements. This information should be used for general guidance; where specific items of equipment are known, check with manufacturers.*

Item	*Outlet*	*Notes*
Personal computer	13 A	May need clean supply
Printer	13 A	
Modem	13 A	
Photocopier	13, 30 or 45 A	Power requirement depends on size. Include neon indicator and ensure easy access for isolation
Shredding machine	13 A	Include neon indicator and ensure easy access for isolation
Foil machine	13 A	
Vending machines	13 A	Include neon indicator and ensure easy access for isolation
Chilled water drinking fountain	13 A	
Macerators	13 A	Include neon indicator and ensure easy access for isolation
External sockets	15 A	Weatherproof, consider lockable cover

Telephones

For budgeting allow one per 5 m^2 (6 yd^2) of office space. See Appendix A.1.b: Corby *et al*[7], 'Communications'[8] and *DTI Interim code of practice on wiring*[20].

Establish:
— system to be used, switchboard position and equipment requirements (space, power, access etc.).
— terminal socket distribution.
— other equipment requiring connection to phone system; modems; facsimile machines.

Data cabling

Establish:

— system to be used and cable specifications; usually single- or multi-core, flat, co-axial, twin-axial or fibre optic.
— cable separation requirements from other wiring.
— connection requirements.
— distribution pattern and junction box positions.

Note that minimum bending radii can be 250 mm (10 in) or more; and that flat cable can be bent in one direction only.
See 2.32.

Plumbing and drainage

Determine requirements for hot and cold water, and drainage installations. Consider:

— position and size of ducts.
— position and space of water tank.
— method of heating water: low-pressure hot water system served from central boiler or storage cylinder with immersion heater etc.
— requirements for boiler room (if needed); also access for maintenance.
— water supply for fire sprinklers and/or hosereels.

See Appendix A.1.b: Haverstock[21].

Fire protection

Establish requirements in terms of national legislation and local by-laws, for example:

— fire resistance of walls and doors.
— limits of floor area, height and capacity of fire compartments.
— means of escape for occupants.

Consider the following precautionary measures:

— dividing main open areas (or areas sub-divided by demountable partitions) into fire-resisting compartments.
— enclosing vertical openings (stairwells, ducts, liftshafts etc.) with fire-resisting materials.
— automatic fire dampers in ducts at all points where they pass through compartments.
— smoke exhaust/extraction system.
— minimising use of combustible equipment and materials: using steel fittings/furniture rather than wood.
— detection systems: sensors actuated by heat, rapid rise in temperature or presence of smoke (distribution should cover possible rearrangements of partitions, voids, ducts etc.).
— extinguishers: automatic sprinkler system using water (wet or dry pipe) or gas (halon or similar) for machine rooms; portable extinguishers for dealing with outbreaks locally.
— alarms: connected to automatic detector system, central indicator panels and electromagnetic fire door hold-open devices were applicable; also, possible direct link to local fire station.

Fire precautions should be discussed with the local fire authority and fire insurers. Although various sources claim that sprinklers should not be installed as they can do more harm than good (water damage greater than damage by fire), evidence would not seem to support this argument. However, in the case of mainframe computer installations this would certainly be the case and gaseous methods should be used. For general information see Appendix A.1.b: 'Thinking About Fire'[5].

Security

Specialist advice should be obtained at an early stage. For detailed information see Appendix A1.b: 'Security in Buildings'[6] and Cummings[18]. In certain cases it may be necessary to take into account the possibility of malicious or even terrorist attack; specialist advice should be sought but in addition avoid designing areas where a person or object could be concealed and ensure that storerooms, plant rooms and access panels are locked. Pay particular attention to spaces such as lavatories where a person could work undetected; consider monolithic ceilings in such areas.

Ascertain requirements for protection of building from possible break-in (including unauthorised entry during normal hours).
Determine overall objectives: what system is required to do; what areas need special protection etc.
Consider both passive and active measures.
Passive measures:

- effect of requirements on general design: planning to facilitate supervision of entry to building; avoidance of dark corners where a would-be thief, vandal or other might operate unobserved; avoidance of the means to gain entry at a higher level up the outside of the building etc.
- ability of elements such as doors, windows etc. to withstand forcible entry: consider strength of materials, fixings, hinges; size of glazed openings; addition of security bars.
- door-locking methods: types, suiting, card or cipher operation.
- special measures for sensitive areas. Consider: floor to soffit solid partitions; acoustic measures to prevent eavesdropping from adjacent spaces; avoidance of possibility of visual snooping.

Active measures:

- forms of detectors: perimeter (on windows and doors); volumetric, heat or acoustic devices etc.
- type of alarm: audible or silent (signalling control centre of alarm company or police) or combination (controlled by microprocessor).
- security lighting.
- closed-circuit television surveillance of entrance(s) and other vulnerable areas.

Cleaning and refuse

Establish how cleaning will be done and at what times; and amount of refuse that accumulates weekly and method and frequency of disposal.
Consider:

- installation of central vacuum-cleaning system and rubbish chutes.
- intermediate storage prior to removal to central collection point.
- special provision for storage of cleaning material, equipment and refuse bins.
- access and routes for the emptying of bins.
- any special needs (noxious materials, compactors where large amounts produced, central shredders etc.).

Flexibility and access

Consider flexibility of services arrangement and ease of access for maintenance, inspection and modification. Establish understanding of actual operations involved to ensure adequate provision in terms of location (avoiding disruption of normal work), space, safety, durability and ease of cleaning means of access and surroundings.

Integration

Consider integration of the services plant and distribution spaces into the structure.

2.25 Building design

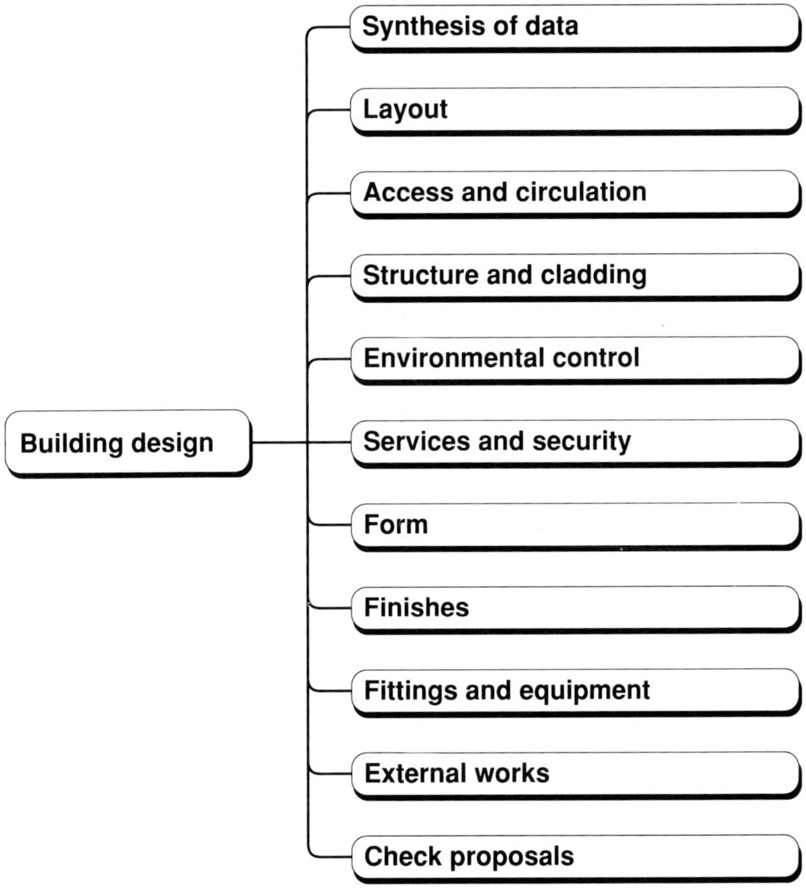

Synthesis of data

Bring together all requirements and constraints in terms of particular aspects of building design. Consider implications of all detailed data with regard to design policies and modify if required. Confirm or adjust space standards to be used for project.

Layout

Develop layout to meet site, circulation, constructional, environmental, statutory, servicing, economic and other requirements.

Consider in particular the effects of:

— phasing.

— service zones and access for change and maintenance.

— growth and change – a design based too rigidly on specific requirements may

See also 2.14. With new information available it may be necessary to change an idea that seemed suitable earlier on.

See 2.22.1–4 for basic information on space planning and relationships between areas.

not be satisfactory for long.
— fixed spaces (lifts, stairs, lavatories, ducts etc.).
— locate in position favourable to future addition and flexibility.
— relationship to any existing, or future, adjacent building which may form part of complex.

Access and circulation

See Appendix A.1.b: *New Metric Handbook*[1], chapters 6 and 16, for general information. Remember that the entrance to a building helps to project the image of the organisation occupying it, and forms the important first impression for visitors.

When deciding location and relationship of spaces, and patterns of circulation, consider:
— access from outside for: staff, visitors, goods delivery/despatch.
— security and control of access.
— internal access to stairs and emergency exits required by fire regulations.
— internal circulation of staff and visitors.
— internal circulation of equipment and materials.
— vertical circulation: stairs, ramps, escalators and lifts for people and goods; shared or separate provision.
— areas requiring limited access and form(s) of control to be used.
— door widths to allow for movement of equipment and furniture and for wheelchair users.

Structure and cladding

See 2.22.1. For more detailed information on column spacings and structural grids see Appendix A.1.b: Duffy *et al*[15]. For general information see Appendix A.1.b: *AJ Handbook of Building Structure*[9] and *AJ Handbook of Building Enclosure*[10].
For information on energy conservation by the design of building fabric see Littler and Thomas[11] and Markus and Morris[12].
Floor loads generally about 3.5–4 kN/m^2 (70–80 lbf/square foot) for office areas; but bear in mind that high concentrations of storage or heavy equipment can lead to local loadings of up to 50 kN/m^2 (1000 lbf/square foot); and that adjustable feet on equipment can lead to very high point loads.

Develop and integrate structural proposals in light of layout. When assessing structure and cladding consider:
— structural grid (column spacing) in terms not only of optimum spacing of office sub-divisions and furniture layouts, but also of cost, height of building, structural system etc.
— live load factors for various parts of the building. If maximum planning flexibility is required, this may involve design of entire structure to maximum live load capacity; otherwise a zoning strategy limiting flexibility will have to be developed.
— sizes of internal columns – these may affect layout and flexibility of furniture arrangements.
— permanent load-bearing internal walls versus demountable or studwork partitioning.
— thermal performance: minimum heat transfer, cost-effective insulation etc. Avoid cold bridges and potential air leaks.
— risk of overheating and condensation.
— services integration – routes of horizontal and vertical ducts, cableways etc. which can seriously affect structure.

Form

See also 2.14.

Develop form of building in light of layout, structural and environmental aspects. Consider in particular:
— compactness: atria or courtyards can greatly lengthen circulation distances.
— extendability: avoid towers or other forms that are difficult to extend.

Finishes

When selecting internal finishes consider:

— wear: both the severity of anticipated wear and the ability of the finish to sustain it.
— ease of cleaning and maintenance using standard techniques.
— colour and surface reflectance (glare and excessive brightness contrasts should be avoided).
— fire resistance where required.
— safety, for example non-slip floors.
— acoustic qualities, for example sound-absorbent ceilings and floors.
— aesthetics.
— cost: initial and long term.

Final selection of materials should be made from large samples in conjunction with other materials to be used in same area, under the type and temperature of lighting to be used in the scheme. See also 2.22.1–4 and 2.34.

Fittings and equipment

Establish client's needs for furniture, fittings and equipment, including:

— existing items to be relocated in the new facility.
— brief for new items required.

Collect information on all items and assess suitability. Determine types, dimensions, position (in relation to access and circulation), loading, fixing, ergonomic factors and purchase and installation procedures and techniques. Consider:

— furniture systems for open-plan and cellular office spaces.
— screens for acoustic and visual separation.
— storage for: filing (check types, sizes and linear run), discs, manuals and other 'book' types of reference, stationery, materials, microfiche pages, coats etc. Survey all client's requirements and estimate capacities needed for all types, including an allowance for expansion.
— special workstation requirements for VDUs, telexes etc.
— seating, assessing needs for each workstation type.
— furniture for all ancillary areas, including conference and meeting rooms, cafeteria, reception etc.
— internal signage allowing for flexibility where necessary.
— miscellaneous items such as ashtrays, interior planting, blinds, pictures and artwork, clocks, fire extinguishers, drinking fountains, vending machines etc.

Identify any items which will need to be purpose designed and made and establish procedure.

Where an assessment of the comparative suitability of competitive furniture systems has to be made, establish which of the following factors are relevant and consider relative merits:

— availability, both immediate, and future for replacement and additional items.

Actual samples of all standard (ready-made) furniture and equipment being considered for the project should be seen – and competing proprietary models compared in detail – before final choice is made.
For detail information see 2.33.
In the UK, leasing furniture and/or equipment can have tax advantages and free capital for other uses. However, tax regulations change frequently, and individual circumstances vary; clients should approach their own accountants for advice.

— cost.
— suitability of worksurface dimensions to tasks, including possible changes in equipment and space required.
— flexibility, both in planning terms and in heights to accommodate varying requirements for keyboard and VDU positions.
— wire management capabilities and capacities, including the ability to accommodate the excess cable often required for flexibility of layout.
— ability to accommodate termination panels, controllers, disc drives etc.
— ability to accommodate air ducting for local cooling of equipment.
— storage capacities and suitability.
— general quality, durability of finish etc.

Systems which allow the individual user to alter heights, angles etc. can create problems due to overuse or mechanical abuse, or simply not be used at all. A managed approach which establishes an individual's requirements with adjustments being made to suit by in-house maintenance staff can avoid such problems.
See also 2.33.

External works

Develop landscape and siting proposals in light of building design proposals, statutory requirements and other factors.
Consider:
— access: roadways, pathways and links to adjacent or adjoining buildings.
— planting and other landscape features.
— parking areas; bicycle racks.
— outdoor lighting and external signs (directional and identifying).
— security aspects.

For car parking allow 20–30 m^2 (24–36 yd^2) per space; for pedal and motor cycles 1.5 m^2 (1.8 yd^2) per space.
For detailed information see Appendix A.1.b: *New Metric Handbook*[1], chapters 7 and 40.

Check proposals

Check that all objectives, resources, constraints, risks and implications of user and other requirements have been taken into consideration in the overall design.
Consider all possible conflicts, trade-offs and balances, for example:
— layout in terms of openness versus privacy, security and internal environmental control.
— flexibility versus form (for example, compactness) and cost-effectiveness of structure and services; also in terms of spatial uniformity, keeping needs of users in mind.
— ability of scheme to cope with possible future changes.
— ratio of nett useable floor area to gross area against original estimates.

2.26 Completion of phase

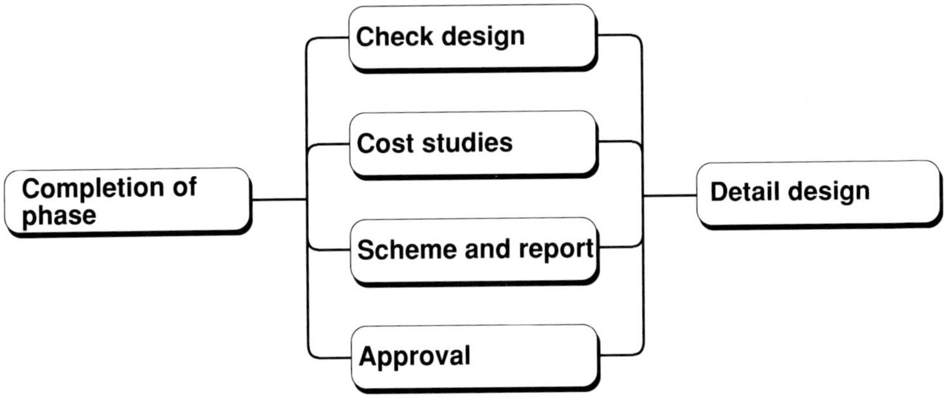

Check design

Check design *proposal* against recorded *requirements*:

— can all *facilities* required by client in fact be accommodated?
— confirm that all *statutory requirements* have been taken into account and verify that proposal meets with approval of all relevant bodies.

Cost studies

Make *detailed cost estimates* of building and services installation, site work etc. Also make estimates of *running costs*, particularly those affected by design proposals, for example maintenance, heating and cooling.
Verify that proposed design can be built within budget: modify if required.

See 2.15 for detailed information on cost studies.

Scheme and report

Present comprehensive proposal to client in clear and concise format:

— drawings, model, sketches.
— independent reports from each consultant with reasons for recommendations and appropriate analytical evidence for the selection of particular proposals.
— cost analysis.

Approval

Obtain client's *approval* before proceeding to detail design.

Note: any changes to the basic design after this point will cause delay and cost money.

Detail design

For general guidance on detail design see Appendix A.1.a: 'Plan of Work', Stage E in *Architect's Job Book;* and Green.

By this stage all major factors in the project should have been considered; this phase is concerned with completing the scheme in increasing depth of detail. To a large extent the process involved is common to all types of building, and it would be beyond the scope of this guide to cover every aspect. However, the following sections offer guidance pertinent to high-technology offices in particular, concentrating on specific details and considerations which might otherwise be missed.

For ease of reference it is sub-divided according to major elements; though it should, of course, be remembered that all elements are interrelated, and no single aspect can be considered in isolation.

2.27 Ceilings

The constraints on ceiling selection and specification should have been established by this stage, making it possible to now determine suitable generic types which may suit the requirements (including the possibility of not have a ceiling at all, i.e. utilising the underside of the slab).

Where a suspended ceiling is required, *performance specifications* should be established, taking into account in particular the following aspects:

— performance in a *fire*.
— *security*.
— *acoustic* performance.
— structural *stability*.
— integration of *services*.
— *access*.
— *finishes*.

Once individual requirements have been established, the performance of different products, materials and constructions can be assessed against the criteria.

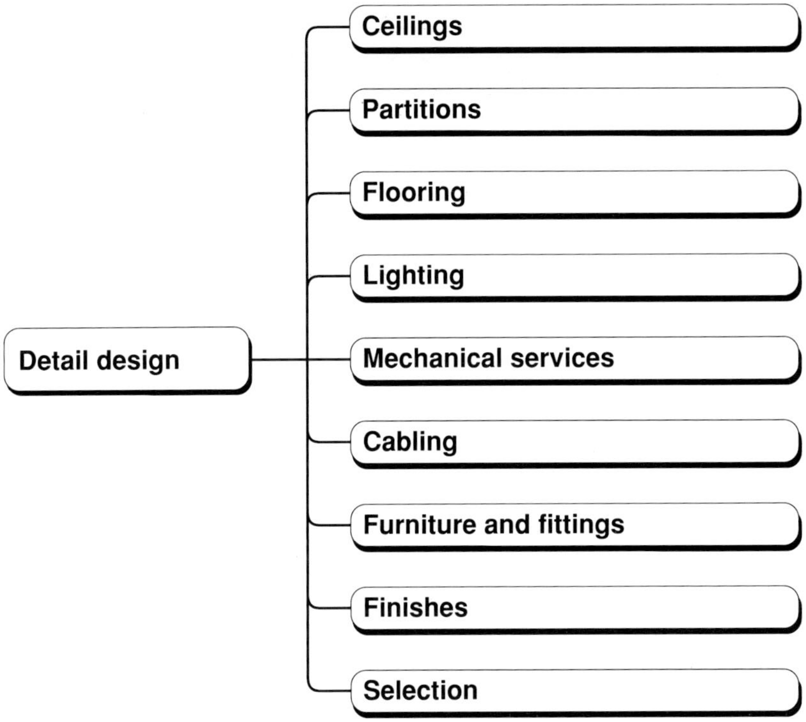

Performance in a fire

Generally, suspended ceilings should be constructed of *non-combustible* materials throughout, including grounds and fixings.

Statutory regulations may permit ceilings to contribute to a required fire resistance for a floor; or may require them to provide a specified degree of resistance to protect the void above. Many proprietary systems can achieve resistance, often by the simple expedient of clipping the panels or tiles to the grid and laying a resistant blanket over the top. However, it should be noted that the integrity of such a ceiling would be lost as soon as sections were removed for access to services etc.; consequently the use of this facility should be restricted to areas with minimal or zero requirement for access.

Surface spread of flame should be class 0 or class 1 to BS 476 *Fire tests on building materials and structures*, Part 7.

Where a *compartmentation* of *escape routes* or other protected areas is a requirement, fire breaks may be needed in the void. With flexible partition layouts it may also be necessary to identify possible future lines of fire-resistant partitions and provide barriers to suit if these would be difficult to add at a later date. Care will be needed where barriers are penetrated by services to ensure that integrity is maintained; this will be made easier by the zoning of services (see 2.10).

Security

Security requirements affecting ceilings may include:

— partitions extending between *floor* and *structural soffit*.
— *confidentiality* afforded by specific acoustic requirements.
— *structural integrity* to resist unauthorised entry.

In public areas, consideration should be given to:
— avoiding suspended ceilings altogether.
— the use of monolithic ceilings.
— access panels with locks or fastenings which require special tools.

Acoustic performance

The acoustic performance of a ceiling needs to be considered from two aspects; sound insulation and sound absorption. The former is a measure of the ceiling's ability to reduce the transference of sound to adjacent spaces whilst the latter affects the quality of sound in the space itself.

Specifying sound-reduction levels through the ceiling construction will not solve the problem of noise transference on its own. Figures quoted by manufacturers are generally produced by testing sections under ideal conditions in a laboratory and may bear little relation to reality.

Sound insulation

The degree to which sound transference through ceilings needs to be reduced will be determined by:
— the *functions* of the areas.
— the *frequency* and *level* of noise in adjacent spaces.
— the level of *background noise*.

For any given ceiling construction its ability to block the passage of sound will vary across the frequency range; and the greater the background noise, the more difficult it will be to discern transferred sound. Subjective appreciation of sound reduction will also be to some extent determined by the absorption characteristics of the source room.

Careful attention must be paid to:
— doors.
— glazing.
— partition construction and perimeter details.
— floors.
— ducts.
— light fittings.
— service pipes/conduit.

Where high levels of acoustic separation are a requirement, approaches involving partitions extending through the ceiling to the soffit should be evaluated against options using insulated ceilings.

Sound insulation performance is dependent on mass, either inherent in the construction, or added in the form of a quilt laid over the top; and consequently the fixings and structure will need to be appraised to ensure that they can carry the additional weight.

Sound absorption

Sound-absorbing ceilings are *lightweight* and thus will be of no use for insulation without additional measures being taken.

Absorption is usually achieved by either:

- tiles or planks manufactured from absorbent material. Where these are perforated, care should be taken to ensure that they can be redecorated without reducing their efficiency.
- perforated tiles or planks with an absorbent blanket laid over. This method may have implications for access to the void.

Where absorbent blankets are used in *air plenums*, they should be *encapsulated* in polythene or a similar material to ensure that no particles enter the air system.

In all cases, it is the *complete installation* which must achieve the required degree of sound performance.

Structural stability

The ceiling, its framework, suspension and fixings must be capable of supporting:

- its own *weight*.
- the *imposed loads* of other attached elements. These may include light fittings, cable trays, a/c grills and trunking, sprinklers, smoke detectors and alarms.
- *vertical* and *horizontal forces* from partitions where applicable. This may require localised strengthening.

The ceiling should remain structurally stable when areas are removed for access, repair or modification.

Integration of services

The manner in which services are unified with the ceiling should be such that *maintenance, repair* and *replacement* can be undertaken with *minimal disruption* to normal office operations. It should be possible in most situations to perform these activities during normal working hours.

Each service facility should follow *logical, consistent recorded* paths and should be co-ordinated so that the access requirements of one are not obstructed by the other.

All *elements* and *fittings* on the underside of a ceiling should be arranged to take into account any future flexibility requirements. *Future changes* to elements should be accommodated either:

- by the use of a system which allows *arrangements* to be *reconfigured* and new elements to be inserted.
- by providing *blanked-off* positions when it is possible to assess future requirements.
- by the use of *exposed* services.

Options should be tested against specific factors for the project, including:

- occupancy *function*.
- *lifespan* of the scheme.
- anticipated frequency and degree of *change*.
- *programme* requirements.
- *cost-effectiveness*.
- *aesthetics*.

Access

Access to the void may be necessary for a number of reasons, including:

— *alterations* to services.
— *maintenance* of services.
— relocating *partitions*.

Establishing the form of the provision must start from an understanding of what is *physically involved* in the operations which will be carried out. From such studies it can then be determined whether full access by means of a demountable system is required, or partial access through local panels.

Access positions should be of a suitable size and correctly positioned and orientated to allow necessary operations to be carried out comfortably and safely. If the form of provision requires the removal of panels or tiles, consideration should be given to how they are handled and where they are placed during operations.

Where full access requires the removal of sections of grid it should be possible to achieve this and the replacement readily and without having to replace components.

All access positions, whether special panels or sections of the ceiling, should be durable so as not to be damaged during the operation, and easily cleaned. If special tools, equipment or procedures would obviate problems of damage or soiling then this should be highlighted to the client.

2.28 Partitions

By this stage suitable generic partition types should have been established, i.e.

— proprietary *relocatable* system.
— *studwork* and plasterboard.
— *solid* (blockwork, brickwork etc.).
— a *combination* of any of the above.

Working from criteria already established, it will now be possible to develop *details* and *performance specifications*, taking into account in particular the following aspects:

— performance in a *fire*.
— *security*.
— *acoustic* performance.
— structural *stability*.
— *ancillary* elements.
— *glazed* partitions.
— *integration* of services.
— *doors*.
— *finishes*.

Once individual requirements have been established, the performance of different products, materials or constructions can be assessed against the criteria.

Performance in a fire

The following aspects must be investigated, considered, quantified and specified:

Fire resistance

Where it has been established that 1/2, 1, 1 1/2 or 2 hours protection is a part of the required performance criteria, the specification should ensure that all elements satisfy the statutory requirements.
Care needs to be taken with detailing to avoid service penetration impairing the performance.

In the UK, statutory requirements are covered by BS 476 *Fire tests on building materials and structures*, Part 8. Separate figures for Integrity, Stability and Insulation should be specified to ensure that the requirements are fully met.

Surface spread of flame

Where it has been established that surface spread of flame characteristics are a part of the required performance criteria, the specification should ensure that elements satisfy the statutory requirements.
Finishes in data processing areas should generally be non-combustible.

In the UK, statutory requirements are covered by BS 476 *Fire tests on building materials and structures*, Part 7, class 0, class 1 or class 3 as required.

Material combustibility

The use of combustible materials in major elements such as partitions should normally be avoided. However, timber studwork clad with plasterboard, or areas of timber framing to glazed partitioning would usually be acceptable.

In the UK, materials should meet the requirements of BS 476 *Fire tests on building materials and structures*, Part 6, where required to by statutory performance criteria.

Glazing

Where glazing is to be incorporated in partitions required to be fire resistant, careful detailing is necessary to ensure that statutory requirements are met. With purpose-designed partitioning, sample panels may have to be submitted for tests to establish compliance; in the case of proprietary systems the manufacturers should already have done this and should be able to provide certification.

In the UK, glazing should satisfy the requirements of BS 5588 *Fire precautions in the design and construction of office buildings*. To achieve compliance, manufacturers must test and prove their systems.

Security

Security requirements affecting partitions may include:

— partitions *extending* between *floor* and *structural soffit.*
— *confidentiality* afforded by specific acoustic requirements.
— *structural integrity* to resist unauthorised entry.

Acoustic performance

The degree to which sound transference through partitions needs to be reduced will be determined by:

— the *functions* of the areas.
— the *frequency* and *level* of noise in adjacent spaces.
— the level of *background noise.*

For any given partition construction its ability to block the passage of sound will vary across the frequency range; the greater the background noise, the more difficult it will be to discern transferred sound. Subjective appreciation of sound reduction will also be to some extent determined by the absorption characteristics of the receiving room and the reverberation characteristics of the source room.

Specifying sound-reduction levels through the partition construction will not solve the problem of noise transference on its own. Figures quoted by manufacturers are generally produced by testing panels under ideal conditions in a laboratory and may bear little relation to reality.

Pay careful attention to:

- doors.
- glazing.
- partition perimeter details.
- ceiling construction.
- floors.
- ducts.
- light fittings.
- service pipes.

Where high levels of acoustic separation are a requirement, approaches involving partitions extending through the ceiling to the soffit should be evaluated against options using insulated ceilings.

In all cases, it is the complete installation which must achieve the required degree of sound reduction.

Structural stability

Three aspects to structural stability have to be considered. Partitions must be:

- *self-supporting.*
- *able to sustain applied loads.*
- able to *resist impact.*

Though interrelated, each aspect has its own characteristics which need to be satisfied:

Self-supporting

The ability to be self-supporting is a product of partition construction and perimeter fixing. Whilst the former is straightforward and well covered by regulations and normal practices, the latter can present problems, particularly with regard to *head fixings.* Unless the partition is extended up to the structural soffit, support will be dependent on fixings to the ceiling grid, and the detailing and specification will have to be considered in unison.

Stability should not be dependent on the presence of ceiling tiles; if areas are removed for maintenance, stability (in all three aspects) must be maintained.

Impact resistance

Partitions should be suitably restrained to resist normal, everyday impacts such as slamming doors, being hit by trolleys etc.

In addition, partitions along *fire escape routes* should be able to adequately resist the sort of pressures which might result from an evacuation of the building.

Applied loads

It is frequently necessary to fix any number of a variety of secondary elements to partitions.

The partition specification and design must be capable of supporting the assessed loads; and of accepting *suitable fixings* in both the *known positions* which such items will occupy and *possible future positions.*

Where heavy items are to be supported off the partitions, the worst case should be considered and the effectiveness of the solution determined, if necessary by structural calculations. For example, in the case of cupboards, the effect of applying the *maximum load to one side* of the partition only should be assessed.

Ancillary elements

A number of elements may have to be supported by or off the partitions, including:

— pinboards.
— whiteboards.
— noticeboards.
— projection screens.
— shelves.
— cupboards.
— signs.
— change machines (in vending areas).
— telephones and hoods.
— CCTV cameras.
— fire extinguishers and safety equipment.
— coathooks.
— doorstops.
— pictures or other forms of artwork.

Alternative methods of fixing include:

— screwing back to suitable *pre-fixed grounds* within the partition.
— *adhesives.*
— clipping to *vertical tracks.*
— suspending from a *horizontal track.*
— *magnetic fixings* where steel partitions are used.

A suitable method will have to be determined for each item, taking account of:

— the *load* to be supported.
— the likelihood of *new positions* being required.
— the likelihood of items having to be *removed* and the fixing position *made good.*

Glazed partitions

Glazed partitions may be used either to provide vision into a room for safety and security reasons, or to create a more spacious feeling.

The required *acoustic performance* will determine whether single, double or triple glazing is needed.

In the UK, specification for glass will be determined by reference to BS 6262 *Code of Practice for glazing for buildings* and BS 6206 *Impact performance for flat glass.*

Where *blinds* are a requirement in conjunction with double glazing, these could be incorporated within the void, provided that one leaf of the glazing can be readily removed for cleaning and maintenance.

Where there is a danger of someone walking into a glazed partition without seeing it, the introduction of some form of *visual interference* at eye level should be considered. Possible methods include:

— *painting* or *printing*.
— *etching* the glass.
— *adhesive* dots or stripes.

Integration of services

Wherever possible, services should not be incorporated in partitions which are likely to be moved.

The manner in which services are unified with the structure should be such that maintenance, repair and replacement can be undertaken with *minimal disruption* to the work process. It should be possible in most circumstances to perform these options during normal working hours.

The individual characteristics of services which may be integrated with the partitions vary considerably. Particular note should be made of *cable separation requirements* and *minimum bending radii*, as these may have significant implications for the means of integration. For further information see 2.24 and 2.32.

Cable routes should follow a *logical, recorded path* and should be arranged so that cables can be readily removed, replaced or added.

Outlet positions should be at a height convenient to their use. Consider method of accommodating future changes, either:

— by the use of *plates* which can be replaced with new to a different configuration.
— by providing *blanked-off* positions when it is possible to assess future requirements.
— by setting outlets within a *panel* which can itself be replaced.
— by the use of *surface-mounted* fittings.

Test options against specific factors, including:

— *occupancy* function.
— *lifespan* of scheme.
— anticipated frequency and degree of *change*.
— *programme* requirements.
— *cost-effectiveness*.
— *aesthetics*.

Doors

Determine whether doors are to be specified as:

— a part of the partition package.
— a separate package.
— a combination of the two.

Arrangements/planning

In corridors and circulation spaces, take account of the need to move trolleys, furniture, equipment etc. through doorways.

The minimum clear *width* through any doorway allowing access for wheelchair users is 875 mm (34 in) (as provided by a standard 926 mm (36 in) leaf in a 1000 mm (39 in) doorset).

Doors into offices and other rooms should normally open against cross-partitions.

The movement of equipment, furniture etc. has implications for both the finishes, which must be durable to withstand the inevitable knocks, and the width, which obviously must be able to accommodate the largest item likely to be moved through the doorway. Where large items are involved, it is wise to check on the space for manoeuvring by means of scale cut-outs on a drawing. In extreme situations it may be necessary to delay the installation of sections of partitioning until after the equipment is in place.

Fire

The procedures described at the beginning of this section will have identified the fire requirements applicable to doors. The acceptability of different methods of meeting requirements will vary according to area and circumstance; attitudes of the relevant authorities to alternative approaches should be established at an early stage.

Determine requirements affecting doors:

— *integrity* (period of resistance to the passage of flame).
— *smoke control.*
— *signage.*
— *ironmongery.*

Manufacturers' literature will state resistance achieved; however, these should be checked against the *Rules for the construction of firebreak doors and shutters*, Fire officers' committee 1985, as small differences in detail may alter the rating.

Meeting the requirements for fire resistance will only control the passage of flames and hot gases; it may be necessary in certain circumstances to ensure that cool smoke will be blocked by the addition of brush or rubber seals to the doors and/or frames.

Vision panels

In addition to statutory requirements, visual access into enclosed offices may be necessary for reasons of safety and security. Consider provision, either:

— by a vision panel in the door.
— or by glazed sidelights.

There may be instances where this general rule is overridden by security considerations where visual access into a room would not be acceptable.

In the design of vision panels take into account:

— *sightlines* from wheelchairs.
— the preservation of *confidential* displays on designated areas of walls within offices.

Security

Security requirements should be defined in the brief, and may include devices such as CCTV, computer monitored door sensors and alarms, and computer controlled access systems.

Ironmongery

All ironmongery selected and specified must perform its required task adequately over the lifetime of the scheme. In choosing ranges the following points should be taken account of:

— statutory and local authority *fire* requirements.
— *safety* requirements.
— *security.*
— *emergency exit* hardware; where required this should be readily operated with one hand.
— hardware should not be positioned so that it is vulnerable to *impact* from trolleys etc; where this is unavoidable, its finish should be durable enough to withstand any impact or wear.

— *lever handles,* where proposed, should be able to maintain the horizontal position for the life of the scheme; and should have returns to avoid catching or snagging clothing.
— *door closers* should be capable of shutting the door against the latch from any position yet without causing undue noise or disturbance to the frame or partitions.

Frames, architraves and skirtings

Frames, architraves and skirtings should be:
— able to withstand *impact* from trolleys and cleaning equipment, particularly in vulnerable positions, and the appearance of the finish should not suffer unduly from such impact.
— *easily repaired* if damaged.

Doorstops

Doorstops should always be provided, and may be fitted either to:
— the *floor* (take care to avoid potential cleaning problems).
— the *partition.*
— the *door* (usually combined with a coathook, can cause strain to the hinges).

Whichever method is adopted, the fixing, its support and the impacted surface must be capable of sustaining the force of the door crashing into it repeatedly.

2.29 Flooring

This section covers detail considerations applicable to the selection, detail of junctions and installation of all types of floor finishes, and includes requirements for:
— sub-floors.
— service traps.
— floor finish junctions.
— stairs and stair nosings.
— entrance matting.
— raised access floors.
— adhesives.
— materials and material selection.
— colour and pattern.
— wastage.
— cleaning and maintenance.

Sub-floor

If floor finishes are to meet expected standards successfully, the sub-floor must be suitably prepared. In particular, it must be:

— *rigid* and *stable* (both physically and chemically).

— *clean, fully cured* and *dry*; dusty surfaces should be sealed.

— *level* and *smooth*; this is particularly critical where thin finishes such as vinyl are proposed.

Tests should be carried out to ensure that the moisture content of screeds is within the range recommended by the manufacturer prior to laying the finish.
If new finishes are being laid over existing finishes (e.g. old vinyl tiles), all traces of polish and surface contaminants must be removed.

Services

The design and selection of service traps and trunking must take the proposed floor finish into account, and vice versa. Traps and access trunking lids should either:

— have *trims* to cover the edges of both the surrounding and the inset floor finish.

— have *raised lips* sufficiently high to protect the edges, without being so high as to impede trolleys etc. being wheeled over them.

Lids, whether access or fixed, must be strong enough to support the point loads which will be imposed without deformation or damage.
Where finishes have a *direction*, inherent as in the case of carpet pile direction or dictated by the pattern, removable lids should be so designed that they can only be replaced in the *correct orientation*.
Care needs to be taken to ensure that the *cable egress*, whether via grommets or upstand pedestals, is well *protected* against damage, without interfering with furniture layouts or with cleaning.
Where the design concept requires flat wire cabling, finishes and fixing methods must be compatible with the requirements for flexibility and adaptation, and be in accordance with the cable manufacturer's recommendations.

See 2.32.

The floor finish must be considered in its relation to internal inspection chambers, manholes, drainage access points and gullies.

Floor finish junctions

Where two different finishes meet, the junction needs to be *protected* by a suitable edging strip. If the finishes are of different thicknesses, the difference should either be accommodated within the screed depth, or bevelled edging strips should be used.
Building *expansion joints* should not be bridged by floor finishes without a break.

Stairs and stair nosings

Non-slip nosings usually should be fitted to all staircases, and finished to give a contrast to the floor to provide a visual aid. In the case of new stairs, fixing lugs should be cast-in; in all cases care should be taken to ensure the security of the fixing.

If these minimum distances cannot be achieved, the frequency of cleaning of adjacent floor finishes will need to be increased.

Entrance mats

Door mats should be provided at all entrances to buildings and should ideally be sufficient to remove all grit and moisture from footwear. However, to achieve this effectively requires a minimum of 7 metres (23 ft) of matting measured in the available directions of travel, composed of 2 metres (6 ft 6 in) of grit-removing and 5 metres (16 ft 6 in) of moisture-absorbent matting, and in many cases this may not be practicable.

Where it is not possible to achieve the requirements within entrance and reception spaces, they can be met by utilising spaces such as lifts and lift lobbies so that the total travel distance over matting before general area carpet is reached totals 7 metres (23 ft).

Raised floors

Finishes to raised floors should:

— be *securely fixed* to prevent movement from rolling loads.
— allow *access* to services – either by removing the finish then lifting the panel, or by removing the finish and panel as one. It should be possible to do this repeatedly without detriment to the finish.
— meet IBM/ICL Electrical Resistance standards – tests should be carried out on the panel and finish combined.

Careful attention should be paid to *ramps* up to raised floors to ensure safety and to protect areas prone to wear. The *gradient* of ramps should not exceed 1 : 12.

Adhesives

Floor finishes should be adhered according to manufacturers' instructions and recommendations to ensure compatibility with the sub-floor and the finish.

Carpets generally should be fixed using a *release type adhesive* to facilitate replacement, except:

— on *stairs* and *ramps* where a permanent bond should be specified for safety reasons.
— on *raised panel floors* where a conducting adhesive, or other suitable bonding method, should be used to ensure adequate electrical contact.

Material selection

Selection of floor finishes should be made against all requirements, taking into account:

— appearance.
— durability.
— cost-effectiveness.
— availability.
— programme.
— maintenance factors.

Selected materials should:
- maintain their *appearance* and *integrity* for the lifespan of the scheme.
- withstand the *concentrated wear* likely in certain areas such as on staircases and through major traffic routes.
- be of such design and colour that *high traffic areas* are not readily visible, and soiling in vulnerable areas is hidden.
- recover adequately from *prolonged static loading* by furniture etc.
- possess adequate *colour fastness* to light, wet and dry rubbing, water and shampoo.

In addition, carpets should not be prone to the shading effects produced by pile reversal.

Colour and pattern

Selection of materials should be made from *large samples* and in conjunction with other materials to be used in the same area. Proposed materials should be selected, and where possible presented to the client, under the type and temperature of lighting which will be used in the scheme.

Consideration should be given to the change in appearance of both colours and patterns with *soiling* and *age*. Where there is doubt about the ability of a particular finish to maintain its appearance, manufacturers could be asked to provide samples demonstrating the expected changes across a range of soiling and wear.

Wastage

Prior to final material selection, *layout drawings* should be produced to avoid undue wastage of material and to ensure that suitable widths are selected.

Cleaning

Proposed materials should normally be capable of being cleaned by *standard cleaning practices*. Particular consideration should be given to floor finishes used in *cafeterias* or adjacent to *vending areas* where colour and design should camouflage residual staining.

2.30 Lighting

This section gives brief guidance on the selection, planning and detailing of lighting, including information on:
- *general considerations* (lamp types and characteristics, heat gains).
- *task* lighting (illuminating the working surfaces).
- *ambient* lighting (general area illumination).
- *aesthetic* lighting (special displays or lighting for effect rather than function).
- *security* lighting (including safety and emergency lighting).

To have some understanding of the principles of lighting design, and to be able to discuss lighting schemes effectively, it is necessary to appreciate some of the terminology and units of measurement. Whilst it is beyond the scope of this book to cover this in any great depth, the following brief definitions may be useful to those with little knowledge of the subject.

Lamp
The light-producing device (incandescent bulb, fluorescent tube etc.).

Luminaire
The light fitting, including reflector, diffuser etc.

Lux
The intensity to which a surface (real, as in a desk top, or imaginary, as in a specified horizontal plane) is illuminated, known as its *illuminance*, is expressed in lux. The surface could be at any angle, but in practice is normally horizontal, usually either the floor or the working plane (850 mm (33 in) above the floor unless a different height is required).
Lux levels can be specified as part of the brief, calculated from manufacturers' data, distribution patterns, heights and reflectance values, and finally measured with a light meter after installation.

Service illumination
The mean illuminance (measured in lux, or foot-candles) of a given area and plan over the life of the installation (taking into account lamp deterioration, and reflectance losses within the fitting and from the walls, with age) is known as the service illuminance.

Utilisation factor
The quantity of light emitted by a lamp is partly absorbed within the luminaire, and partly by the surfaces within the room. The ratio of the quantity of light reaching the working plane to the quantity of light emitted by the lamp is the utilisation factor. Being a product of the room as well as the luminaire, it is dependent on the proportions and reflectance values of the surfaces, and will also change with time.

Daylight factor
Daylight factor expresses the level of illuminance, provided by daylight alone, on a given plane inside the building as a percentage of the level of illuminance on a similar plane outside the building. To standardise the measurement, and to ensure that levels are achieved on dull days, the sky is taken as being overcast and providing an illuminance of 5000 lux (465 ft-candles). Consequently, in a room with a stated daylight factor of 5 per cent, the illuminance would be 250 lux (23 ft-candles).
For more detailed information on lighting measurement, levels, characteristics and design see Appendix A.1.b: *New Metric Handbook*[1] chapter

43, also *The IES Code: recommendations for lighting building interiors/IES Lighting Handbook*[22]
For information on lighting levels for different areas see 2.22 and 2.23.

Fig 2.28 *Lamp types and characteristics.*

Lamp type	*Lamp reference letter*	*Lamp designation and code (capital letters denote BS colours)*	*Constructional and operational characteristics*	*Lamp colour appearance*	*Approximate correlated colour temperature (K)*	*CIE colour rendering group*
Tubular fluorescent (MCF)	A	NORTHLIGHT; COLOUR MATCHING	Tubular fluorescent lamps are low-pressure linear light sources with differences of colour appearance and colour rendering due to the use of different phosphor coatings. Generally, efficacy decreases as colour rendering improves. Immediate light output when switched on cold or hot. Light output affected by ambient temperature. Can be dimmed if used with special control gear. All lamps have universal operating positions. Smaller wattage lamps are available	Cool	6500	1
	B	ARTIFICIAL DAYLIGHT		Cool	6500	1
	C	DAYLIGHT		Intermediate	4300	3
	D	NATURAL		Intermediate	4000	2
	E	"Kolor-rite; Trucolor 37		Intermediate	4000	1
	F	Colour 84		Intermediate	4000	2
		Plus-White			3600	2
	G	de luxe Natural		Intermediate	3600	1
	H	WHITE		Intermediate	3500	3
	I	WARM WHITE		Warm	3000	3
	J	de luxe Warm White; Softone 32		Warm	2700 3000	2
High-pressure discharge	K	Mercury halide (MBI)	High-pressure mercury lamp with metal halide additives in fused silica arc tube; clear outer bulb. Some ratings available in reflector form. Run-up period to full light output about 5 min. Re-ignition about 10 min; less if special circuits are used.	Intermediate	4200	1
		Mercury halide (MBIL)	MBI lamp in linear form, normally with outer bulb. Horizontal operation only		4200	2
		Mercury halide fluorescent (MBIF)	MBI lamp with fluorescent costing on inside of outer bulb		4000	2
	L	Mercury fluorescent (MBF)	High-pressure mercury lamp with fused silica arc tube and outer bulb with fluorescent coatings to increase proportion of red light. Run-up and re-ignition times as for MBI	Intermediate	4000	3
		Mercury fluorescent reflector (MBFR)	As for MBF but with internal reflector		4000	3
		Mercury-tungsten fluorescent (MBTF) (blended)	An MBF lamp with tungsten filament in series with arc tube to act as ballast and increase red light emitted		3600	3
	M	High-pressure sodium (SON)	High-pressure sodium lamp with arc tube in diffuse outer bulb. Run-up period to full light output 2 min. Re-ignition can take place within 1 min if external ignitor is used	Warm	2100	3
		High-pressure sodium (SONT)	SON lamp with clear tubular outer envelope		2100	3
		High-pressure sodium (SONL)	Linear SON lamp with clear slim tubular outer enveloped. Enables higher degree of light control to be achieved if required		2100	3
		High-pressure sodium (SONR)	SON lamp with internal reflector bulb		2100	3

Colour rendering characteristics (based on visual assessment)	*Typical applications*
Similar to north skylight; emphasises blues and, to a lesser extent, greens	Applications where colour rendering similar to north sky daylight is needed. Appears cold at low illuminances
Similar to Northlight/Colour Matching, but emits more ultra-violet radiation to conform with natural skylight	As above, but for use where critical colour matching to BS 950 Part 1 is required
Emphasises yellows strongly and, to a lesser extent, greens; subdues reds	Factories. Light blends well with daylight
Emphases yellows and, to a lesser extent, greens and blues. Reds shift slightly towards orange	Offices, department stores
Equal emphasis given to all colours	Display lighting. Shops, hospitals (clinical areas), museums
Emphasises oranges, greens and blue-violets, but subdues yellows and deep reds	Offices, department stores
Emphasises yellow, oranges and greens; subdues deep reds. Blues shift towards violet	Offices, department stores
Equal emphasis given to blues, greens and yellows, but more to reds	Shops
Emphasises yellows and, to a lesser extent, greens. Subdues reds and, to some extent, blues which shift towards violet	General-purpose use where high efficacy is primary requirement
Emphasises yellows and, to a lesser extent, greens. Reds slightly subdued. Subdues blues which shift towards violet	General-purpose use where high efficacy is primary requirement
Emphasises yellows and, to a lesser extent, greens. Subdues blues which tend towards violet	Hotels, restaurants, homes
Equal emphasis given to greens and blues; more to yellows. Reds rendering variable according to lamp type and manufacturer	Industrial and commercial applications, e.g. high-bay factories, area lighting, shops and offices
As for MBI	As for MBI
As for MBI	As for MBI
Emphasises yellows and blues which shift towards violet. Subdues reds	Industrial and commercial applications, e.g. shops, and offices, high-bay factories and area lighting, roadways
As for MBF	As for MBF
Emphasises yellows and blues which shift towards violet. Subdues reds to some extent	May be used as direct replacement for some GLS incandescent lamps, particularly where long life is important and access for maintenance is difficult
Emphasises yellows strongly, reds to lesser extent. Greens acceptable. Blues, which shift towards violet, strongly subdued	Industrial and commercial applications, e.g. public buildings, high-bay factories, area lighting, roadways
As for SON	As for SON
As for SON	As for SON
As for SON	As for SON

Figure continues overleaf.

Lamp type	*Lamp reference letter*	*Lamp designation and code (capital letters denote BS colours)*	*Constructional and operational characteristics*	*Lamp colour appearance*	*Approximate correlated colour temperature (K)*	*CIE colour rendering group*
Incandescent	P	Tungsten halogen (T/H)	Compact tungsten filament lamps with clear or diffusing silica tube or bulb containing halides or halogens which prevent blackening and increase life and/or efficacy which is relatively low. Linear types restricted to horizontal operation only	Warm	2900	1
	Q	Tungsten – General lighting service (GLS)	Tungsten filament in clear or diffusing glass bulb filled with inert gas. Relatively low efficacy. Immediate full light output. Light output sensitive to voltage variations. Easily switched and dimmed	Warm	2700	1
		Tungsten reflector	Tungsten filament in internally metallised blown or pressed bulb. Available in a range of reflector controus		2700	1

Published by courtesy of the I.E.S.

General considerations

Lamp characteristics

Care is needed in selection with regard to the audible sound level of ballast and with the possibility of its radio frequency interfering with screen images – consult manufacturers.
For more information on colour selection see 2.34.

When selecting suitable lamp types, consider in particular:

— *colour*: the spectrum range of a lamp is indicated by its colour temperature (K) and therefore its effect on a particular colour scheme. Figure 2.28 gives information on typical lamp types.

— *size*: with fluorescent lamps in particular, problems can arise with lengths; tubes are available in lengths of 300, 600, 900, 1200, 1500 and 2400 mm (12, 24, 36, 48, 60 and 96 in), which with the extra dimensions for the fittings puts them either just longer or well shorter than usual ceiling module dimensions. This can be overcome by using surface-mounted fittings, using a recessed continuous luminaire (ignoring the grid in one direction), or by alternating luminaires with air diffusers or blank panels to create the effect of a continuous fitting.

Great care should be taken when mixing different lamp types in the same space; different colour rendering qualities can have peculiar effects on colour schemes. The same problems can occur where daylight is supplemented by artificial light; remember that daylight is not constant and that the aspect will affect the colour rendering qualities.

Heat gain

See also 2.31.

The lighting levels required by offices will produce heat gains which must be dealt with, by:

— minimising the effect by careful selection of lamp types.

— ventilation; this will be particularly effective if air is extracted through the luminaires.

Colour rendering characteristics (based on visual assessment)	*Typical applications*
Emphasises reds strongly, yellows and greens to lesser extent. Blues strongly subdued	Display and area lighting
As for T/H	Hotels, restaurants, homes
As for T/H	Display and accent lighting

Task lighting

Suitable lighting at the worksurface can be achieved either:

— by overhead lighting which also provides general illumination; the layout must be carefully co-ordinated with the workstation planning.

— by supplementing the background illumination with individual fittings at the workstation.

In either case the problems of glare and reflections will have to be addressed.

Overhead lighting is probably more cost-effective, but requires great care to avoid problems with glare and reflections, and can inhibit future flexibility for layouts; task lighting provides a great deal of individual control and flexibility, but will generally require a greater frequency of lamp replacement, make actual levels of illumination difficult to calculate, and limit the possibilities for energy management.

Glare

Visual fatigue will be caused where glare becomes excessive, and happens when contrasts become too great. This will be more likely in brightly lit spaces.

Glare can either be direct from the light source (luminaire or window), or from reflection. Complete avoidance of glare is difficult to achieve, because it is dependent on a number of interrelated factors; consider minimising the risk by:

— fitting blinds to windows (vertical louvre, venetian or diffusing roller).

— careful co-ordination of light-distribution patterns of luminaires, fixing height and length of room (the risk of glare increases with lower mounting heights and with distance as light fittings come within field of view).

The light distribution pattern of a luminaire is indicated by the BZ value given in manufacturers' data; a high value indicates most light distributed sideways, a low value most distributed downwards. See Fig. 2.29.

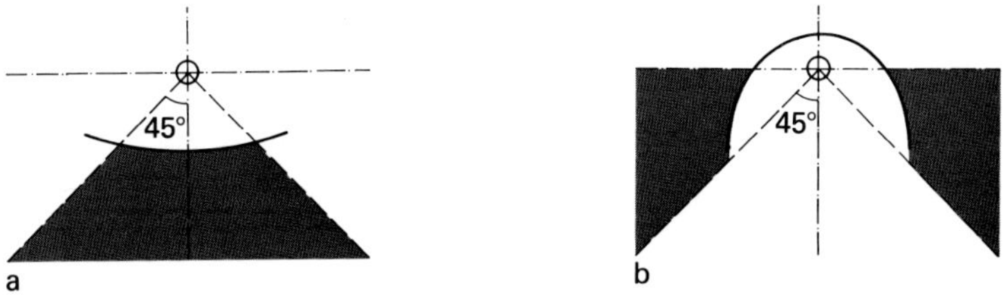

Fig. 2.29 *Luminaire light distribution patterns; luminaires with high BZ ratings emit most of their light upwards and sideways; those with low BZ ratings emit most light downwards.*

— selecting luminaires with diffusers to prevent direct view of the lamp.
— avoiding dark finishes adjacent to light sources.
— using matt or semi-matt finishes, particularly around and within the workstation.
— maintaining the reflectance values of surfaces adjacent to workstations between 30 and 70 per cent.
— maintaining the luminance (brightness) ratio between the keyboard and screen, the worksurface and adjacent surfaces as close as possible to 1 : 3 : 10. As far as possible, the luminance of the keyboard should match that of the screen.

Reflections
Reflections on screens can be a serious cause of eye strain and fatigue, amplified by operators having to work with over-bright screens to try and combat them. Their occurrence can be minimised by:
— arranging luminaires parallel to windows, with screens parallel to both wherever possible.
— the use of indirect ambient lighting.
— fitting filters to the screens.
— using luminaires which can be rotated through 90°.
Additional problems will be encountered where equipment incorporating light-emitting diodes or liquid crystal displays (LEDs or LCDs) is to be used; too high a level of illuminance will render these difficult to read.

Ambient lighting
Satisfactorily answering the problems of task lighting will not in itself achieve a room that is pleasantly lit. The lighting will also need to ensure that the walls and ceiling receive sufficient light whilst maintaining good three-dimensional modelling with adequate shadowing. This will be aided by:
— light-coloured finishes.
— windows (as opposed to rooflights).
— luminaires which emit a proportion of light sideways.
— using uplighters to provide ambient lighting combined with feature and task lighting.

Satisfactory uplighting giving an acceptable spread of light without the lamps being visible normally requires a minimum ceiling height of 2,750 m (9 ft). Defects in the ceiling will be highlighted; consider any remedial action which may be required.

However, it should be noted that achieving the desired effect requires a delicate balance of daylighting, luminaire and lamp specification, room proportions and finishes. In normal circumstances this can be achieved through the application of rules of thumb and experience; in more complex situations the advice of a lighting specialist should be sought.

Aesthetic effect
Usually there is little scope in offices for the use of lighting purely for effect, the requirements of function and safety being overriding in most areas. However, most projects will provide the opportunity for at least a small amount of special treatment; and using light in this way can be a very effective and economical way of

creating interest and drama. Possibilities might include:

- lighting the building for external effect at night.
- creating variety within ancillary areas (cafeterias, for example).
- lighting display areas or adding interest to circulation routes, dead-end corridors and reception spaces.

  Using lighting for effect is generally best confined to secondary areas: achieving dramatic effect and satisfying the demands of working spaces are unlikely to be successful.

Safety lighting

Safety lighting includes:

- minimising the risk of accident – on stairs, ramps etc.
- security – lessening the danger of theft, attack etc.
- emergency – aiding the evacuation of the building.

For the first two aspects, ensure that all areas of the building are adequately lit, inside and outside, including external stairs and ramps, rear entrances, car parks etc. Leave no dark corners; lighting is one of the most effective, and cheapest, forms of deterrent; but remember that it is only effective when lit; cables and fittings, particularly externally, should not be vulnerable to interference.

Emergency lighting takes two forms:

- *maintained*: with all lamps operating all the time; the advantage being that faults with the circuit or lamp will be obvious.
- *non-maintained*; operating only when an emergency occurs; with the disadvantage of having to be checked regularly.

Three different means of powering emergency lighting are available:

- from a generator; this is often unsuitable because of the start-up time involved.
- from central batteries: these require separate, ventilated space and cabling to each luminaire position.
- from self-contained batteries within the luminaire. Although the individual units are more expensive than the second option, the removal of the need for cabling means that they often prove cheaper overall, and they are becoming the most commonly used system.

Maintenance and operation

The maintenance and operation of a building after completion are becoming increasingly complex, and the needs of those whose job it will be should be considered throughout the design process. When selecting and positioning luminaires, take account of:

- the ease with which it will be possible to clean and maintain them.
- lamp life and replacement cost.
- access to the luminaires.

In addition, ensure that the specification requires:
- all cables, circuits, fuses etc. to be identified and labelled.
- that a schedule of lamps and fuses be provided.

In addition it may be wise to insist on a package of replacement lamps being provided by the contractor for the client.

2.31 Mechanical design

This section provides limited guidance on the detail design of the mechanical systems for high-technology offices insofar as they impinge on the responsibilities of the building designer; it does not attempt to provide the sort of information which will be required by the mechnical consultant. Topics covered are commonly encountered problems and situations, including:
- zoning.
- plant rooms.
- water storage.
- air pressurisation.
- filtration.
- controls.
- diffusers.

Zoning

See also 2.23.

Ensure that the zone separation of systems allows:
- areas with different working periods to operate independently.
- capacity to be utilised in the most critical areas after partial breakdown.

Plant rooms

Where there is a possibility of noise nuisance being caused to the neighbourhood, measure ambient sound levels at the site boundary so the effect can be determined

See also 2.23.

Confirm that siting and screening will prevent any noise nuisance.

Where gas-type fire protection is being installed in plant rooms, consider providing a manually operated air-purging system to clear the gases.

Where equipment containing toxic refrigerants is being used in enclosed spaces, consider installing an extract system able to cope with a major leakage.

Provide facilities for all maintenance and access requirements, including:
- adequate lighting.
- lifting facilities for major items where necessary.
- gantries and access ladders to high-level equipment.
- walkways where service routes are laid across the floor.

Water storage

Ensure that:
- dosing facilities are provided for water for humidifiers, cooling towers and chilled water storage tanks.
- water storage for cooling tower supplies are sufficient to allow critical areas to operate at full load for a suitable period of time after mains supplies are cut off (agree length of time with client).

Air pressurisation

Air-conditioned buildings will normally be pressurised with a difference of approximately 10 per cent between the supply and extraction rates. Check whether any special requirements apply to specific areas (for example, clean rooms will need to be positively pressured relative to surrounding spaces as well as the outside; kitchens should be negatively pressured to prevent the spread of cooking smells).

Filtration

Ensure that:

— standard-size filters are used wherever possible for ease of replacement.
— adequate space for maintenance is provided, including room to withdraw the old filters.

Controls

Confirm how the system adapts to cope with different operating conditions:

— through all the seasons of the year.
— at night and at weekends (including occasional) or permanent times of working).
— in the event of frost.
— in the event of power failure.

Identify means of protection provided against total system shut-down in the event of one component failing.

Determine exact location of sensors and confirm positions:

— provide representative conditions unaffected by draughts, direct radiation from sun or other heat sources etc.
— confirm that sensors do not clash with any other elements.

Diffusers

Diffuser location is critical to the effective distribution of air, and because of the pattern of light and dark provided by the slots, they inevitably form a strong visual element. Check that the detailed design conforms to the scheme design and is visually acceptable, yet:

— provides full circulation and avoids pockets of stale air or hot spots (for example, under desks or in corners).
— avoids short-circuits of air from the supply diffusers to the extract.
— provides sufficient air at seated head level without causing draughts at standing head height.

For detailed information on mechanical services to machine rooms see 2.22.3.

Miscellaneous considerations

Check that the detailed scheme includes the following, where applicable:

— water conservation measures (spray taps to wash hand basins, urinal flushing governed by sensor monitoring water flow to wash hand basins etc.).

— services are colour-coded, and that all valves, stopcocks etc. will be labelled, coded and cross-referenced to drawings on completion.
— facilities for landscape watering (consider collection of rainwater).
— mains water supply to vending machines.
— pipework insulation which does not produce toxic fumes in the event of a fire.

2.32 Cabling

This section provides guidance on the commonly encountered problems with cable management. The intention is to assist the designer to anticipate potential difficulties and resolve them with the appropriate specialist consultant whilst avoiding over-detailed discussion of the rapidly changing field of cable technology itself.

In particular, the following aspects are discussed:
— *general* items, including gas detection, access and power variations.
— *distribution,* including methods, cable separation and circuit identification.
— *final interface,* including outlets, wire management in screens and furniture, floor boxes etc.

General

Power supply variations

Common tolerances to power supply variations (in the UK) are:
- Voltage:

Three phase 415 V	373–448 V
Single phase 240 V	216–258 V

- Frequency:

50 Hz	49.5–50.5 Hz

Some equipment, particularly mainframe computers, may be susceptible to variations in electrical power supply. Where this is the case, check that the system includes alarm devices which monitor some or all of the following:
— power failure.
— emergency power operation.
— changes in voltage and frequency outside pre-set limits.
— temperature changes outside pre-set limits.
— telephone switching system faults.

Ensure that the alarms provide visual and audible signals allowing appropriate action to be taken, without causing an automatic shut-down of the computer systems.

Access

See also 2.27, 2.29 and 2.31.

Ensure that all positions requiring periodic access are identified at an early stage. Form of access must be determined from an understanding of the nature of the work to be performed. For example, where access is required to cables in the ceiling void, check that:
— the location of the access point is such that minimal disruption will be caused to normal work.
— the opening is large enough for a man carrying any necessary tools, spares etc.

— the cables are fixed at a height which can be reached easily from stepladders.
— where access is via removable ceiling panels, there is somewhere clean that the panel can be placed, that it is not susceptible to damage, and that dirty finger-marks can be cleaned.

In all cases, ensure that:
— any fire ratings are maintained.
— the integrity of the surrounding floor, wall or ceiling is maintained when panels are removed.
— security requirements are not compromised (lockable panels).
— positions are identified, on drawings where necessary, and *in situ* (where access is via removable ceiling panels, indicate the particular panel(s) with a small dot or similar identifying mark).

Gas detection

Where fire-alarm systems are being installed, consider the addition of gas-detection sensors, linked to the system, located at all low-level service entry points to the building, and at any other positions where gas might collect (sumps, cellars etc.).

Telecommunications: liaison with authorities

Early liaison with telecommunications authorities is essential to avoid the common problem of surface-fixed wiring appearing all over a newly completed interior. Establish:
— division of responsibilities.
— service entry position and requirements (normally a hole immediately outside the perimeter of the building with a plastic pipe passing through to the inside to act as a conduit; provision of this is the customer's responsibility.
— wiring routes, frame room requirements (where applicable), switchboard position and requirements, junction box positions and termination positions.
— programme.

In the UK, it is now common for British Telecom to provide the service only to a terminal box or frame room inside the building, with all further equipment and wiring provided by specialist contractors (or the electrical subcontractor in simple installations). This can make the process of controlling wiring routes and junction box positions simpler.

Distribution

Methods

Primary and secondary distribution methods and routes will already have been determined (see 2.24). Detail considerations will depend on method(s) adopted.

Ceiling distribution

Ceiling distribution systems depend for their success on the ability to satisfactorily arrange secondary distribution. Examples of possible routes include:
— through partition walls in cellular arrangements.

— down columns (surface-fixed conduit or trunking, or concealed behind cladding).
— via power poles. (These often have a rather crude appearance, and can create a cluttered 'forest' in large areas; these problems can be obviated where groups of workstations can be served by one purpose-designed pole visually and physically linked to the furniture.

Within ceiling, ensure:
— adequate fixings for cable tray, including weight of additional cables allowed for expansion.
— co-ordination with other services, particularly at cross-over points and access positions.
— that fire barriers are suitably stopped where perforated.

Raised floor distribution

Raised floors provide the greatest flexibility for routes and distribution. Ensure that:
— primary routes are positioned to allow access without disrupting normal work.
— outlets are positioned adjacent to, but not under, equipment or workstation positions.

Perimeter distribution

Perimeter distribution can be at skirting or dado height, either in exposed trunking or conduit, or concealed beneath cladding. Where exposed, great care needs to be taken with the detailing to ensure a satisfactory appearance. To achieve control of the final result:
— examine all components of the proposed system, including fixings, junctions and outlets.
— establish how different finishes can be applied, where required, prior to final selection.
— draw large-scale elevations identifying and positioning all elements. Superimpose adjacent furniture, equipment and all wall-fixed items to avoid clashes.

Cable separation

Ensure that cable manufacturers' and authorities' requirements for separation are met.

Some communications cables carry digital signals of a lower amplitude than is assumed for normal guidelines, and may therefore require greater separation from power cables than would usually be provided. Consult equipment manufacturers for guidance.
Where metallic screening is not provided (around the cable itself, or within trunking), a minimum distance of 150 mm (6 in) should be maintained between data cables and other wiring.

Identification

With the proliferation of cables being installed in buildings, it is imperative that cables are properly identified for reasons of safety and efficiency, and to allow redundant cables to be removed in the future.

Ensure that the specification defines a method of coding all cables, at both ends.

Final distribution

Outlets

Ensure that all outlet positions are suitable for their usage, and that all clashes with other elements are resolved. Fully co-ordinated drawings will be required to check in particular for:

— floor boxes/outlets occurring under table legs, pedestals, screens or seating positions.
— outlets under raised floors positioned where they cannot be accessed without moving equipment or furniture.
— positions requiring unacceptably long lengths of flex.

In addition, where floor boxes are to be used, check that they provide adequate protection for the flexes, and that the actual plugs to be used will fit within the space (some power plug tops, for example, have a moulded ring as part of their design which will not fit into most floor boxes).

For more potential problems with floor boxes, see 2.29.

Cables in screens and furniture

Where cables are carried within screens or furniture, consider measures to prevent them being moved while still connected.

See also 2.33.

Ancillary outlets

Ensure that all ancillary requirements are met, and co-ordinated with other elements. For example:

— public address system (where required) power, cabling and speaker positions.
— power in WCs for shavers and macerators.
— external power outlets for maintenance etc.
— clocks: power, wiring and positions.
— security system wiring (including all sensor positions).
— telephones in lifts.
— payphones where required.

2.33 Furniture and fittings

This section looks at some of the factors to be assessed when selecting, specifying or designing furniture and fittings. For clarity it is divided by type: desks, screens, storage and chairs. It should be remembered, however, that items cannot be considered in isolation but should be judged as to how well they work together, and with the rest of the building.

In most cases selection and specification of furniture will follow the pattern of identifying functional needs, assessing available standard products, establishing other criteria (cost, delivery etc.) and making the final choice on the basis of all criteria. Occasionally it will be found that standard products do not fulfil the requirements and purpose-made items will have to be designed. Basic functional requirements will have been established by this stage; other criteria to be determined and assessed include:

- modularity: how well do the dimensions of the product accord with the building and services module?
- adaptability: how easily can a particular configuration be changed, or dismantled and relocated?
- range of items: can the different needs be met from within one product range?
- co-ordination with existing furniture, where necessary (consider refurbishments and alteration of existing furniture where possible).
- manufacturer's back-up: delivery (both initial and future), installation, likely product continuity, spares etc.
- aesthetics: how well does the product conform with the rest of the design?
- costs: now and future.

In addition the response of employees should be sought and assessed. Operator stress in using VDUs etc. can be alleviated by good ergonomics, but ergonomics is not an exact science; being predisposed to like a chair, for example, will colour any assessment of its comfort.

Where possible view existing installation and check the condition of the furniture after several rearrangements have taken place. Discuss the practicalities of the system with those responsible for replanning and maintenance.

Desks

Despite the claims made to the contrary by many manufacturers, the function of a desk has never changed radically and it remains, at its simplest, a table. The value of add-on features should be assessed in this light, for over sophistication can be self-defeating.

However, the demands of offices and technology means that some features may be useful. Arguably, some of these would be better incorporated within the equipment itself, and in the case of some manufacturers, they are; but this is not always so and individual needs will have to be assessed. Facilities which will be offered, and aspects of them which should be considered, include:

- wire (or cable) management: at its simplest, a hole in the desk top; more sophisticated versions include routing through hollow leg sections and cable trays concealed under hinged flaps in the top. Consider: the relationship at the floor (a choice of entry positions affords greater flexibility), capacity, safety (particularly the possibility of damage at entry and exit positions), separation characteristics (plastic dividers may mean that more expensive, screened data cables have to be used) and the ease with which cables can be added or removed (the need to thread wiring should be avoided; take particular note that some equipment comes complete with moulded plugs, complete with ring-pull sections in the case of IBM, which may make threading impossible).
- adaptability: features which allow furniture to be tailored to individual

In the UK, wire management systems should conform to BS6396: 1983 *Requirements for electrical systems in office furniture*.
Separation distances between cables of a minimum of 50 mm will obviate the need for screening or ducting (although this may still be desirable for protection).
Consider whether any special arrangements will be required to deal with surplus cables: some systems incorporate spaces where these can be 'dumped'.

needs are useful provided that adjustments can be made simply. Check that desk-top height adjustments can be performed without removing equipment and that extensions can be handled without requiring additional components.

— equipment support facilities: where features such as keyboard recesses, split-level tops, document holders, turntables, telephone stands etc. are a requirement, ensure that they are tested with the actual equipment to be installed, and seek user reactions (see section on mock-ups below).

Dealer desks

The density of equipment and cables, and the manner of operation, combine to make dealing desks a special case. In addition to the general requirements covered in 2.22.2, consider the following points:

— overall height should not exceed 1100 mm (43 in) to allow visual contact across the desk.
— dealer boards are sometimes located in the flat desk top; this can lead to problems with objects accidentally being dropped onto the board and operating switches, and problems from spilt coffee.
— consider wiring telephone handsets from the front edge of the desk to avoid problems with wires trailing across the desk.
— coffee spillage is a perennial problem; ensure that liquid on the desk top will not reach equipment or wiring, and that provision is made for coffee cups (recesses or something similar).
— desk arrangements are likely to be reconfigured; consequently access to equipment and cables must be from the front (operator position).

Screens

Screens may be required to fulfil a number of functions:

— providing acoustic and visual privacy.
— carrying services.
— supporting furniture and/or lighting.
— providing display space.

In addition to confirming that these functional requirements are met, at detail design stage ensure that:

— the planned arrangements will be stable (where shelving or cupboards are to be supported, consider the effect of eccentric loading).
— cable-carrying facilities allow for planned expansion, are properly separated and meet statutory requirements. Check in particular that there is no danger of damage to wiring at screen junctions or at ingress/egress positions.
— visual awareness of the whole space is not unnecessarily restricted; consider screens of different heights.
— the display facilities allow for personalisation of the workstation.

Storage

Check that all aspects covered in 2.22.2 are covered. Confirm suitability of proposed products by testing actual samples of client's stored items in a mock-up (see below).

Chairs

Assessment of comfort characteristics is very much a matter of personal choice; other characteristics can be judged on a more objective basis. Select a shortlist of possible chair ranges by considering:

— durability: where possible view old installations; take wear characteristics into account.
— suitability of range: ensure that all required chair types (desk, visitors, conference etc.) are covered by the range, or, if not, that compatible products are available.
— range of adjustment: ideally height of seat, arms and back; tension of back.
— safety: five-star bases, 'give' in seat to absorb impact.
— movement: castors, swivel and tilt.
— maintenance: availability of spare parts (castors, gas-lift mechanisms etc.) and ease of recovering.
— implications of long-term use: ease of adjustment to vary position, avoidance of cutting off circulation at front edge of seat.

Once a short-list has been determined, arrange tests and establish means of assessing user feedback. Tests can either be conducted in a mock-up (see below), or preferably by arranging longer-term use in the existing offices.

Sometimes existing chairs will have to be incorporated in the new scheme. They will usually benefit from re-upholstering prior to being installed in the new location: arrange a phased programme of batches to avoid unnecessary disruption.

Mock-ups

In any sizeable project, establishing a mock-up covering all major elements should be considered prior to final selection. The mock-up could be installed on-site, where possible, or in any other suitable building with sufficient space and height. The installation should be treated as a design exercise in itself; and needs to be carefully arranged to demonstrate all elements and their interactions as realistically as possible.

A typical installation might consist of three cellular offices and a small area outside, complete with raised floor and finish, ceiling, lighting, air-conditioning grills etc. In a more elaborate situation the external walling and glazing might be included.

Mock-ups are useful for testing many aspects of the design, including:

— making final selection from two or three alternatives (ceiling tiles, partitions, raised floors etc.).
— checking the effectiveness of details at the junctions of elements.
— checking the lighting design: by arranging the installation as a working

environment any problems with glare or reflections can be foreseen.

— judging alternative ranges of furniture.

— presenting the final design to the user in a form which can be easily comprehended.

Where the programme allows, the main contractor should be made responsible for the installation, as this will assist with his understanding of the design, and help him to foresee any constructional problems.

Where alternative products are being considered, manufacturers may be persuaded to contribute materials in view of the competitive situation.

2.34 Finishes

Confirm the suitability of proposed finishes, taking into account the following factors:

— *wear* (both the severity of anticipated wear and the ability of the finish to sustain it).

— *repair* (the ease with which repairs can be effected on-site using standard techniques).

— *fire resistance* (where required).

— *aesthetics*.

Typically, the less sophisticated a material is, the more susceptible it will be to damage; but conversely, the simpler it will be to repair. The correct balance for a particular situation will be a product of degree of exposure to damage, delivery periods on replacement components where applicable, skills available and cost-effectiveness.

Selection of finishes should be made from large samples and in conjunction with other materials to be used in the same area. Proposed materials should ideally be viewed (and where possible presented to the client) under the type and temperature of lighting which will be used in the scheme.

2.35 Selection

The final selection of any solution (whether it be a detail, material or a finish) must take account of the original problem, its ability to address the problem, and the balance between various criteria. The criteria might include:

— ability to satisfy the *brief*.

— ability to satisfy the *functional* requirements.

— ability to satisfy *statutory regulations*.

— availability from a number of different *sources*.

— availability as a *standard product*.

— ability to *integrate* with other building elements.

— simplicity of *installation* and *maintenance* techniques.

— *spares* stockholding carried by suppliers.

— *cost effectiveness*.

— availability to meet *programme*.

— *quality* assurance.

Figure 2.29 shows an example of an evaluation checklist for options being considered for any element. Use of a checklist similar to this will ensure that a consistent approach is applied to all elements, and that all aspects are considered before final selection is made.

Fig. 2.29 *Example of performance evaluation checklist*

Subject:	*Rating values:*
Options – brief description	*1 = fails to meet criteria* *2 = meets criteria* *3 = exceeds criteria*
Selection criteria	*Options* *A* .... *B* .... *C* ....
1 Satisfies brief:	
2 Satisfies function:	
3 Satisfies statutory regulations:	
4 Multiple source:	
5 Standard product:	
6 Integration ability:	
7 Installation and maintenance techniques:	
8 Spares stockholding:	
9 Cost-effectiveness:	
10 Availability:	
11 Quality assurance:	
12	
13	
Recommendation:	

A.1 References and sources of information

a. References: section 1

1 Jones, J. Christopher, *Design Methods: Seeds of human futures*, Chichester: Wiley, 1981.

2 Palmer, M. A., *The Architect's Guide to Facility Programming*, Washington: American Institute of Architects, 1981.

3 Preiser, W.(ed.), *Facility Programming: methods and applications*, Stroudsburg, Pa.: Dowden, Hutchinson & Ross, 1978.

4 Sanoff, H., *Methods of Architectural Programming*, Stroudsburg, Pa.: Dowden, Hutchinson & Ross, 1977.

5 Alexander, C. *et al.*, *A Pattern Language: Towns, Buildings, Construction*, New York: Oxford University Press, 1977.

6 Elder, A. J., *Guide to the Building Regulations 1985* (2nd edition), London: Butterworth Architecture, 1988.

7 Speaight, A. & Stone, G., *The AJ Legal Handbook* (3rd edition), London: Butterworth Architecture, 1982.
The Architectural Press, 1982.

8 Mazria, E., *The Passive Solar Energy Book:* (Expanded professional edition), Emmaus, Pa: Rodale Press, 1979.

9 Koenigsberger, O. H. *et al.*, *Manual of Tropical Housing and Building*, Part 1: Climatic Design, London: Longman, 1973.

Other useful general references:

An Introduction to Cost Planning, London: The Royal Institution of Chartered Surveyors, 1976.

Architect's Job Book, compiled by L. Beaven and D. Dry (4th edition), London: RIBA Publications, 1983.

Bathurst, P. E. & Butler, D. A., *Building Cost Control Techniques* (2nd edition), London: Heinemann, 1980.

Cartlidge, D. P. & Mehrtens, I. N., *Practical Cost Planning*, London: Hutchinson, 1982.

Cross, N. & Roy, R., *Design Methods Manual* (*Man-made Futures:* Units 13-16), Milton Keynes: The Open University, 1975.
Ferry, D. J., *Cost Planning of Buildings* (4th edition revised by T. Brandon), London: Granada, 1980.
Green, R. *The Architect's Guide to Running a Job* (Fourth edition), London: Butterworth Architecture, 1989.
Kemper, A. M., *Architectural Handbook: environmental analysis, architectural programming, design and technology, and construction*, New York: Wiley, 1979.
Lacy, R. E., *Climate and Building in Britain*, London: HMSO, 1978.
Longmore, J., *BRS Daylight Protractors*, London: HMSO, 1968.
Lynch, K., *Site Planning* (2nd edition), Cambridge, Mass.: MIT Press, 1971.
Powell, J. (ed.), *Handbook of Architectural Practice and Management* (4th edition), London: RIBA Publications, 1980.
Seeley, I. H., *Building Economics: appraisal and control of building costs and efficiency* (2nd edition), London: Macmillan, 1976.
Stone, P. A., *Building Design Evaluation: costs in use* (3rd edition), London: Spon, 1980.

b. References: section 2

1 Tutt, P. & Adler, D. (eds.), *New Metric Handbook*, London: Butterworth Architecture, 1979.
2 Lawson, F., *Restaurants, Clubs & Bars*, London: Butterworth Architecture, 1988.
3 'Energy Primer', *The Architects' Journal*, vol. 175, 19 May, 26 May and 9 June 1982.
4 Goldsmith, S., *Designing for the Disabled* (3rd edition), London: RIBA Publications, 1976.
5 'Thinking About Fire', *The Architects' Journal*, vol. 176, 11 August, 18 August and 8 September 1982.
6 'Security in Buildings', *The Architects' Journal*, vol. 171, 28 May 1980 *et seq*.
7 Corby, M., Donohue, E. J. & Hamer, M., *Telecomms Users' Handbook*, London: Telecommunications Press, 1982.
8 'Communications', *The Architects' Journal*, vol. 176, 4 August 1982.
9 Hodgkinson, A., *AJ Handbook of Building Structure* (2nd edition), London: Butterworth Architecture, 1980.
10 Vandenberg, M. & Elder, A. J. (eds.), *AJ Handbook of Building Enclosure*, London: Butterworth Architecture, 1974.
11 Littler, J. & Thomas, R., *Design with Energy* – the conservation and use of energy in buildings, Cambridge, New York and Melbourne: Cambridge University Press, 1984.
12 Markus, T. A. & Morris, E. N., *Buildings, Climate and Energy*, London: Pitman, 1980.
13 ASHRAE *Handbook of Fundamentals*, New York: The American Society of Heating, Refrigerating and Air Conditioning Engineers, Inc. 1981.

14 Martin, P. L., and Oughton, D. W., *Faber and Kell's Heating and Air Conditioning of Buildings* (7th edition), London: Butterworth Architecture, 1989.

Green, R. *The Architect's Guide to Running a Job* (Fourth edition), London: Butterworth Architecture, 1988.

London: RIBA Publications 1980 (under revision 1989–90)

15 Duffy, F., Cave, C. & Worthington, J. (ed.), *Planning office space,* London: Butterworth Architecture, 1976.

16 Mynors, C., *Planning applications and appeals,* London: Butterworth Architecture, 1987.

17 Chappell, D., *Report writing for architects,* London: Butterworth Architecture, 1984.

18 Cumming, N., *Security,* London: Butterworth, 1987.

19 UK: *IEE Wiring Regulations* (15th edition), The Institute of Electrical Engineers.

USA: *National Electrical Code* (enacted into local regulations, sometimes with variations).

20 *DTI Interim Code of Practice on Wiring*: Telecoms Division Branch 4, Department of Trade and Industry.

21 Haverstock, H., *The Building Design Easibrief,* London: Morgan Grampian Plc, 1987.

22 UK: *The IES Code: recommendations for lighting building interiors,* London: The Illuminating Engineering Society, 1977.

USA: *IES Lighting Handbook* (5th edition), New York: The Illuminating Engineering Society, 1972.

23 'Development Economics: Offices', *The Architects' Journal,* vol. 183, 23rd April 1986 *et seq.*

24 'Space for Services', *The Architects' Journal,* vol. 183, 12th February 1986 *et seq.*

Other useful references:

Pulgram, W. L. & Stonis, R. E., *Designing the Automated Office,* New York, Whitney Library of Design, 1984.

Klein, J. G., *The Office Book*, London, Quarto Marketing Ltd., 1982.

Neufert, E. (ed.), *Architects' Data,* London: Granada Publishing Ltd, New York: Halsted Press, 1980.

Rush, R. D. (ed.), *The Building Systems Integration Handbook,* New York: The American Institute of Architects/John Wiley & Sons, 1986.

Harris, D. A. *et al*, *Planning and Designing the Office Environment,* New York: Van Nostrand Rheinhold Company, 1981.

c. Sources of information (general): UK

Ordnance Survey
Romsey Road
Maybush
Southampton SO9 4DH
Tel. 0703-775555
The central survey and mapping organisation in the public sector. Produces and maintains up-to-date basic surveys at 1:1,250 for major urban areas, and at 1:2,500 (minor towns and cultivated areas) or 1:10,000 (mountain and moorland) for the remainder of the country; also a range of special maps and services. Catalogues and various leaflets are available from address given; maps obtainable through booksellers and OS agents.
The need to reproduce OS publications in whole or part is provided for by a scale of royalty charges and a series of licences designed to meet the needs of various authorities, organisations and the professions. Full information is given in OS leaflets No. 8 and No. 23.

Institute of Geological Sciences
Geological Museum
Exhibition Road
South Kensington
London SW7 2DE
Tel. 01-589 3444
also
Murchison House
West Mains Road
Edinburgh EH9 3LA
Tel. 031-667 1000
Geological survey maps are available at a scale of 1:63,360 (1 in.) (when reprinted these sheets are generally being replaced by sheets at 1:50,000, new sheets are published at 1:50,000 only) with special areas available at 1:25,000 and 1:10,560 (6 in.). Memoirs describing the geology, including details of sections, bore holes and other data, have been published for many of the sheets. A catalogue of maps is available from the Institute who provide advisory services on a wide range of economic and environmental topics.
The museum contains a collection of building stones from most quarries now working stone in the UK, as well as marbles and other ornamental stones from most countries of the world. The library contains material covering the geological sciences literature of the world and is open to members of the public for reference purposes.

Meteorological Office
London Road
Bracknell
Berkshire RG12 2SZ
Tel. 0344-20242
also:
231 Corstorphine Road
Edinburgh EH12 7BB
Tel. 031-334 9721
and:
Tyrone House
Ormeau Avenue
Belfast BT2 8HH
Tel. 0232-28457

Weather information for sites in the UK (and abroad) to help with analysis and design; also provides a range of services including CLIMEST, a quick-reply service to assist the construction industry.
Various publications available (listed in leaflet No. 12). Library is open to the public and contains material covering, amongst other things, all aspects of meteorology and climatology and a large collection of world-wide data.

Department of the Environment
Air Photographs Unit
6th Floor
Prince Consort House
Albert Embankment
London SE1 7TP
A large range of aerial photography – photographs, negatives and microfilm – and a Central Register of Air Photography which contains, amongst other things, information on the coverage and scale of commercial photography.
Copies of material are available for sale.

Department of the Environment
Map Library
5th Floor
Prince Consort House
Albert Embankment
London SE1 7TP
The map library holds an extensive collection covering many aspects of town and country planning and local government, mostly of England and Wales. Selected maps are for sale – details and prices available on application.

Aerofilms Ltd
Gate Studios
Station Road
Boreham Wood
Herts WD6 1EJ
Tel. 01-207 0666
Oblique aerial photography to order; from a library collection (covering a variety of subjects including meteorology, geology, building construction, architecture) in black and white, and colour. Free proofs submitted on request; print prices and reproduction fees supplied on request. Stereo pairs available as paper prints, 35 mm slides and overhead projector transparencies.

Office of Population Censuses and Surveys
St. Catherine's House
10 Kingsway
London WC2B 6JP
Tel. 01-242 0262

Library contains population census and vital statistics reports from most countries. Open to general public (preferably by appointment).

Building Research Establishment
1) Building Research Station
Bucknalls Lane
Garston
Watford
Herts WD2 7JR
Tel. 09273-74040
2) Fire Research Station
Borehamwood
Herts WD6 2BL
Tel. 01-953 6177
3) Princes Risborough Laboratory
Princes Risborough
Aylesbury
Bucks
Tel. 084-44 3101

also:
BRE (Scottish Laboratory)
Kelvin Road
East Kilbride
Strathclyde G75 OR2
Tel. 03552-33941

The BRS covers building design and construction, environmental design etc., the Fire Research Station is concerned with fire extinction and prevention, structural aspects of fire in buildings, means of escape etc.; the Princes Risborough Laboratory deals with the use of timber, wood-based and other materials in building.
Details of advisory services and publications are available from each station.

British Services Research and Information Association
Old Bracknell Lane West
Bracknell
Berks
Tel. 0344-25071
A non-profit-making association. The provision of information and advice is one of its main functions. Membership includes consulting engineers, contractors, manufacturers and others concerned with mechanical and electrical services of buildings.

British Standards Institution
2 Park Street
London W1A 2BS
Tel. 01-629 9000
Recognised body for the preparation and promulgation of standards including performance and constructional specifications and codes of practices. Enquiry service and publications available. The library contains complete sets of British Standards as well as foreign and international standards. It is open to the general public.

Fire Protection Association
Aldermary House
Queen Street
London EC4N 1TJ
Tel. 01-248 5222
Central advisory organisation (set up by insurers) covering all aspects of fire prevention and control. Provides an information service and will give technical and general advice on fire protection both at design stage and in the maintenance of buildings. Library facilities may be used by the public (preferably by appointment). A list of publications is available.

HM Stationery Office
Atlantic House
Holborn Viaduct
London EC1P 1BN
Tel. 01-583 9876
Produces hundreds of publications each year for Parliament, Government departments, museums and other public institutions in the UK.
The most useful guides are the sectional lists. These, and all HMSO publications, can be obtained from HMSO bookshops (London, Edinburgh, Manchester, Birmingham, Cardiff, Bristol and Belfast) or from booksellers appointed as stockists.

National Association of Building Centres
26 Store Street
London WC1E 7ET
Tel. 01-637 1022
Represents all building centres in the UK and Ireland with the object of co-ordinating their functions and services. The individual centres usually have a permanent exhibition of building products and provide an enquiry/advisory service. Information on the individual centres may be obtained from the National Association.

Central Council for the Disabled (Access for the Disabled)
34 Eccleston Square
London SW1
Tel. 01-821 1871
Provides a full advisory service on the design of buildings for the disabled. A list of publications on the subject is available.

Centre on Environment for the Handicapped
126 Albert Street
London NW1 7NF
Tel. 01-267 6111
Provides an advisory and information service on the design of buildings for the handicapped and for elderly people.

d. Sources of information (general): USA

US Geological Survey (Department of the Interior)
Topographic maps and indexes: benchmark locations, level data, and tables of elevations; streamflow data; water resources; geologic maps; horizontal control data; monument location.
Topographic maps available in 7½-minute (latitude and longitude) quadrangle size plotted to scales of 1:24,000 and 1:31,680 and in 15-minute quadrangle size plotted to a scale of 1:62,500.

Geologic map of the US to a scale of 1:2,500,000.
Geologic quadrangle maps in various scales.
Mineral resource maps are also available.
An index map identifying published maps and publication date is available free from:
Map Information Service
US Geological Survey
12201 Sunrise Valley Drive
Reston, VA 22092

State Geological Surveys or equivalent state agencies
Geologic maps of most states to a scale of 1:500,000.
Mineral resource maps.

Army Map Service (Department of the Army)
Topographic maps in 7½-minute quadrangle size plotted to a scale of 1:25,000; in 15-minute quadrangle size plotted to a scale of 1:50,000; and in 30-minute quadrangle size plotted to a scale of 1:125,000. Maps covering larger areas are prepared on scales of 1:250,000 and 1:500,000.

US National Ocean Survey (Department of Commerce)
Topographic maps; coastline charts; topographic and hydrographic studies of inland lakes and reservoirs; benchmark locations, level data, and tables of elevations; horizontal control data; seismological studies.

Soil Conservation Service (Department of Agriculture)
Local Soil Conservation Service Offices
or
Information Division
Soil Conservation Service
Washington DC 20250
Soil surveys generally covering one county (may cover several small counties or only parts of a large one) are published for all counties except Illinois. In this state the University of Illinois Agricultural Experimental Station publishes them. Surveys usually consist of maps that show the distribution of soils in the area, description of the soils, some suggestions as to their use and management, and general information about the area. An index is available.

Bureau of the Census
Census maps containing summarised population data are available for many different types and sizes of areas, for example, county, urbanised area, metropolitan and place maps. These are all available either from the Government Printing Office or the Central Users' Service.

Sanborn Map Company Inc.
Pelham NY
Sanborn fire insurance maps: these detailed maps of street layouts, building locations etc. are used by insurance companies, governmental agencies, utility companies, banks etc. Local fire insurance agents are equipped with Sanborn maps of their respective cities and towns; principal offices maintain complete nationwide files.

Bureau of Land Management
Township plots, showing land divisions, state maps, showing public land and reservations; survey progress map of the USA, showing the progress of public-land surveys.

Mississippi River Commission (Department of the Army)
Hydraulic studies and flood control information.

US Forestry Service (Department of Agriculture)
Forest reserve maps including topography and culture and vegetation classification.

US Postal Service
Rural free delivery maps by counties, showing roads, streams etc.

Local municipalities: county, city, town, village.
Street maps, zoning maps, drainage maps, horizontal and vertical control data, utility maps.

US Department of Commerce: National Technical Information Service
Provides information on Government-sponsored research in different fields. Good reference material on earthquakes from annual bulletin: 'United States Earthquakes'.

US Weather Bureau and local weather stations
Historic data on weather conditions and maps of US climatic conditions.

Superintendent of Documents
Government Printing Office
Washington DC 20402
Daily weather maps published by the National Oceanic and Atmospheric Administration's Environmental Data Service. Also soil surveys, census maps etc.

Agricultural Stabilisation Conservation Service (US Department of Agriculture):
Aerial Photography Division
Eastern Laboratory
45 French Broad Avenue
Asheville
North Carolina 28802
also:
Western Laboratory
2505 Parley's Way
Salt Lake City
Utah 84109
The ASCS has a larger coverage of aerial photographs than any other single agency in the USA. An index showing which agency holds pictures of a required area can be obtained from the Map Information Service of the US Geological Survey (see address above).

'Photogrammetric Engineering'
Magazine of the American Society of Photogrammetry
An informative guide to the organisations that provide photogrammetric aerial maps.

e. Standards and regulations

Where appropriate, equivalent standards are given for the USA; however, local variations make it impossible for this to be achieved universally. Regional standards are usually based on one of the following:

Uniform Building Code
International Conference of Building Officials, Inc.
5360 South Workman Mill Rd.
Whittier California 90601

Standard Building Code
Southern Building Code Congress International Inc.
900 Montclair Rd.
Birmingham, Alabama 35212

Basic Building Code
Building Officials and Code Administrators International Inc.
17926 South Halstead Street
Homewood, Illinois 60430

National Building Code
American Insurance Association
Engineering and Safety Service
85 John Street
New York, New York 10038

Life Safety Code NFPA 101
National Fire Protection Association
470 Atlantic Avenue
Boston, Massachusetts

A.2 Site survey/ analysis

Natural factors

A. Geology and soil

Data required:
(a) Underlying geology, rock character and depth.
(b) Soil type and depth: determine value as an engineering material (for example, safe bearing capacity) and as plant medium; also suitability for septic tanks, excavation, corrosion and frost heave potential; shrink/swell characteristics.
(c) Check drainage characteristics and for signs of fill, slides and subsidence.
(d) Possible use as a building material: adobe, brick, stone.

Materials, processes, sources:
Soil survey maps and reports; geologic maps; aerial photographs. See Appendix A.1.c:
ERTS (Earth Resources Technology Satellite) images.
Trial holes (either dug pits or boreholes) with visual and tactile identification and/or laboratory testing of soil samples.
Building surveyor of local authority (UK).
Report from a geologist.

Limitations/danger signals:
— Swelling clay or peat.
— High salt content in soil.
— Signs of past landslides.
— Evidence of creep (slippage).
— Known earthquake faults.
— Volcanic areas.
— Underlayers of impermeable materials.
— Signs of erosion.
— Rock lying close to surface.
— Made up ground (filling) or undermining.

B. Topography

Data required:
(a) Height above sea level and geographical north point.
(b) Pattern of land forms.
(c) Contours, bench marks.
(d) Slope analysis, for example, orientation.

Materials, processes, sources:
ERTS images.
Topographical maps (useful for preliminary reconnaissance). See Appendix A.1.c.
Geologic maps.
Aerial photographs: preferably in stereo pairs so that site can be viewed three-dimensionally.

Site survey by architect or land surveyor.
Computer-drawn illustrations can be useful to communicate the visual feeling of a land area.

(e) Visibility analysis.
(f) Circulation analysis.
(g) Unique features.

Limitations/danger signals:

— Steep slopes (over 15 per cent).
— Undesirable slopes: west orientation, or slopes which block sun. Small buildable area. Possible problem of affecting sun-rights on adjacent properties.

Materials, processes, sources:
Geologic maps.
Aerial photographs (infra-red is best for distinguishing between land and water).
ERTS images.
Local hydrological studies.
Trial holes (either dug pits at least 2 m deep or boreholes) dug during wet season.
Local health department for testing of water samples.
Visual inspection of existing structures.

C. Hydrology

Data required:
(a) Existing water bodies: fluctuation and purity; flood levels.
(b) Natural and man-made drainage channels: flow, capacity, purity.
(c) Surface drainage pattern: amount, blockage, undrained depressions.
(d) Water table: elevation and fluctuation, springs.
(e) Underground water supply: quantity and quality.
(f) Potential for catching and storing surface water run-off in surface holding basin or underground tanks. Watersheds.

Limitations/danger signals:

— High water table.
— Underground stream.
— Undrained areas: waterlogging.
— Site or portion of site located in flood plain (below known flood level).
— Streams or water bodies polluted by sewage or industrial waste.

Materials, processes, sources:
Report from a landscape architect; ecological survey.
Aerial photographs (infra-red is valuable for distinguishing between different types of vegetation and identifying areas of plant disease).
Geologic and topographic maps.
ERTS images.

D. Vegetation/ecology

Data required:
(a) Dominant plant/animal communities: location and relative stability.
(b) Their dependence on existing factors, self-regulation and sensitivity to change.
(c) Mapping of general plant cover, including wooded areas.
(d) Specimen trees to be retained: their location, species, height and spread, and diameter at base.

Limitations/danger signals:

— Unique landscapes or those with fragile quality.
— Rare or unique flora or fauna.
— Habitat for wildlife or breeding ground.
— Migratory rest stops.
— Presence of insects (for example, mosquitoes, termites) or rodent breeding places.
— Poisonous reptiles and plants.

Data required:

(a) Regional data on:

— monthly mean maximum and minimum temperatures.

— monthly mean maximum and minimum relative humidities.

— total average precipitation for each month; maximum rainfall for any 24-hour period; likelihood of driving rain and intensity.

— direction and force of prevailing winds; seasonal changes.

— sky conditions; cloudiness.

— average daily amounts of solar radiation for each month; sun angles – path of daily and seasonal sun.

— average annual and monthly snowfalls.

(b) Local microclimates: warm and cool slopes, air drainage, wind deflection and local breezes, shade, heat reflection and storage, plant indications.

(c) Noise levels, smell, atmospheric quality.

(d) Regional hazards: hail, tornadoes, lightning, sand and dust storms.

Materials, processes, sources:

Published weather data for region.
Data obtained from nearest weather station.
Solar charts, for example, cylindrical sun chart. See Appendix A.1.a: Mazria[8]; Koenigsberger[9].
Solar radiation calculator and sliding calculator. See Appendix A.1.a: Mazria[8].

Limitations/danger signals:

— Lack of vegetation.

— Severe conditions (extreme heat or cold, strong winds, severe frost).

— Site situated in natural hazard belt.

— Odours, smoke and dust from industrial or other sources.

— Noise and vibration from traffic or trains; industrial or recreational sources etc.

— Cold pockets in low-lying areas.

— Excessively windy, for example, crest of hill.

— Cold winter winds and wind funnels.

F. Natural amenities

Data required:

(a) Character of visual spaces.

(b) Viewpoints, vistas.

(c) Quality and variation of light, sound, smell, feel.

Limitations/danger signals:

— Undesirable views or unpleasant character of one kind or another: barren, bleak, depressing, dirty, unfriendly etc.

Man-made and cultural factors

A. Site values, rights and restraints

Materials, processes, sources:
Local authorities/agencies (county and/or city): building department, engineering department, transport and roads department, health department, town-planning department.
Private or public utilities, for example, post office.
Deeds office (county assessors – USA).
Factory inspectors.
Local authority building by-laws/regulations.
Organisation providing for building funding, for example, building society.
Insurance company.
Licensing authorities.
Fire brigade.

Data required:

(a) Determine municipal valuation, market price.

(b) Obtain existing drawings if available; dimensions, shape and area of site; exact position of boundaries.

(c) Status of property: form of ownership, easements, restrictions, rights of way, rights of access, zoning, density, floor space index, building lines, height restrictions, parking requirements, consents already received.

(d) History of site: rights of public and adjoining owners; public and private intentions for future use of site; possible conflicts; boundaries and party walls and fences (ownership and condition); preservation orders on existing buildings or trees.

(e) Ascertain what consents are required and from which authorities they must be obtained; demolition requirements.

Limitations/danger signals:

— Adjacent sites that enjoy any easements against the site in question, for example, relating to drains and sewers or possibly a right to draw water from a well on the site.

— Possibility that planning permission for the project in question may not be given by the local authority or any other body from which consent must be obtained.

— Size or shape of site not suitable for type of proposed development and/or possible future expansion.

B. The surrounding area

Materials, processes, sources:
City and county land use and street maps.
City future development plans.

Data required:

(a) Existing land uses and functions; possible future changes; historic trails and passageways; historic buildings; conservation areas.

(b) Relationship to surroundings; adequacy of local facilities: transport, schools, shops, postal service, housing etc. What is within walking distance?

(c) Relationship to users, labour force, markets, existing sources of supply and services.

(d) Quality/character of neighbourhood and suitability for proposed project; effect of project on neighbourhood.

(e) Existing street layout and possible future changes; accessibility for all purposes; parking facilities.

(f) Possibility of extending site in future if necessary, for example, possibility of purchasing adjoining land.

Limitations/danger signals:

- Future motorway or highway schemes that might affect project.
- Undesirable features in vicinity: tanneries, airports, railway sidings, highways or roads carrying heavy traffic, refuse dumps, radioactivity, high tension wires etc.
- Lack of public transport.
- Lack of diversity.
- Lack of schools, police, libraries, amusement, employment.
- Socially unattractive area.

C. Adjacent properties and existing buildings

Data required:

(a) Outline, location, elevations, type, condition and use of buildings on adjacent properties.
(b) Possible fire hazards; possible restraints, for example, unwanted shadows.
(c) Plans, elevations and construction details of existing buildings.
(d) Investigate condition and structural defects: signs of dry rot, beetles, damp patches, settlement cracks, loose plaster; condition of services and possibility of extension.

Materials, processes, sources:
Visual observation; site and area survey.

Limitations/danger signals:

- Buildings and trees on adjacent properties casting unwanted shadows particularly during colder months when sun is low.
- Existing buildings in vicinity showing signs of structural cracking.
- Undesirable views.
- Adjacent vacant or underused land which is vulnerable to change.

D. Services

Data required:

(a) Position, size and depth of public sewers and stormwater drains.
(b) Utility services available, for example, gas, water, electricity and telephone; positions, sizes, pressures, type of connections and type of supply (overhead or underground).
(c) Authority responsible for utility services; special requirements; costs for service and installation.
(d) Availability of and access to special services: rubbish removal, fire protection and other emergency services, street maintenance (for example, snow removal) etc.
(e) Potential for use of natural energy sources, for example, solar, wind and water.

A.3 Photographic illustrations

The following series of photographs will help to illustrate some of the aspects of office design. There are, however, many aspects such as lighting, air-conditioning effectiveness, acoustic qualities, finishes etc. which contribute to successful design but which cannot be illustrated photographically. These aspects can only be experienced, fairly examined and evaluated within the reality of the building itself. For this reason the images concentrate on the workstation, where the design impinges most directly on the user.

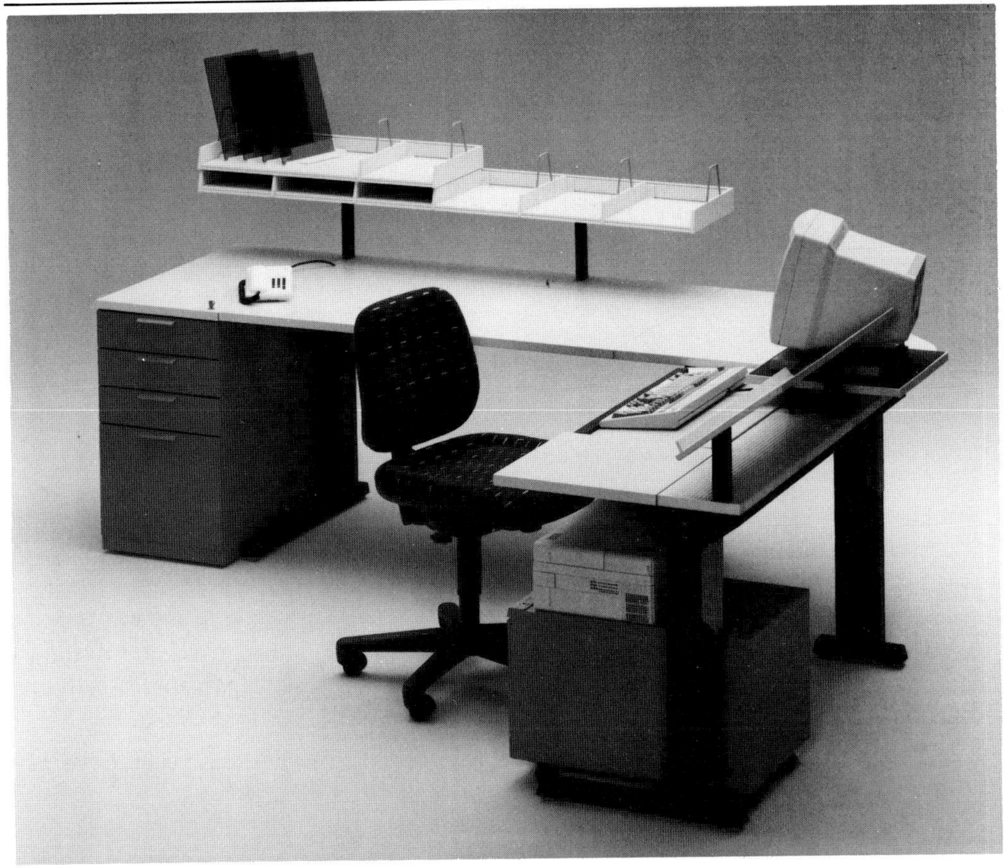

3.1

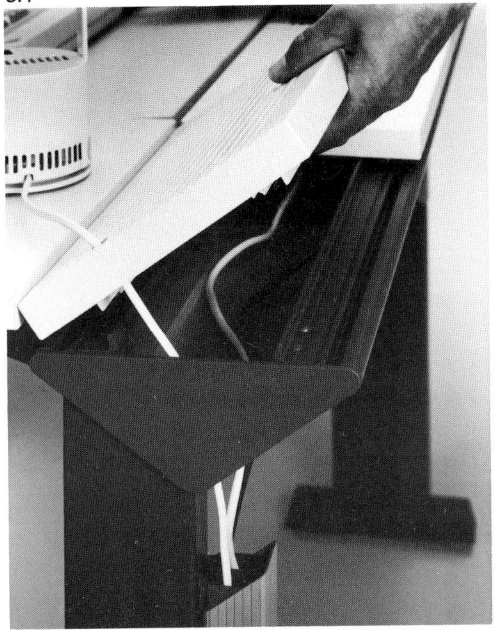

3.2

3.3

Fig. 3.1 *A typical workstation set-up, with one leg accommodating VDU, processor, keyboard and reference space, and the other more traditional functions with storage space over. (Martela, Amfi system)*

Fig. 3.2 *The cable management feature of the system shown in Fig. 3.1 with cables carried in trunking attached to the leg section and through a 'V'-shaped trough at the rear of worksurfaces to equipment positions. (Martela, Amfi system)*

Fig. 3.3 *Features designed to accommodate printers, keyboards etc. should be tested with the client's own equipment to ensure compatibility, ease of use and comfort. (Scott Howard)*

Figs 3.4 and 3.5 *With some systems the means of accommodating the wiring and equipment becomes a major determinant of the appearance; sometimes to such an extent that it will be a dominant factor in the overall quality of the interior. In such cases a decision on furniture selection will need to be taken at an early stage to allow co-ordination of the whole scheme. (Martela, Cre-Activ system)*

3.4

3.5

3.6

3.7

3.8

3.9

Figs 3.6 and 3.7 *Many systems accommodate cabling and equipment within a more traditional appearance. In this case wires run through the leg panels to a tray section under the worksurface. The tray is hinged, dropping down (as shown) to facilitate wiring. Access to terminals is through a hinged flap at the rear of the desk. (Lucas Furniture Systems)*

Fig. 3.8 *Simple and straightforward wire management in a conventional table-based system. In this case cables are clipped within a recess in the leg section, emerging at the worksurface via a sliding capping piece. (Scott Howard)*

Fig. 3.9 *The variety of shapes and sizes of equipment needed in a dealing desk do not always lend themselves to a neat and tidy appearance. However, the frequency of replacement or addition of items means that apparently* ad hoc *solutions can often be the most effective. (Scott Howard).*

Fig. 3.10 *The bare essentials of the desk in Fig. 3.9 showing the deep central core to accommodate cables, equipment and cooling ducts. (Scott Howard).*

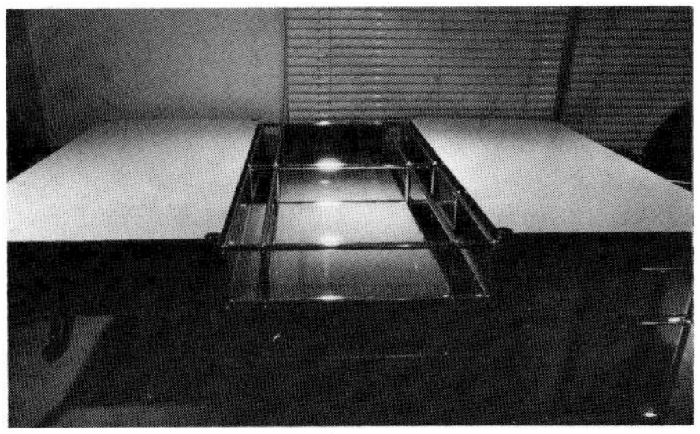

3.10

Fig. 3.11 *Some systems facilitate angles other than 90°, allowing greater flexibility in planning. (Scott Howard)*

Figs. 3.12 and 3.13 *Most systems allow a choice of storage facilities within a standard module. (Lucas Furniture Systems/Scott Howard)*

Fig. 3.14 *A novel use of the space at the rear of a desk with a lift-up flap revealing a small amount of filing storage. (Lucas Furniture Systems)*

Fig 3.15 *Uplighters used with low ceilings will give dramatic effects, but will need to be combined with other means of illumination to be effective. (Scott Howard).*

3.11

3.12

3.13

3.14

3.15

A.4 The main consultants

a. Architects

Only persons appropriately qualified and registered under the Architects' Registration Acts may use the title architect. Although this may be a guarantee of a certain level of competence, it is certainly no more than that. Architects vary greatly in their outlook and approach: some are general practitioners, others are specialists; some are artists, others are businessmen. It is, therefore, very important for a client to find the right architect for the specific project in question.
One way of doing this is by approaching the Clients' Advisory Service of the RIBA (see 'Professional bodies' below) for advice. When the field has been narrowed to a few firms it is wise to visit each one to meet and talk to the partners and to see how each office is organised as well as examples of the firm's work before making a final decision.
In the USA there is a new way of matching client with designer: the public sector has recently been obliged by legislation to advertise its requirements for architectural services to which interested architects may respond. As a result the American Institute of Architects has been forced to abandon its prohibition of competitive bidding for projects by member practices. Without radical changes in Government policy this could not happen in the UK.

Responsibilities and services

The architect's primary professional responsibility is to act as the client's adviser and additionally to administer the building contract fairly between client and contractor. Architects generally provide a variety of services to meet the special requirements of their clients. The work normally undertaken during the course of a building project is described by the RIBA as 'basic services' and it may be summarised as follows (the work described is usually undertaken together with other appointed consultants):

1 Preliminary services which include: discussing, reviewing and evaluating the client's brief; providing advice on how to proceed and on the need for other consultants' services; site visit and initial appraisal; and preparation of outline timetable.

2 Analysis of requirements and preparation of feasibility studies.
3 Outline proposals and an estimate of construction cost for the client's preliminary approval.
4 Development of a scheme design together with cost estimate; attending to applications for planning permission.
5 Detail design and co-ordination of design work done by other consultants and specialists; attending to applications for building approvals.
6 Advising on and arranging for tenders and contract.
7 Contract administration and site supervision up to completion of the works.

Details of these and other services which architects may be called upon to provide, either to augment the basic services or as a separate service, for example, the preparation of the brief (which in many cases is considered an additional service) may be obtained from the RIBA.

Fees

Until recently architects' fees were based on a set of standard mandatory figures prepared by the RIBA. Various fee options are now available and which is used depends on factors including the service to be provided, the size and type of project and negotiations between client and architect. The three basic options used are:

1 Percentage of total construction cost. The RIBA has separate recommended fee scales for new works and works to existing buildings. These consist of sliding scales for different classes of work – the higher the cost of the project and the less complex the building type, the lower the percentage.
2 Time charges based on hourly rates for principals and other technical staff.
3 In certain cases architect and client may agree on a lump sum.

Professional bodies

The Royal Institute of British Architects (RIBA)
66 Portland Place
London W1N 4AD
Tel. 01-580 5533

The Royal Incorporation of Architects in Scotland (RIAS)
15 Rutland Square
Edinburgh EH1 2BE
Tel. 031-229 7205

The Royal Society of Ulster Architects
2 Mount Charles
Belfast BT7 1NZ

The American Institute of Architects
1735 New York Avenue, NW
Washington DC 20006

Most architectural firms in the UK are members of the RIBA and are governed by its code of professional conduct. The services which can be provided by architects, the conditions of appointment and the scale of fees charged by them for particular services are described in *Architect's Appointment* and in the *Directory of Practices* which also includes the names and addresses of member practices and the types of work they undertake. These and other publications produced by the RIBA are available from their bookshop at the London address. The Institute provides a client's advisory service. Their library contains a comprehensive collection of publications on architecture and is open to the general public for reference.

b. Building surveyors

Services

A chartered building surveyor is qualified by examination and experience as a member of the Royal Institution of Chartered Surveyors, and can provide an advisory or consultancy service on various aspects of the construction and economics of buildings. This includes:

1. the diagnosis of building defects and advice on remedial work;
2. the planning and implementation of maintenance work;
3. project management; and
4. structural surveys of all types of property.

Fees

Fees are often based on the time involved but in some cases, such as the supervision of building work, they may be based on a percentage of the overall cost of the project. The Royal Institution of Chartered Surveyors publishes *Conditions of Engagement for Building Surveying Services* which sets out in detail the type of work carried out. Potential clients should consult this publication, and a fee for the service to be provided should be agreed prior to instructions being given.

Professional body

The Royal Institution of Chartered Surveyors (RICS)
12 Great George Street
Parliament Square
London SW1P 3AD
Tel. 01-222 7000
and:
7 Manor Place
Edinburgh EH3 7DN
Tel. 031-225 7078

c. Engineers

Services

There are two main groups of engineers: civil and structural, and services engineers. The first group form part of the design team to assist with the design and calculations for elements such as foundations, retaining walls, columns, beams, slabs and roofs whether these are of reinforced concrete, steel or timber. On some projects (for example, those consisting largely of structural elements) the engineer may be employed as the principal designer.

Services engineers are appointed as members of the design team to assist with the design of environmental control aspects such as lighting, heating and air-conditioning, and mechanical services. As these items can represent a high proportion of building costs, the appointment of the required consultants at an early enough stage for them to participate in the briefing process and feasibility studies is to be recommended.

Fees

For details of fees in relation to services provided contact the Association of Consulting Engineers or the appropriate institution.

Professional bodies

The Association of Consulting Engineers
1st Floor
Alliance House
12 Caxton Street
London SW1H 0QL
Tel. 01-222 6557

This is a professional association of independent consulting engineers. It provides an advisory service and, if requested to do so, will nominate suitable members for particular purposes. Publications are produced describing the services provided by consulting engineers, the conditions of engagement and the scale of fees.

The Chartered Institution of Building Services
Delta House
222 Balham High Road
London SW12 9BS
Tel. 01-675 5211

The Institution promotes the science and practice of heating, ventilation, air-conditioning, domestic hot water engineering and all other building services. Enquiry and advisory services are available.

The American Institute of Consulting Engineers
345 E 47th Street
New York
NY 10017

d. Interior designers

Services

These professionals generally provide the same design and technical services that an architect provides but restrict their work to interiors only.

An interior designer may work on a project in association with other professionals (as part of a design team), or may in certain cases (non-structural refurbishment) be the sole consultant. In all cases the interior designer may be appointed by agreement for one or more of the following progressive stages:

1 A study of the client's requirements and the scope of work; ascertaining feasibility and advising on the need for other specialist consultants. The preparation of preliminary proposals including initial assessment of cost and programme.

2 The preparation of detailed proposals and the necessary working drawings and specifications required for determining the contract cost. The invitation of tenders from approved contractors.

3 The submission of a report on tenders; and advising on the selection of contractors etc., supervision of the contract.

An interior design consultant may also be commissioned in an advisory capacity or for part of the whole normal service including the preparation of feasibility studies and reports, detail surveys etc.

Fees

There are three primary ways in which consultancy services are charged:

1 a percentage basis where an agreed percentage figure (usually on a sliding scale and between 15 and 10 or less per cent) is applied to the whole cost of the works plus remuneration for expenses;

2 a time basis where agreed time rates are levied plus expenses (small jobs are usually done on this basis); or

3 a lump sum basis where a total fee is agreed for the services specified.

Professional bodies

The British Institute of Interior Design
Lenton Lodge
Wollaton Hall Drive
Nottingham NG8 1AF
Tel. 0602-701205

This is a professional organisation of interior designers, designers in related disciplines, crafts persons/designers and persons who provide a service in one or more specific areas within the interior environment. The Institute can supply details of services, fee scales etc., and will supply clients with a short list of interior designers of appropriate experience for specific projects.

The American Institute of Interior Designers
730 5th Avenue
New York
NY 10019

Chartered Society of Designers
29 Bedford Square
London WC1B 3EG
Tel. 01-631-1510

e. Landscape consultants

The term landscape consultant refers to the following three groups of professionals:

1 Landscape architects who are trained in the planning and design of all types of outdoor spaces. They use knowledge of the natural elements of the landscape, its materials and components, to create the spatial and aesthetic elements of the new environment. Many practitioners are also qualified in other disciplines such as horticulture, planning or architecture. They may develop projects into contracts and supervise their execution on site.

2 Landscape scientists who are concerned with the physical and biological principles and processes which underlie the planning, design and management of natural resources. They have the ability to relate their scientific knowledge to the practical problems of landscape work which can range from small-scale site surveys to ecological assessments. Landscape scientists usually have a science background such as ecology, often with specialist skills such as soil science, hydrology or botany.

3 Landscape managers are specialists employing management techniques in the long-term care and development of new and existing landscapes. They usually have a degree in horticulture, forestry or agriculture together with further training in land management or other related disciplines.

Services

The landscape consultant's work involves both the existing landscape and the design and implementation of new landscapes and is generally associated with other professionals such as architects, planners, ecologists and engineers. The scale of work undertaken can vary considerably from designing a small courtyard or settings for all kinds of buildings to designing recreation facilities and preparing landscape plans for large areas.

The services provided may take the form of purely advisory work or may include surveys, appraisal, implementation and management. When engaged on a typical commission related to building work the landscape consultant may perform some, or all, of the following services:

1 the appraisal of site conditions;

2 the survey of the site to provide accurate information about the nature of the land and soil, including the existing features, the condition and lifespan of trees and shrubs, and the types of plants already growing or likely to grow;

3 the preparation of preliminary sketch plans and approximate estimates for the client's approval;

4 the preparation of all drawings and specifications required for the execution of the work;

5 the preparation of contract documents (other than bills of quantities); also obtaining and advising on tenders;
6 the administration of the contract and supervision of the work on site;
7 checking and certifying accounts (but not measurement and valuation of the work); and
8 the submission of plans for necessary approvals by public bodies.

Fees

There are two main methods of determining remuneration: on the time basis or on the percentage basis, with reimbursement for expenses being added to the fee in both cases. Full details may be obtained from the Landscape Institute.
The percentage basis is only applied to a contract costing £10,000 and over and is calculated from two components: a percentage figure is read off a graph against the cost of the project (that is, the higher the project cost the lower the percentage). This figure is the 'norm' which is adjusted by a coefficient based on either the form of contract or the type of job (and therefore its complexity). Some services (for example, site surveys) are specifically excluded from those within the percentage 'norm' and are charged for additionally on a time basis or negotiated sum.

Professional bodies

The Landscape Institute
12 Carlton House Terrace
London SW1Y 5AH
Tel. 01-839 4044
The Institute can provide information on conditions of engagement and professional charges and will nominate practices for commissions at the request of clients. It operates a reference library and publishes a quarterly journal, *Landscape Design*, which is available to non-members on subscription.

The American Institute of Landscape Architects
501 E San Juan Avenue
Phoenix A285012

f. Land surveyors

Services

In a world of rapidly changing technology, the services offered by land surveyors are constantly adapting and expanding to meet the needs of a wide variety of clients. The major advisory and/or consultancy services offered to those involved in new construction work include:
1 property boundary surveys;
2 area or site surveying;

3 architectural surveys, to record new and existing buildings in plan, by section or in elevation;
4 setting out of building and construction work; and
5 aerial photography and photogrammetry – orthophotomaps or the recording of historic buildings and monuments etc.

Fees

There is no fee scale for land surveying services and information on ranges of fees for specific services may be obtained from the Royal Institution of Chartered Surveyors or directly from member firms.

Professional body

The Royal Institution of Chartered Surveyors (RICS)
12 Great George Street
Parliament Square
London SW1P 3AD
Tel. 01-222 7000
and:
7 Manor Place
Edinburgh EH3 7DN
Tel. 031-225 7078
The Institution has an information centre which runs a nomination service for clients and will always give guidance on services offered or transfer a client to the appropriate divisional secretary. Various publications are available including the *Directory of Land and Hydrographic Survey Services in the United Kingdom.*

g. Quantity surveyors

Services

The quantity surveyor is the expert professional trained to assist clients and architects with construction costs, construction management and construction communications. This consultant is an important member of the briefing and design team and should be appointed at an early stage to provide some, or all, of the following services:

1 preliminary cost advice including recommendations on most economical layout, materials and methods of construction; also estimates of future maintenance and running costs;
2 estimates of the costs of alternative proposals;
3 cost planning – a specialist technique used to help all the members of the design team to arrive jointly at practical designs for a specific project and stay within the agreed budget. Also assessment of the cost implications of changes;
4 advising on contractual methods;

5 preparing bills of quantities which are used for competitive tendering and as an important element in effective cost control during construction;
6 negotiating tenders for projects planned from the outset with a single contractor. It is advisable to consider appointing an independent quantity surveyor for advice on the financial and contractual aspects when embarking on a package deal;
7 financial management and valuing of work during construction; and
8 preparing final accounts, statements of expenditure for tax or accountancy purposes etc.

Fees

Recommended scales of fees related to the cost and complexity of the project are published by RICS. Chartered quantity surveyors will always provide estimates of their fees and RICS will give advice when necessary.

Professional body

The Royal Institution of Chartered Surveyors (RICS)
12 Great George Street
Parliament Square
London SW1P 3AD
Tel. 01-222 7000
and:
7 Manor Place
Edinburgh EH3 7DN
Tel. 031-225 7078

The Institution has an information centre which runs a nomination service for clients and will always give guidance on services offered or transfer a client to the appropriate divisional secretary. Various publications are available including leaflets describing the main services offered, and package contracts.

A.5 Briefing and design methods

There are a number of briefing and design methods which can be used to help produce different kinds of information (see Fig. A.1). Each of these techniques or tools is a separate activity for collecting, exploring, communicating, analysing, organising or evaluating information and ideas, and it is a question of not only determining whether one or more of them will be appropriate to a specific project, but also matching them with information needs. The methods used for a particular design situation will depend, amongst other things, on the people involved, on the stage one is at, on what is already known and on what one is trying to find out.
A few of the most basic, and perhaps more useful, methods are described here in broad outline. For more detailed information refer to Appendix A.1.a:

a. Literature search

To locate and retrieve published information which will not only help to lay the foundation for further investigation and for preliminary conclusions, but will also provide some of the required design data.

1 Identify the purposes for which the information is required and ascertain priorities.
2 Determine the degree of detail required – bare essentials may be sufficient initially.
3 Identify likely sources of reliable, up-to-date and relevant information. In many cases (for example, where those involved have previous experience of the relevant building type) the process may simply involve updating knowledge from literature already available in one's own library.

Literature search can be time-consuming. It is advisable to determine a timetable taking into account, not only by when the information will be required, but also a deadline beyond which the search will be discontinued. The penalty of insufficient information at a given time must be balanced against the cost of obtaining it.

Group activity = Indicates method which is generally a group activity

Users = Indicates method which generally involves users

	Methods	Kinds of action / categories of information: Exploring design situations and/or data gathering	Searching for or generating ideas	Exploring problem structure (analysis & organisation)	Evaluation
Group activity, users	**Stating objectives**	●			
	Literature search	●	○		
Users	**Interview**	●	○		
Users	**Questionnaire**	●	○		
Users	**Observation**	●	○		
	Visit/study existing buildings	●	○		
Users	Data logs	●		○	
	Standardised data forms	●		●	
Group activity	**Brainstorming**		●	○	
Group activity	Synectics		●	○	
Group activity, users	Role playing		●	○	
Group activity, users	Gaming		●	○	
	Interaction matrix			●	
	Correlation diagrams			●	
	Functional innovation			●	
Users	**Pattern language**	○	●	●	○
	Classification			●	
	Checklists	●		○	●
	Selecting criteria				●
	Ranking and weighting				●
	Cost planning			●	
	Life cycle cost analysis			●	●
	Value analysis			●	●
	Cost benefit analysis			●	●
	Energy accounting			●	○
Users	Post occupancy appraisal				●

Fig. A.1 *Chart indicating some of the many methods that can be employed during the briefing and design process as well as the kinds of actions for which they may be used (● = primary use, ○ = secondary use). The methods in heavy type are described in outline in this Appendix.*

The choice of sources and the applicability of data being collected must be continuously evaluated. Literature search should be stopped as soon as sufficient useful data to answer the stated questions has been gathered. Accurate references should be kept of all publications that are found to be useful for easy retrieval at a later date, and collected data should be stored in a flexible way so that new information can be readily added.

b. Interviews

This is the most common and direct method of obtaining specific and detailed information from clients and users. Interviews serve the same purpose as questionnaires but have the advantage of direct and immediate interaction between interviewer and client or user.

Interviews may be unstructured or structured. The former – in which no

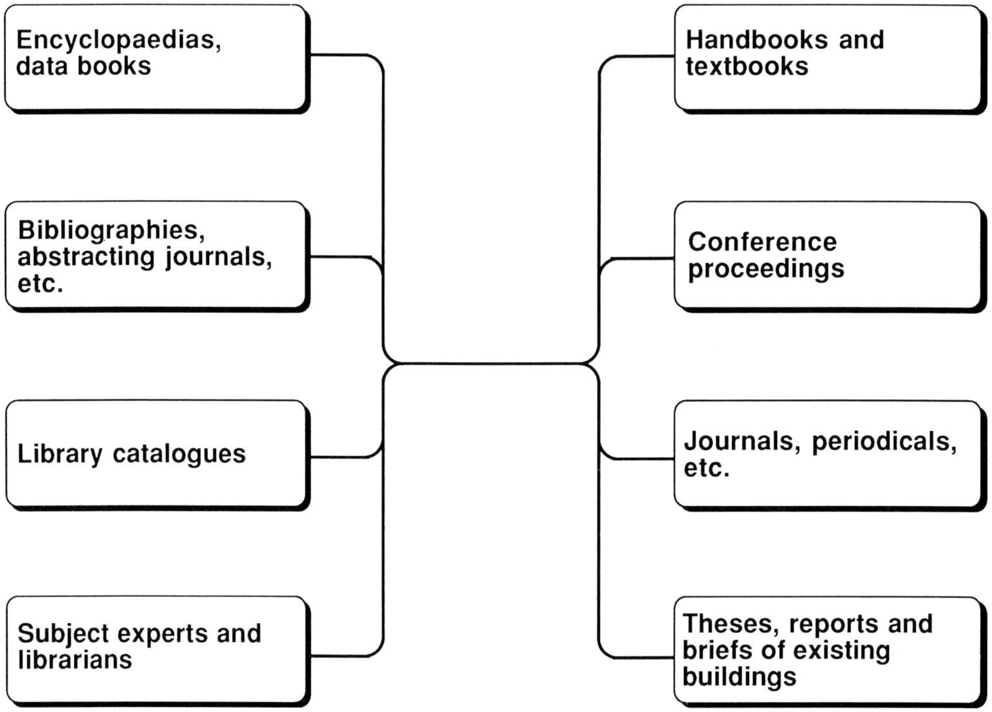

predetermined format is used – tends to be exploratory in nature and is often employed with the aim of gaining a general understanding of a problem or situation; and also of identifying the right questions to include in a questionnaire or structured interview. Structured interviews, on the other hand, follow a pre-arranged format in order to generate quick responses to specific questions.

1 Identify the kinds of information needed.
2 Identify the different types of people involved in the user situations that require exploration: client, managers, operators, consumers etc. Each type will usually have different impressions, needs, attitudes, values, preferences and problems, some of which will almost certainly be in conflict with those of the other types or groups.
3 Establish contact with and obtain the co-operation of the various groups involved.
4 Prepare a set of questions or a checklist: it is only common sense to obtain expert advice.
5 Decide who will be interviewed and make the necessary arrangements. Allow sufficient time for the predetermined questions to be answered and/or for free discussion.
6 Those interviewed should be allowed to talk spontaneously about any aspects of the activities in which they are involved that seem important to them, and encouraged to expand on those which are particularly relevant to the design situation being explored. This should be possible even in a structured interview.

7 Responses, comments and suggestions must be accurately recorded together with relevant circumstantial information: the ages, sex and expertise of those interviewed etc.

8 It is generally useful for the interviewer to have some experience of the actual user-situation being explored, and the interviews may be preceded, or followed up, by one of the observation techniques.

9 Interviewers should try to remain neutral and remember that the views and interests of the *interviewee* are being sought. (Interviewers may well have to listen to views with which they totally disagree and must not get carried away by their own points of view.)

c. Questionnaire

This serves basically the same purpose as an interview – of which it may form part – but takes the form of a written set of questions which generally require a written response. It is used to obtain a variety of usable information from large numbers of people.

1 Identify the kinds of information needed to meet specific objectives.

2 Identify the different types/groups of people involved and consider which would be most helpful in obtaining the information required.

3 Consider the types of questions which will be most suitable to get the information required: factual, informative, opinion/attitude and/or self-perception. Also consider how the answers are to be analysed.

4 Consider the form in which answers are to be given: questions can be unstructured – open-ended, encouraging descriptions of likes, dislikes, attitudes, values, behaviour and settings – or can require a fixed response: choice between two possibilities (yes/no; good/bad etc), multiple choice or ranking of set of alternatives. Although the fixed response method is obviously easier to analyse and to feed into a computer, both types of questions are often used in a single questionnaire.

When formulating questions, keep in mind that they should be short and use language that makes the meaning clear to all respondents. They should be free from any possible bias (assumptions and prejudices of the questioner), and should elicit definite, short, simple and useful answers.

Consider the design of the questionnaire: it should be laid out so that it is easy to understand and use, and does not take too long to complete. The following sequence, with questions designed to flow naturally from one to the next, is widely used:

1 Short introduction: explanation of purpose and instructions.

2 Easy-to-answer preliminary questions.

3 The main questions or body of the questionnaire.

4 Questions eliciting personal data.

Establish how the questionnaire is to be circulated, for example, in interviews, by post or at a meeting. If sent by post an accompanying explanatory letter should be enclosed.

It is essential, if the exercise is to have any validity, to draw up and circulate a pilot questionnaire to test the questions and answers, and the method of analysis, before drafting the final document.

d. Observation

It is often helpful – and sometimes essential – for designers to expose themselves to the complexities of the real situation they are designing for. The various observation techniques can be employed to get useful information about people's behaviour in a specific environment/setting: patterns of behaviour and use, space requirements and relationships, the use of furniture and equipment, dysfunction etc. Other methods (for example, interviews) will be needed to get information on the users' opinions and attitudes.

1 Identify the kinds of information needed, for example, details of the activities that take place – the different kinds as well as their frequency, duration and sequence; physical and other characteristics of the space or setting; details of the various interactions among users and between them and the setting; general data on the users involved.

2 Consider whether the study will be exploratory – to gain a general understanding; or structured – to collect specific detailed information.

3 Identify the various types of users and settings involved and consider which are to be observed: in the case of data collection for an airport design, for example, one will need to know something about the behaviour/use patterns of not only travellers but also visitors, flight crews, ground staff, administrators etc.

4 Determine what method(s) will be used:

— Direct unobtrusive observation. This may be best if users are likely to modify their actions when knowing they are being watched.

— Direct observation with the co-operation of users. It is sometimes useful to observe not only experienced users but also volunteers inexperienced in the use of the space or setting, noting their reactions and difficulties while attempting to achieve a predetermined objective.

— Participation by the observer: several sessions may be required to experience different user situations/perspectives.

— Other: tracking, behaviour-mapping etc. See Appendix A.1.a: Jones[1], Palmer[2], Sanoff[4] and Cross & Roy.

5 Obtain the necessary permission and/or co-operation needed to carry out the proposed study.

6 Decide how data – actions, difficulties, problems, impressions, ideas etc. – will be recorded. Consider the possibility of using mechanical methods such as tape recording, still or time-lapse photography, videotaping or cine-filming.

Note: It must be pointed out that interviews, questionnaires and observations are research-based methods on which there is a great deal written and still some controversy. Even those trained in these methods can make mistakes and can draw the wrong conclusions from the data collected. One must, therefore, not only get expert help/advice, but also remember that while the results from these methods may give good indications of attitudes, they should be treated circumspectly and certainly not as 'the answer'.

e. Visit/study existing buildings

Before embarking on a project, a great deal can be learnt by architect, client and selected users through visits to similar organisations and buildings. There is no better way to keep abreast of new developments and obtain an insight into the problems of a particular building type, while also becoming aware of, experiencing and evaluating the many alternative solutions. While a careful study of the literature of the subject is a good introduction it is not, generally speaking, by itself sufficient.

1 Go through published information on the building type in question (in architectural journals and other professional publications).

2 Draw up a list of possible buildings to visit. When making a final selection, remember:

— It is useful to visit a few buildings that will be reasonably comparable in size and character to the one being planned and, ideally, those that offer a wide range of alternative approaches in terms of layout, construction, finishes and equipment.

— Buildings which appear to be most attractive in photographs and which are widely publicised are not necessarily the ones that function best for occupants and users. Although much can be learned from both good and bad examples, the greater the number of successful solutions one can visit the better.

— Do not attempt to visit too many buildings. It is generally advisable to keep the number down to between six and eight that can be examined carefully enough to make the exercise worthwhile.

3 Decide who will go on the visits: client, architect, selected staff and/or users. A small group made up of people with different backgrounds will provide a variety of points of view. If a specialist building consultant has been appointed his presence will be helpful as he will be able to point out satisfactory solutions of problems as well as failures. This consultant would almost certainly be able to suggest some buildings worth visiting.

4 Prepare a programme for the proposed visits allowing enough time (between a half and a full day) to study each building, see visual demonstrations and ask questions. Contact the organisations in question to arrange for the visits and for appointments with the people who should be seen.

5 Draw up a checklist of things to be looked at, points to be discussed and questions to which answers are needed:

— How was the project organised: Who prepared the brief? What sort of consultants were used? Who made various design decisions and why were they made? What would be changed with hindsight?

— Who uses the building and what kinds of functions does it house? What were the user requirements and client objectives? How well are these met by the building in question?

— How were decisions made about the interior design? What space standards were used? Is it easy to find one's way about? Are layouts of spaces satisfactory or unacceptable? Do some areas seem unduly congested and are there others where space is obviously wasted?

— What system is used – structural grid, depth of spaces etc. – and how well does this suit the functions? What is the relationship of service ducts and vertical circulation to the structure? What are the ceiling heights? Are they satisfactory for the various activities involved? How practical are the materials used for floors, walls and ceilings in terms of function, quality, appearance, maintenance, sound and cost?

— What form of lighting is used and is the quality of light satisfactory for the tasks to be performed? What system is used to provide power/communication outlets? How flexible is it? What were the acoustic criteria? Is there any sound disturbance?

— What kinds of furniture and equipment are used? How were they selected? How well do they meet the criteria of function, flexibility, quality, appearance, maintenance and cost?

— To what extent has flexibility/adaptability and possible future extension been provided for? How has it been done?

— What methods will be used to collect the data required: by interviewing those involved in the briefing, by talking to staff, from observation etc.?

6 Take notes during each visit. These will be helpful during subsequent discussions and for the preparation of a written report which is a useful way of organising information and ideas, and of making them available to others. It may be worthwhile taking photographs during visits to illustrate, and remind one of, specific points.

7 If it is not possible to visit some important buildings they should at least be carefully examined, ideally by studying the original brief and, if at all possible, any published post-occupancy appraisal (or evaluation as it is called in the USA). Where such material is available it is well worth studying even if the building has been visited because it provides useful supplementary information.

Post-occupancy appraisal, especially from clients' and users' points of view, has great value both as a first step in the development of a building brief – it offers the potential for obtaining the type of feedback needed to avoid past mistakes and improve the design process – and as a final step in assessing user satisfaction when it may be used for fine-tuning of the building. Although there is a growing awareness of the need for this type of study, there is at present relatively little published material available. Appraisals published in the architectural press, which range from very general descriptions to detailed case studies, do not generally attempt to examine how users relate to the building and the reasons why the building may be satisfactory or have failed in use.

f. Standardised data forms

These are used to collect, record and organise various types of routine or repetitive data (room requirements, descriptions of existing facilities, user activities, energy consumption etc.). They are an ideal way of presenting detailed design information consistently for each space, system or activity in a building brief.

1 Identify the type of data that is to be collected and recorded, for example, requirements for each of the spaces in the building.

2 Determine the various categories of information that are needed, for example, activities/functions to be performed in the area, number of occupants/users, furniture and equipment, floor area, relationship to other spaces, environmental conditions, special finishes.

3 Decide on the most suitable method of recording the different types of data and prepare a layout for the form accordingly, for example, form may allow blocks within which the necessary data is filled in or may be organised as a checklist. Where possible the form should be kept to a single sheet (see Fig. A.3).

4 When a satisfactory form has been developed and drawn up have sufficient copies printed/duplicated. It may be advisable/necessary for the designers to produce a draft form after completing other studies (questionnaires, interviews, observations etc.) and discussing it with the client and users before it is finalised.

5 Determine how these forms are to be completed and by whom. Forms may, for example, be attached to a questionnaire to be completed by users and the client, and finally evaluated by the designers.

g. Brainstorming

This is an extremely fast and versatile group technique which may be used at all stages of the briefing and design process to generate a large variety of ideas and/or information (sources of information, questions for interviews etc.).

1 State problem clearly and simply.

Fig. A.3 *Example of standardised form for collecting room requirements of a new building. In this case a section of the form has been organised as a checklist. In certain circumstances the whole form may best be compiled in this way.*

Space Requirements for: (Project name/job number etc)	Department: Space name/number:

Function of space and activities Main: Secondary:	Number of occupants/users Max: Average: Types:	No of similar rooms required:

Access and relationship to other spaces Main: Secondary:	Floor area:	Ceiling height:

Furniture and equipment		Finishes	Services	Environmental	Other
Desk		Floor:	Plumbing:	Heating, ventilation and air-conditioning:	Doors:
Counter					
Table			Electrical:		
Chairs					Windows:
Bulletin board		Walls:			
Bookshelves				Lighting:	
Storage cupboards			Fire:		Colours:
Typewriter		Ceiling:			
VDU			Communications:	Acoustics:	Storage:
Duplicating equipment					
Switchboard					

2 Select a group of people – small groups of between four and twelve people generally work best – to participate. Group members should ideally have some relevant knowledge/experience. No previous experience of brainstorming is necessary.

3 Select a chairman/group leader who will be able to control the session, keep the pace going and encourage a relaxed, creative atmosphere. Someone may be required to record verbal responses.

4 Decide on a time-limit for the session which should not continue for too long – between 30 and 60 minutes seems to produce the best results.

5 The following should be made clear to the participants:

— There must be no criticism or analysis of ideas.

— As many ideas as possible must be generated within the predetermined time period: the more ideas there are the more chance there is of finding some that are really useful.

— They must not worry about ideas being practical or not: responses must be spontaneous and uninhibited.
— They should feel free to combine or build on the other ideas put forward.

6 Decide on method of recording spoken ideas, for example, on a blackboard or large roll of paper. An alternative method is to allow a preliminary period for participants to write their initial ideas down, and each then reads an idea in turn. Further ideas are written on separate cards as the session proceeds.

7 Sort ideas into groups and evaluate them. The ideas themselves may not be the most valuable output: the different groups (or categories) may be used to expose a range of possible solution areas from which a serious search for a final answer can start.

h. Interaction matrix

A frequently used and most useful method for determining and/or visualising the patterns of interactions or relationships between a number of elements in a problem, for example, the connections/adjacencies required between the spaces/rooms in a building.
A matrix, in its most basic form, is a simple two-way grid on which all possible combinations, by pairs, of the elements are recorded and ranked. The matrix itself does not determine the interactions – it is rather a framework within which the information is set out and which assists the search for relationships (space, activity, organisational, functional etc.) within a set of several elements.

1 Define the terms element and interaction/relationship as they apply to the specific problem, for example, room/space and adjacency/proximity.

2 Decide what, if any, form of ranking (scale of preference/priority) is to be applied, for example, in the case of adjacency of rooms the following scale may be used: 0 = not necessary, 1 = desirable or some, 2 = essential.

3 Draw up a matrix which sets out the complete range of possible interactions between every pair of elements and check for each pair whether or not interaction occurs (see Fig. A.4).

4 It is often not necessary to use both halves of a matrix, for example, when determining required adjacency between rooms – unless the direction of door swings is to be determined – and a so-called half-matrix may be used (see Fig. A.5).

5 Try to keep the number of elements to a maximum of 20 or 25 – in a very large project it is usually possible to group the elements in sub-sets. It can be difficult to complete all the judgements involved when a matrix contains large numbers of elements, and the possibility of errors is greatly increased.

Fig. A.4 *In matrix (A) relationships between pairs of activities are simply marked in the grid: no ranking is used. The totals at the foot of the vertical columns give the number of relationships, and thus the importance of each element. In example (B) a closeness ranking is indicated in one half of the grid (E = especially important, I = important, O = average satisfies, U = unimportant and X = undesirable) and the reason governing this is indicated in the other half (1 = use of typing pool, 2 = noise, 3 = number of visitors, 4 = movement of paper, 5 = use of supplies).*

A.

	A	B	C	D	E
A			●	●	
B					
C	●			●	
D	●		●		●
E				●	
	2	0	2	3	1

B.

	President	Purchasing	General sales and administration	Accounting	Production planning	Data processing	Mail and supply room	Reception
President		U	I	U	U	X	U	E
Purchasing			U	O	U	U	U	E
General sales and administration	1			I	O	E	I	I
Accounting		4	4		U	E	O	U
Production planning			4			I	U	U
Data processing	2		4	4	4		U	U
Mail and supply room			5	5				U
Reception	3	3	3					

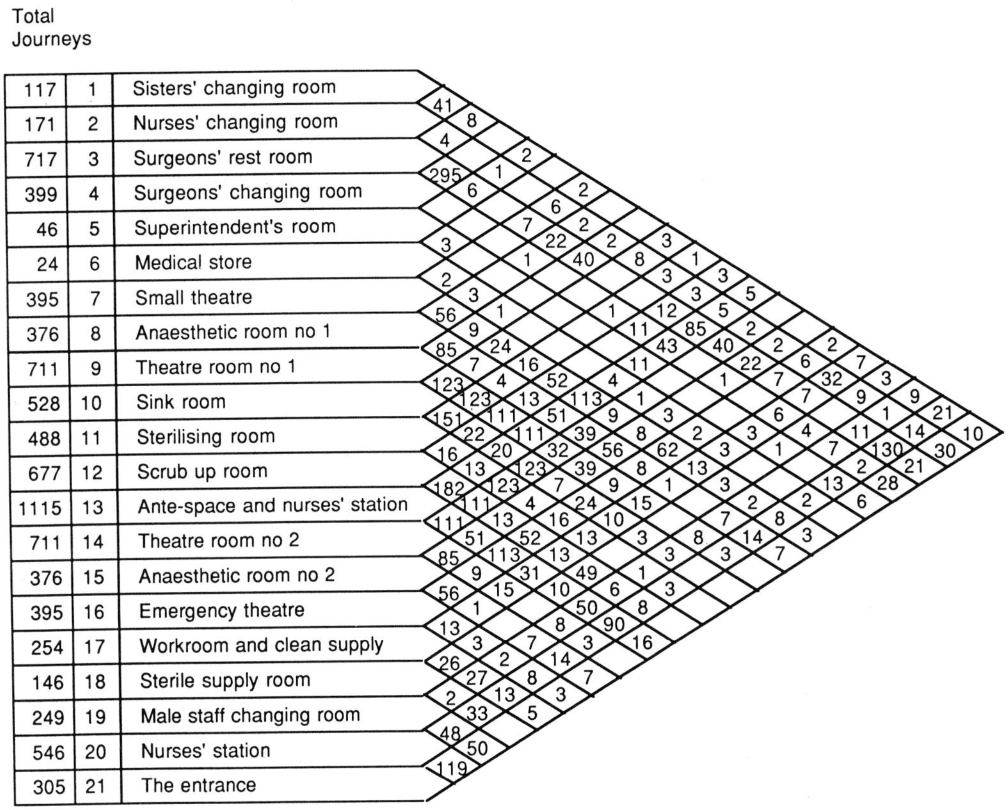

Fig. A.5 *Matrix illustrating journeys between rooms by people working in a typical existing operating theatre suite. This can be used to decide what modifications are needed to reduce movement to a minimum and to combine the units in the most satisfactory way from all known points of view. (From* The Architects' Journal, *17 June 1964, p.1375).*

i. Correlation diagrams

There are a variety of techniques (interaction nets, bubble and block diagrams, flow diagrams etc.) which are used for displaying spatial or other relationships between elements within a design problem. Such diagrams are widely used as an intermediate step for generating the actual plan layout of a building, and for visualising all the factors and variables that have a bearing on the design process.

1 Collect and analyse data. It is generally advisable to use an interaction matrix to determine relationships/interactions.

2 In the case of the interaction net technique a preliminary diagram is drawn with elements (for example, functions or spaces) represented by symbols and arranged in a circle. Relationships/interactions are indicated by linking elements with lines which may be varied in weight (thickness) to show the relative importance of the connections. The diagram is then adjusted with elements rearranged to minimise the crossing of lines (considering the essential links first and, once these have been sorted out, the secondary ones) and to clarify the pattern of interaction, looking for strong sub-groupings or clusters of elements (see Fig. A.6).

3 Bubble diagrams are usually sketched freehand with bubbles (representing elements drawn within each other, overlapping or separated by a link (line) depending on the relationships and connections. Lines may be used to indicate the distance between elements, the pattern of movement between elements, and/or the importance of the connection between each of them (see Fig. A.7).

4 Block diagrams, which are similar to bubble diagrams, consist of squares or rectangles – representing each space – that are drawn to scale (proportionally sized to the amount of floor area required). Each of the blocks can be cut out of paper or cardboard and shuffled around to test various arrangements.

5 A form of flow chart can be used to visualise or externalise all the factors and variables having a bearing on a particular design project. A roll of newsprint or brown paper attached to a wall can be used for this purpose. One approach is to:

- **a** draw up a classification of the main sub-components (elements) which are to be investigated (activities, materials etc.);
- **b** list all the points that can be thought of, putting each under the classification that seems to make most sense;
- **c** establish relationships. By studying the chart, connections may be found where none seemed to exist before. For example, in preparing a chart for a children's playground the list under activities may include climbing, running, sliding, jumping; under the heading of materials one may have listed heavy canvas, which, when stretched and supported is buoyant and comparatively resilient. Thus, a link may be established between this and 'jumping', suggesting a trampoline-like structure;

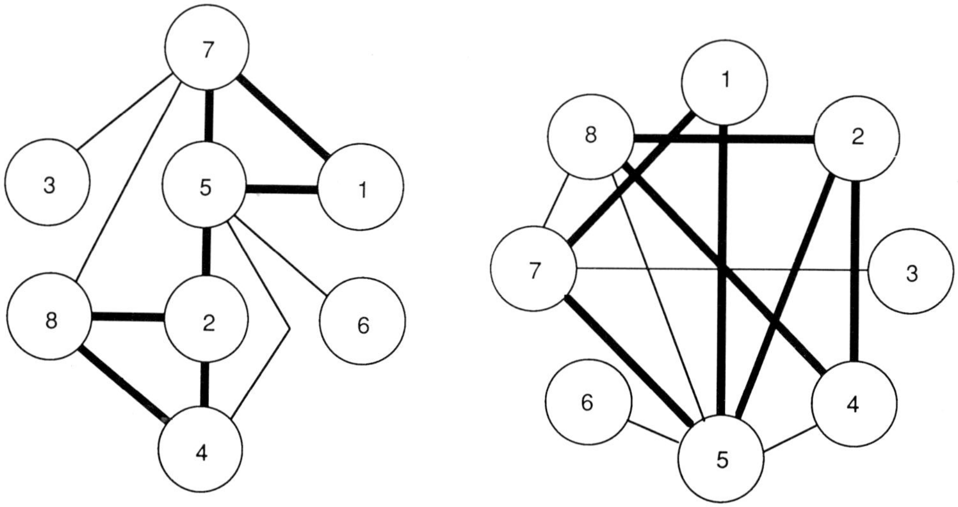

Fig. A.6 *The two basic stages of an interaction net illustrated very simply.*

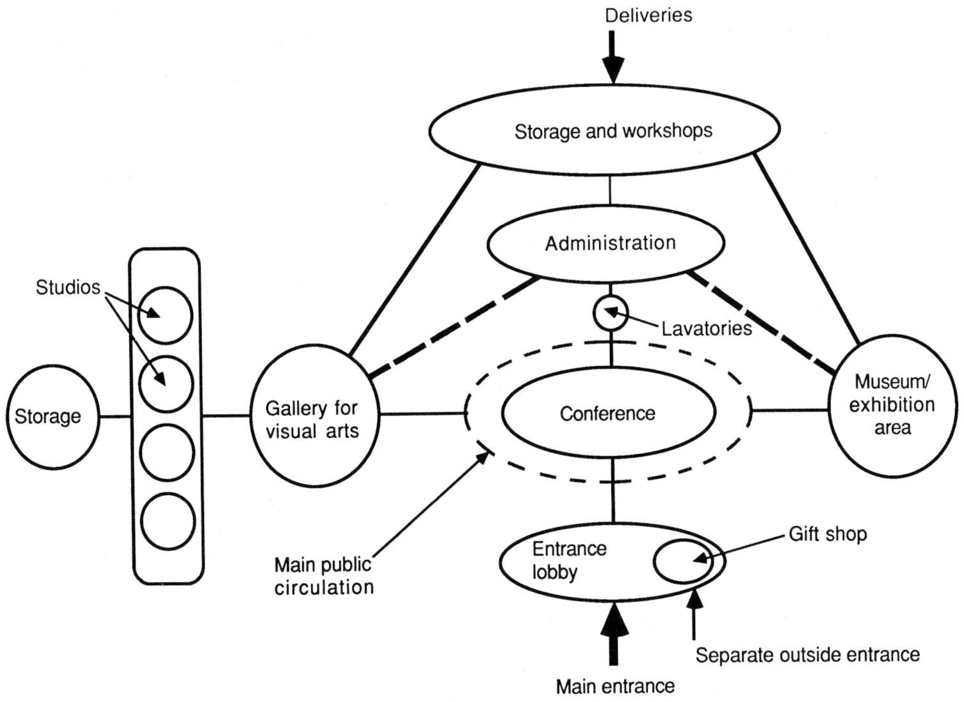

Fig. A.7 *Bubble diagram used as a first step for generating actual plan layout of a building.*

d draw lines to connect relationships and possible things to do as a result of the connections (for example, design a trampoline-like structure), as they are established. New concepts, categories, relationships and solutions/things to do are filled-in as they come to mind during the briefing/design process; then

e once this part of the chart has been more or less fully developed (it will never be complete) a second half consisting of implementation (who does what, when and how) can be added. The chart remains on the wall being altered and amended until the work has been completed.

j. Pattern language

This is a method developed by Christopher Alexander and his associates at the Centre for Environmental Structure at Berkeley, California, which is, theoretically, supposed to allow everyone to design for themselves the places they live and work in, while simultaneously giving order to the whole environment. The language consists of a 'dictionary' containing a set of patterns each of which suggests how a specific problem, which happens over and over again in an environment or a building, can be solved (see Fig. A.8). By selecting relevant patterns from Alexander's dictionary, generating others to suit local culture and conditions, and then combining them according to the specific needs of the project in question, a design can be created.

Although it may be naive to believe that the complex buildings and environments of today's industrialised society can be designed by users working with pattern books and without the aid of professional designers, there is a great deal of value in Alexander's work. For the purposes of education, the generation of ideas, the development of awareness, and involvement during the briefing and design process, Alexander's book of patterns can be an invaluable tool not only for designers but also for clients and users.

Fig. A.8 *The main points of three patterns, adapted from* A Pattern Language.

Positive outdoor space
Outdoor spaces which are merely 'left over' between buildings will, in general, not be used.

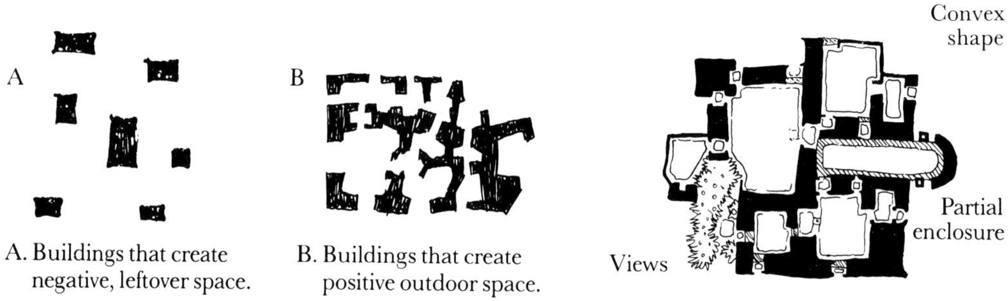

Therefore:

Make all the outdoor spaces which surround and lie between your buildings positive. Give each one some degree of enclosure; surround each space with wings of buildings, trees, hedges, fences, arcades, and trellised walks, until it becomes an entity with positive quality and does not spill out indefinitely around corners.

Cascade of roofs
Few buildings will be structurally and socially intact, unless the floors step down towards the end of the wings, and unless the roof, accordingly, forms a cascade.

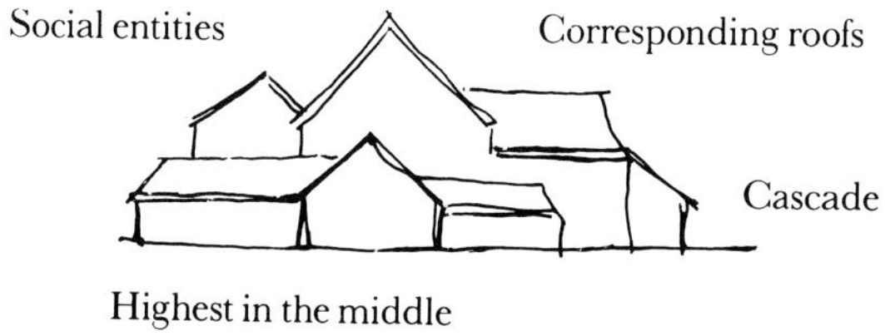

Therefore:

Visualize the whole building, or building complex, as a system of roofs. Place the largest, highest, and widest roofs over those parts of the building which are most significant; when you come to lay the roofs out in detail, you will be able to make all lesser roofs cascade off these large roofs and form a stable self-buttressing system, which is congruent with the hierarchy of social spaces underneath the roofs.

Intimacy gradient

Unless the spaces in a building are arranged in a sequence which corresponds to their degree of privateness, the visits made by strangers, friends, guests, clients, family, will always be a little awkward.

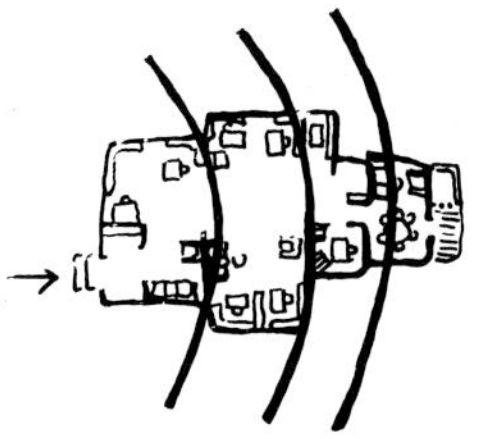

Office intimacy gradient

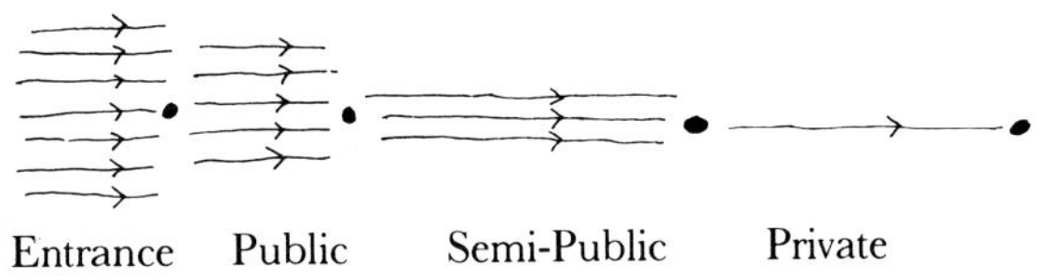

Therefore:

Lay out the spaces of the building so that they create a sequence which begins with the entrance and the most public parts of the building, then leads into the slightly more private areas, and finally to the most private domains.

k. Cost planning

The object of cost planning (see Fig. A.9) (usually the responsibility of the appointed quantity surveyor) is to ensure that the final cost of a building project does not exceed the client's original budget figure.

A start should be made on analysing and controlling costs as early as possible in the briefing and design process. This will avoid the costly and time-consuming changes that result when it is discovered that costs exceed the budget *after* a design has been prepared.

1 Establish cost limitations at the start of the project: the client often stipulates a limit in his initial statement (preliminary brief).

2 Prepare a realistic preliminary estimate as early as possible (usually during the feasibility phase) either to confirm that the cost limitation is realistic in terms of the stated requirements, or to enable those involved to begin the inevitable trade-offs.

3 The preliminary estimate must often be based on the requirements defined during the development of the brief:

— Space: the floor area required.
— The use to which the space will be put.
— Quality: the standard of finishes, fittings and equipment required.
— External works.
— The maintenance and running costs the client is prepared to meet.

The estimate is generally calculated by using a cost per m^2 of floor area, based on an analysis of costs of the same, or similar, requirements in actual construction of a particular building type. Other techniques, for example, unit method in certain building types, may be used. The figure will be adjusted to suit local conditions and to take inflation into account. Included in the estimate will be all, or some, of the following:

— professional fees;
— administration and other expenses of the client (for example, legal fees);
— cost of the site and/or demolition;
— finance costs (mortgages etc.); and
— risk and profit element (for example, if the building has to provide an economic return).

It is not an easy task for the quantity surveyor to prepare a realistic estimate as, amongst other things, much depends on his ability to detect the degree of buildability in the designer's proposals. A more detailed estimate is prepared once there is a final scheme design to work from.

— As work proceeds the quantity surveyor will prepare cost studies of alternative solutions, test economic viability, and check regularly that requirements and proposals will not result in expenses that are likely to exceed the cost limit.

— Once a realistic estimate is agreed a cost plan is generally prepared. This plan establishes how the approved estimate will be spent by allocating parts of the sum to individual elements: roof, external walls, wall finishes, heating installation etc . Costs are allocated on a quality basis, usually related to an analysis of completed buildings rather than to specification decisions made for the project in question (these usually happen later in the process). The plan is not a design straightjacket but a framework influencing decision-making and within which the detailed design and specification must be developed. Adjustments can be made as the work proceeds but must be done systematically and under control, so that additional expenditure on one element is balanced by savings on others.

— There are various methods of cost evaluation (not described here), such as life-cycle cost analysis, value analysis and cost-benefit analysis, that may be used to assist in making briefing and design decisions.

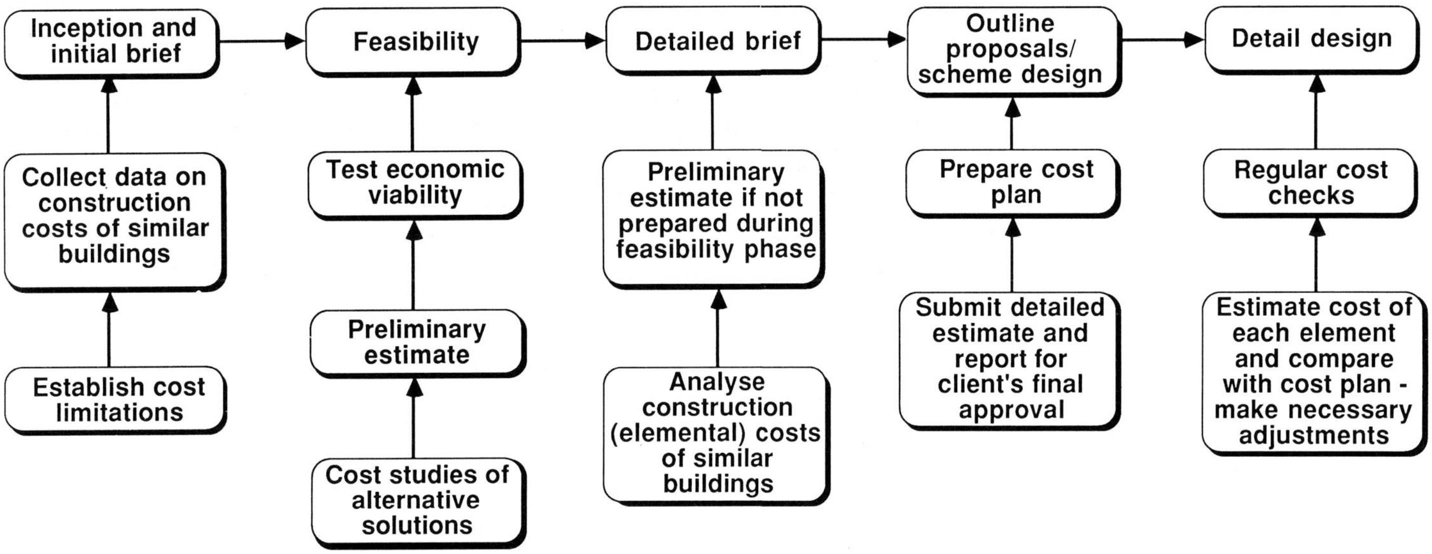

Fig. A.9 *Chart indicating basic cost planning procedures in relation to the main briefing and design phases.*

A.6 Glossary

The following glossary covers some of the words commonly encountered when dealing with technological equipment in offices. It is not intended as a comprehensive guide to computer jargon; rather to simply assist communication between all concerned by concentrating on the hardware which the designer may have to accommodate, and some of the computer-speak words which have a more general application.

architecture	confusingly, used in computer terms to describe the basic concept of a system.
bug	a defect in the operation of a computer caused by a fault in the program or the hardware, or by an electrical variation.
co-axial cable	cable formed with a single, central conductor surrounded by another (usually braided copper).
configuration	a collection of machines interconnected to act as one system.
database	an organised system of related information.
hard copy	computer-generated information in printed form, as opposed to stored on disc, tape etc.
host computer	the controlling computer in a network, or a computer used to prepare programs for operation on other machines.
interactive	system which operates asking questions of the user, and responding to the answers.
interface	the operating link between two items in a system, usually two pieces of hardware (computer to printer, for example) but sometimes used to describe the means by which the user interacts with the computer.

loop	programming term describing the repetition of a set of instructions a predetermined number of times or until a certain state is reached.
mainframe	large computer, usually remote from its terminals.
menu	list of options shown on the screen for selection by the operator.
modem	device linking computers to the telephone system by converting digital signals to analogue for transmission and vice versa to receive.
network	describes the interconnection of geographically separate pieces of equipment. A local area network (LAN) connects hardware within a small area; a remote area network those widely separated.
node	any piece of hardware connected to a network.
noise	unwanted signals producing errors.
off-line	used to describe equipment not directly connected to the main computer.
on-line	used to describe equipment with direct interactive links to the main computer; also devices connected to a telephone line (facsimile, modem etc.).
optical character reader (OCR)	scanning device capable of reading text and converting it to digital signals for input into a computer.
plotter	converts data to drawings on paper.
real time	processing information immediately, as opposed to storing it for action later, is described as acting in 'real time'.
software	the programs which allow computer hardware to operate.
stand alone	used to describe software which can operate without the need for any supporting program.
terminal	equipment through which data is entered into or extracted from a computer.
video/visual display terminal/unit (VDT/VDU)	the device incorporating a screen which displays information. Usually a cathode-ray tube (similar to a television screen), but sometimes light-emitting diode (LED) or gas-plasma display type.
write	to transfer data to a storage device (disc, tape etc.) or to a display.

Conversion Factors and Tables

The system of measures used in this book is 'Système International d'Unités' known in all languages as SI units which are based on the following:

Quantity	Name of unit	Unit symbol
Length	metre	m
Mass	kilogram	kg
Time	second	s
Electric current	ampere	A
Thermodynamic temperature	kelvin*	k
Luminous intensity	candela	cd

* The degree Celsius (°C) is used for all practical purposes.

Quantity	Conversion factors	
Length	1.0 mm	= 0.039 in
	25.4 mm (2.54 cm)	= 1 in
	304.8 mm (30.48 cm)	= 1 ft
	914.4 mm	= 1 yd
	1 000.0 mm (1.0 m)	= 1 yd 3.4 in (1.093 yd)
	20.117 m	= 1 chain
	1 000.00 m (1 km)	= 0.621 mile
	1 609.31 m	= 1 mile

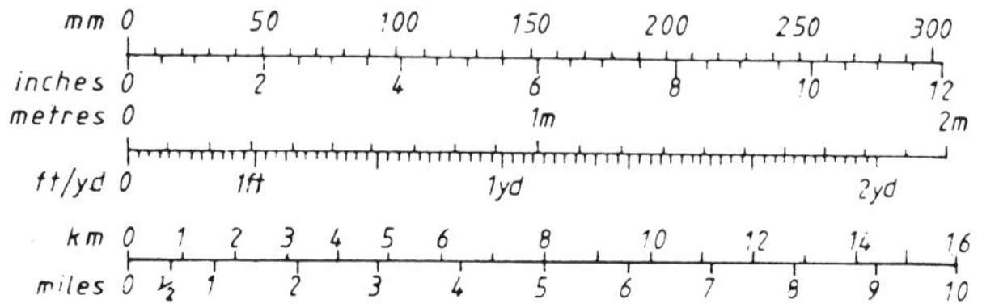

Area	100 mm^2 (1.0 cm^2)	= 0.155 in^2
	645.2 mm^2 (6.452 cm^2)	= 1 in^2
	929.03 cm^2 (0.093 m^2)	= 1 ft^2
	0.836 m^2	= 1 yd^2
	1.0 m^2	= 1.196 yd^2 (10.763 ft^2)
	0.405 ha (4046.9 m^2)	= 1 acre
	1.0 ha (10 000 m^2)	= 2.471 acre
	1.0 km^2	= 0.386 mile^2
	2.59 km^2 (259 ha)	= 1 mile^2
Temperature	X°C	= (⁹⁄₅X + 32) °F
	⁵⁄₉ × (X − 32) °C	= X°F

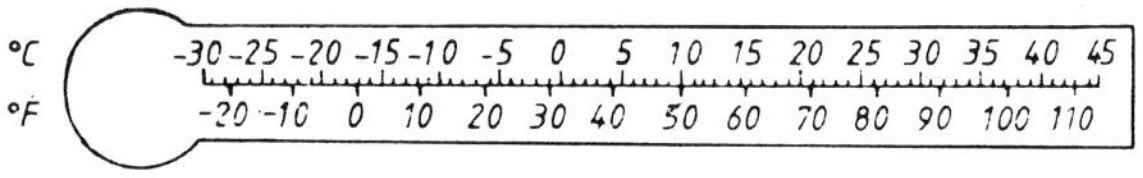

Illumination	1 lx (1 lumen/m^2)	= 0.093 ft-candle (0.093 lumen/ft^2)
	10.764 lx	= 1.0 ft-candle (1 lumen/ft^2)
Mass	1.0 g	= 0.035 oz (avoirdupois)
	28.35 g	= 1 oz (avoirdupois)
	454.0 g (0.454 kg)	= 1 lb
	1 000.0 g (1 kg)	= 2.205 lb
	45.36 kg	= 1 cwt US
	907.2 kg (0.907 t)	= 1 ton US
	1 000.0 kg (1.0 t)	= 1.102 ton US
Force	1.0 N	= 0.225 lbf
	1.0 kgf (9.807 N; 1.0 kilopond)	= 2.205 lbf
	4.448 kN	= 1.0 kipf (1 000 lbf)
	8.897 kN	= 1.0 tonf US
Force per unit length	1.0 N/m	= 0.067 lbf/ft
	14.59 N/m	= 1.0 lbf/ft
	175.1 kN/m (175.1 N/mm)	= 1.0 lbf/ft

Tables

Length

mm ⟷ in

mm		in	mm		in
25.4	1	0.04	254.0	10	0.39
50.8	2	0.08	508.0	20	0.79
76.2	3	0.12	762.0	30	1.18
101.6	4	0.16	1016.0	40	1.57
127.0	5	0.2	1270.0	50	1.97
152.4	6	0.24	1524.0	60	2.36
177.8	7	0.28	1778.0	70	2.76
203.2	8	0.31	2032.0	80	3.15
228.6	9	0.35	2286.0	90	3.54
			2540.0	100	3.93

m ⟷ ft

m		ft	m		ft
0.3	1	3.28	3.05	10	32.8
0.61	2	6.56	6.1	20	65.62
0.91	3	9.84	9.14	30	98.43
1.22	4	13.12	12.19	40	131.23
1.52	5	16.4	15.24	50	164.04
1.83	6	19.69	18.29	60	196.85
2.13	7	22.97	21.34	70	229.66
2.44	8	26.25	24.38	80	262.47
2.74	9	29.53	27.43	90	295.28
			30.48	100	328.08

Area

m^2 ⟷ ft^2

m^2		ft^2	m^2		ft^2
0.093	1	10.76	0.93	10	107.64
0.19	2	21.53	1.86	20	215.28
0.28	3	32.29	2.79	30	322.92
0.37	4	43.06	3.72	40	430.56
0.46	5	53.82	4.65	50	538.2
0.56	6	64.58	5.57	60	645.84
0.65	7	75.35	6.5	70	753.47
0.74	8	86.11	7.43	80	861.11
0.84	9	96.88	8.36	90	968.75
			9.29	100	1076.39

Volume

m^3 ⟷ ft^3

m^3		ft^3	m^3		ft^3
0.03	1	35.32	0.28	10	353.15
0.06	2	70.63	0.57	20	706.29
0.08	3	105.94	0.85	30	1059.44
0.11	4	141.26	1.13	40	1412.59
0.14	5	176.57	1.42	50	1765.73
0.17	6	211.89	1.7	60	2118.88
0.2	7	247.2	1.98	70	2472.03
0.23	8	282.52	2.27	80	2825.17
0.25	9	317.83	2.55	90	3178.32
			2.83	100	3531.47